Lecture Notes of the Institute for Computer Sciences, Social Informatics and Telecommunications Engineering 365

More information about this series at http://www.springer.com/series/8197

Lourdes Peñalver · Lorena Parra (Eds.)

Industrial IoT Technologies and Applications

4th EAI International Conference, Industrial IoT 2020
Virtual Event, December 11, 2020
Proceedings

 Springer

Editors
Lourdes Peñalver ⓘ
Universitat Politècnica de València
Valencia, Spain

Lorena Parra ⓘ
Instituto Madrileño de Investigación y
Madrid, Spain

ISSN 1867-8211   ISSN 1867-822X (electronic)
Lecture Notes of the Institute for Computer Sciences, Social Informatics
and Telecommunications Engineering
ISBN 978-3-030-71060-6   ISBN 978-3-030-71061-3 (eBook)
https://doi.org/10.1007/978-3-030-71061-3

This Springer imprint is published by the registered company Springer Nature Switzerland AG
The registered company address is: Gewerbestrasse 11, 6330 Cham, Switzerland

Preface

We are delighted to introduce the proceedings of the fourth edition of the European Alliance for Innovation (EAI) International Conference on Industrial IoT Technologies and Applications (Industrial IoT 2020). This conference brought together researchers, developers, and practitioners around the world who are leveraging and developing the Internet of Things for a smarter industry. The aim of the conference is to stimulate interaction and convergence among researchers active in the areas of control, communications, industrial robotics, industrial cloud, smart sensors and actuators, informatics, mobile computing, and security. All topics are in the context of the Industrial IoT.

The technical program of Industrial IoT 2020 consisted of 14 full papers organized in 4 technical sessions. Aside from the high-quality technical paper presentations, the technical program also featured one keynote speech given by Prof. Dr. Pascal Lorenz from the University of Haute Alsace, France.

Coordination with the steering chairs, Imrich Chlamtac, Jiafu Wan, Min Chen, and Daqiang Zhang, was essential for the success of the conference. We sincerely appreciate their constant support and guidance. It was also a great pleasure to work with such an excellent organizing committee team for their hard work in organizing and supporting the conference. In particular, the Technical Program Committee, led by our TPC Chair Lei Shu, who completed the peer-review process of technical papers and made a high-quality technical program, Jesus Tomas and Oscar Romero, as Local Chairs, Francisco Martinez-Capel as Workshop Chair, Sandra Sendra as Publicity & Social Media Chair, Lorena Parra and Lourdes Peñalver, as Publications Chairs, Jose M. Jimenez as Web Chair, Paulo Gondim as Panels Chair, José Pelegrí as Sponsorship & Exhibits Chair, Mohammed Atiquzzaman as Tutorials and Keynote Speakers Chair, and the Chairs of the proposed workshops, Miguel Ardid and Victor Espinosa for MARSS 2020, Sandra Sendra and José Miguel Jiménez for SSPA 2020, and Pedro V. Mauri and Lorena Parra for TECROP 2020. We are also grateful to the Conference Manager, Barbara Fertalova, for her support and to all the authors who submitted their papers to the Industrial IoT 2020 conference and workshops.

We strongly believe that the Industrial IoT conference provides a good forum for all researchers, developers, and practitioners to discuss all scientific and technological aspects that are relevant to smart grids. We also expect that future Industrial IoT conferences will be as successful and stimulating, as indicated by the contributions presented in this volume.

Jaime Lloret

Conference Organization

Steering Committee

Chair

Imrich Chlamtac   Bruno Kessler Professor, University of Trento, Italy

Members

Jiafu Wan   South China University of Technology, China
Min Chen   Huazhong University of Science and Technology, China
Daqiang Zhang   Tongji University, China

Organizing Committee

General Chair

Jaime Lloret   Universitat Politècnica de València, Spain

TPC Chair and Co-chair

Lei Shu   Nanjing Agricultural University, China

Local Chairs

Jesús Tomás   Universitat Politècnica de València, Spain
Óscar Romero   Universitat Politècnica de València, Spain

Workshops Chair

Francisco Martinez-Capel   Universitat Politècnica de València, Spain

Publicity and Social Media Chair

Sandra Sendra   Universidad de Granada, Spain

Publications Chairs

Lorena Parra   IMIDRA, Spain/Universitat Politècnica de València, Spain
Lourdes Peñalver   Universitat Politècnica de València, Spain

Web Chair

José Miguel Jiménez   Universitat Politècnica de València, Spain

Panels Chair

Paulo Gondim   Universidade de Brasília, Brasilia, Brazil

Sponsorship and Exhibits Chair

José Pelegrí   Universitat Politècnica de València, Spain

Tutorials and Keynote Speakers Chair

Mohammed Atiquzzaman   University of Oklahoma, USA

MARSS 2020 Workshop Chairs

Miguel Ardid   Universitat Politècnica de València, Spain
Víctor Espinosa   Universitat Politècnica de València, Spain

SSPA 2020 Workshop Chairs

Sandra Sendra   Universidad de Granada, Spain
José Miguel Jiménez   Universitat Politècnica de València, Spain

TECROP 2020 Workshop Chairs

Pedro V. Mauri   IMIDRA, Spain
Lorena Parra   IMIDRA, Spain/Universitat Politècnica de València, Spain

Technical Program Committee

González, Pedro Luis   Universidad Central, Colombia
Abdullah, Miran Taha   University of Sulaimani, Kurdistan Region, Iraq
Basterrechea, Daniel Andoni Universitat Politècnica de València, Spain
Rocher, Javier   Universitat Politècnica de València, Spain
Mirza Abdullah, Saman   Koya University, Kurdistan Region, Iraq
Pathan, Al-Sakib Khan   International Islamic University Malaysia (IIUM), Malaysia
Westphall, Carlos Becker   Federal University of Santa Catarina, Brazil
Lorenz, Pascal   University of Haute Alsace, France
Wu, Jinsong   Guilin University of Electronic Technology, China
Han, Guangjie   Hohai University, China
Ghafoor, Kayhan   Koya University, Kurdistan Region, Iraq
Araujo, Alvaro   Universidad Politécnica de Madrid, Spain
Chen, Fulong   Anhui Normal University, China
Lin, Kai   Dalian University of Technology, China

Contents

Session 4

Session 1

Session 1

Crowd Anomaly Detection Based on Elevator Internet of Things Technology

Chunhua Jia, Wenhai Yi, Yu Wu, Zhuang Li, Shuai Zhu$^{(\boxtimes)}$, and Leilei Wu

Shanghai Elevator Media Information Co., Ltd., Shanghai, China
{jiachunhua,yiwenhai,wuyu,lizhuang,zhushuai,wull}@zailingtech.com

Abstract. A work-flow which aims at capturing residents' abnormal activities through the passenger flow of elevator in multi-storey residence buildings is presented in this paper. Firstly, sensors (hall sensor, photoelectric sensor, gyro, accelerometer, barometer, and thermometer) connected with internet are mounted in elevator to collect image and data. Then computer vision algorithms such as instance segmentation, multi-label recognition, embedding and clustering are applied to generalize passenger flow of elevator, i.e. how many people and what kinds of people get in and out of the elevator on each floor. More specifically so-called GraftNet is proposed for fine-grained multi-label recognition task to recognize human attributes (e.g. gender, age, appearance, and occupation). Thirdly, based on the passenger flow data, anomaly detection of unsupervised learning is hierarchically applied to detect abnormal or even illegal activities of the residents. Meanwhile, based on manual reviewed data, Catboost algorithm is implemented for multi-classification task. Experiment shows the work-flow proposed in this paper can detect the anomaly and classify different categories well.

Keywords: IoT · Anomaly · Computer Vision · Machine learning · Big Data · Cloud computing

1 Introduction

In modern city, most people live in apartments of multi-storey buildings, due to the complexity of structure and high density of residents, public safety [1] as well as the management of urban residential community effective is challenged [2]. Thanks to technologies based on Artificial Intelligence (AI) [3] and Big Data and Internet Of Things (IoT), which make it possible to capture or predict direct or potential safety hazard on real-world activities [4,5]. On the other hand, the patterns of behaviors or activities vary from one to one and change continuously [5,6], it is particularly difficult to give a specific definition on residents' activities which would put their own safety in danger. Considering all the aspects above, the elevator could be the most feasible and suitable [7] environment to take operation on because it is legal and reasonable to deploy public surveillance

© ICST Institute for Computer Sciences, Social Informatics and Telecommunications Engineering 2021
Published by Springer Nature Switzerland AG 2021. All Rights Reserved
L. Peñalver and L. Parra (Eds.): Industrial IoT 2020, LNICST 365, pp. 3–17, 2021.
https://doi.org/10.1007/978-3-030-71061-3_1

and people take elevator widely and frequently enough. By real-time collecting, processing and analyzing the video flow in the elevator, important information including the state of the elevator, the states of people can be obtained [8]. Based on IoT, it is not difficult to capture elevator malfunction (e.g. stuck) in real-time through setting several different sensors in elevator [9]. A camera is used to automatically check if any passenger is trapped in elevator box when malfunction happens through Computer Vision (CV) algorithm, e.g. pedestrian detection [10].

Some researchers focus on predictive maintenance based on the detection of abnormal usage of an elevator, taking advantage of sensors information [11]. Common Internet Of Things (IoT) solution can only detect hardware malfunction, however, it is unable to describe the behavior of residents. Video surveillance fits this task better. Through the design of software and hardware, a work-flow is proposed in this paper. Camera and some other sensors including barometers, thermometers, accelerometers and so on mounted in the elevator, which helps to collect real-time data including video, velocity, temperature, pressure and so on. A distribution Powerline Carrier (PLC) Communication Systems [12] is constructed which achieves a stable and high speed transmission and satisfies the demand of data transmission. Once real-time data was collect, computer vision algorithm can be used for objection detection [13,14] and multi-classification model, named GraftNet, to distinguish the attributes and the number of the people, the body area of the people, the distances between people and the moving trajectories of the people in the elevator. Collected data is uploaded and stored in cloud based on Hadoop [15] and the artificial intelligence models are deployed and managed by Kubernetes [16]. The system introduced above is deployed on more than 100000 elevators currently.

The proposed system has the following parts:

- Power line Carrier (PLC) Communication Systems is used to create a smart elevator, which defined as a box equipped with numerous sensors and actuators, e.g. camera, barometers, thermometers, accelerometers. PLC systems are also 24 h a day connected and they have a relative small bandwidth compared to traditional modem communication systems. These properties make PLC systems a good alternative for low bandwidth intensive Internet services such as remote monitoring.
- Data collected from sensors including pictures and time series data are saved in cloud for the flexibility and cost-saving, user trust, privacy and security are also concerns.
- Cloud computing provides the architecture for creating Clouds with market-oriented resource allocation by leveraging technologies such as Virtual Machines (VMs). All the AI models including computer vision, anomaly detection and multi-classification are deployed on cloud.
- More specially, multi-classification model named GraftNet is proposed. GraftNet is a tree-like network that consists of one trunk and several branches and analyses the passenger flow of elevators in residence building.

The rest of the paper is organized as follows. The related work of IoT, computer vision and anomaly detection is briefly discussed in Sect. 2. We explain the infrastructure of internet of things and how to capture and analysis computer vision for passenger flow. The proposed multi-classification model named Graft-Net is also described in Sect. 3. Then, based on the collected and analyzed data, hierarchical anomaly detection for abnormal activity is utilized, we discuss this part in Sect. 4. Finally, in Sect. 5, we describe the experiments of our system, conclude our findings and suggest opportunities for future work.

2   Related Work

There were surveys conducted to anomalous events detection which utilize video surveillance. Recognizing human activities of daily living [17], which is an important research issue in building a pervasive and smart environment.

A survey [18] was given visual surveillance of object motion and behaviors, review recent developments and general strategies of all these stages, and proposed a general processing framework including several stages such as environment modeling, motion segmentation, object classification, understanding and description of behaviors, which all belong to computer vision domain. The possible research directions were given, e.g., occlusion handling, a combination of two and three-dimensional tracking. Videos Surveillance system should become more intelligent, crucial, and comprehensive to deal with the situations under which individual safety could be compromised by potential criminal activity. Surveillance systems provide the capability of collecting authentic and purposeful information and forming appropriate decisions to enhance safety [19]. Three generations of contemporary surveillance system and the most recent generation is decomposed into multi-sensor environments, video and audio surveillance, and distributed intelligence and awareness. A novel framework [20] was developed for automatic behavior profiling and online anomaly sampling/detection without any manual labeling of the training data set, which aims to address the problem of modeling video behavior captured in surveillance videos for the applications of online normal behavior recognition and anomaly detection. A real-time computer vision and machine learning system for modeling and recognizing human behaviors in a visual surveillance task were describe [21]. The system was particularly concerned with detecting when interactions between people occur, and with classifying the type of interaction. A novel approach to understand activities from their partial observations monitored through multiple non-overlapping cameras separated by unknown time gaps was propose [22]. Dynamic Probabilistic Networks (DPNs) [23] were exploited for modeling the temporal relationships among a set of different object temporal events in the scene for a coherent and robust scene-level behaviour interpretation.

Human detection and tracking [24] were tasks of computer vision systems for locating and following people in video imagery. Some object detection and object instance segmentation model were very popular at that time. For example, a simple fully-convolutional model for real-time instance segmentation was proposed in Yolact [13] and Mask R-CNN [14]. Some models offer a probabilistic model that allows us to predict the user's next actions and to identify anomalous user behaviours. Predicting the behavior of human participants in strategic settings was an important problem in many domains [4]. Deep learning architecture based on long short-term memory networks (LSTMs) was created [3], which models the inter-activity behaviour. By employing a deep learning approach, Deep Neural Network (DNN) framework was introduced, which has the capability for both modeling social influence and for predicting human behavior [6]. Social Influence Deep Learning (SIDL) [5] is a framework that combines deep learning with network science for modeling social influence and predicting human behavior on real-world activities.

A key goal of surveillance was to detect behaviors that can be considered anomalous [25]. Anomaly detection [26], which is also known as outlier or novelty detection, was a widely studied topic that had been applied to many fields including medical diagnosis, marketing, network intrusion, and to many other applications except for automated surveillance. There were different outlier detection models. A distance-based outlier detection method that finds the top outliers in an unlabeled data set [27]. Proximity-Based methods [28] consider the task of performing anomaly detection in highly noisy multivariate data. Statistical anomaly detection typically focuses on finding individual data point anomalies [29,30]. Neural networks, including Variational Auto-Encoders (VAEs) have shown great potential in the unsupervised learning of data distributions [31]. Outlier detection as a binary-classification issue by sampling potential outliers from a uniform reference distribution was approached [32]. Anomalies are data points that are few and different, as a result of these properties, anomalies are susceptible to a mechanism called isolation. Isolation Forest (iForest) [32] detects anomalies purely based on the concept of isolation without employing any distance or density measure—fundamentally different from all existing methods. An open-source Python toolbox [33] for performing scalable outlier detection on multivariate data contains different kinds of anomaly detection models.

To capture activities with potential public safety hazard, anomaly detection of unsupervised learning was the choice from algorithm perspective because the definition of safety hazard on people's activity was ambiguous and such activities were relatively rare. By real-time collecting, precessing and analyzing the video flow in the elevator and using background subtraction algorithm and human tracking algorithm, some important information including the state of the door of the elevator, the states of people can be obtained [8].

The previous work tried to analysis the video with the help of computer vision algorithms (see, [3,4,24]) which inspired our job. A work-flow is proposed based on the results of computer vision as well as some other sensors. Combined the different information of sensors, unsupervised learning (for example, Isolation Forest) and multi-classification, are given to make the conclusion which is valuable for the management of property management company. Our system can detect the anomaly directly and based on the passager flow data, we can easily distinguish the normal residence, group rental, apartment, office, decoration, dormitory and so on.

3 Structure of Our System

In this section, the architecture of the proposed work flow is given, the related computer vision algorithms will be discussed as well. In the first part, the IoT system will be described. The second part discusses how to calculate the number of person in/out the elevator. The proposed GraphNet for fine-grained multi-label classification recognizes different attributes of elevator passengers. With the help of PLC networks, connecting is much more reliable and efficient.

3.1 Infrastructure of Internet of Things (IoT) for Data Collection

Camera and several kinds of sensors (Hall sensor, photoelectric sensor, gyro, accelerometer, barometer, thermometer, etc.) are mounted in or on the elevator as the deployment of our system. Our work flow is a solution which is easy to promote with low cost and does not require access to the elevator's ECU, which means our solution could be deployed without influence of the elevators. Once the sensors is properly setup, we are able to monitor the trace of elevator running. Images captured from the camera help to collect passenger data. One snapshot is taken once the elevator moves from one floor to another. Alongside with the image, time stamp and floor numbers of start/end are also collected. Images with extra information are uploaded and stored on cloud for further analysis. The mechanism of snapshooting is based on one simple assumption: people get in or out of the elevator only when it stops at certain floor, and thus we can generalize how many and what kinds of people get in and out by comparing images successively captured, as shown in Fig. 1.

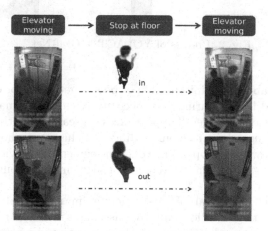

Fig. 1. Comparison of two images successively taken.

As shown in Fig. 1, by comparing the stage change of two images snapshooted serially. Conclusion a person in or out special floor can be easily make.

3.2   Instance Segmentation, Embedding and Clustering

Considering occlusion is inevitable when there are several passengers in the elevator at the same time, for feature extraction on each individual passenger, instance segmentation is needed. Different from object detection, instance segmentation can accurately segment all objects at pixel level and minimize the impact of occlusion and background. It could be considered as a pre-process similar to attention mechanism, so that other CV models could focus on human target itself completely.

YOLACT [13], a representative one-stage method which was proposed to speed up instance segmentation, is utilized to segment target person from background and other non-targets as shown in Fig. 2.

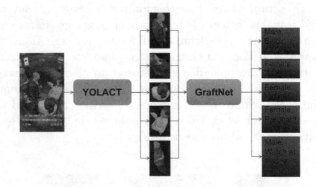

Fig. 2. Process of YOLACT + GraftNet.

As mentioned above, the information of people getting in or out of each floor could be generated by comparing two successively captured images. We assume the variance of passengers' overall appearances is greater than that of their faces, so FaceNet [34] designed for face embedding and clustering should be sufficient to identically represent the appearance of each segmented individual. As a result, FaceNet is re-trained with our own dataset of segmented passengers and utilized as feature extractor.

As shown in Fig. 3, there are M passengers in image $p1$ captured right before the elevator stops at certain floor, and N passengers in image $p2$ captured right after the elevator leaves that floor. All those segmented passengers are fed to FaceNet and corresponding feature vectors are returned. Then we build an association matrix D with order $M * N$. The element d_{ij} represents the Euclidean distance between the feature vectors of passenger i in $p1$ and passenger j in $p2$. Minimal value searching on each row (or column) with a threshold t is carried out on D to get the best match for each passenger (no match found if the minimal value is greater than t). The passengers in $p2$ without any match from $p1$ are considered as "get out of that floor" and those in $p1$ without match from $p2$ are considered as "get into the floor". Then attributes recognition are only applied on above two kinds of passengers for each floor.

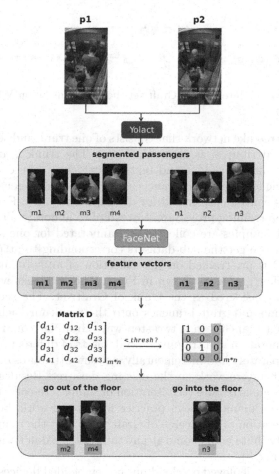

Fig. 3. Segmentation, embedding and clustering to generalize passenger flow of each floor.

3.3 GraftNet: A Solution for Fine-Grained Multi-label Classification

To analyse the passenger flow of elevator in residence building, data with more descriptive information is needed, e.g. gender, age, occupation, appearance, etc. GraftNet is proposed, which id a solution for fine-grained multi-label recognition task, i.e. to recognize different attributes of elevator passengers.

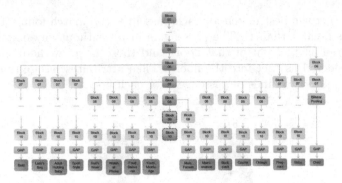

Fig. 4. Architecture of GraftNet (based on Inception V3).

GraftNet is a tree-like network that consists of one trunk and several branches corresponding to attributes, as shown in Fig. 4. The trunk is used to extract low-level features such as shapes and textures, which can be commonly represented with generic features. And branches is mainly used to generate high-level features and thus can be customized for different attributes. For GraftNet, we propose a two-step training procedure. Instead of to annotate all samples for all attributes overall, samples are collected and annotated for one single attribute separately, so that we get the sub-datasets corresponding to attributes. In first step, InceptionV3 is pre-trained on the collection of all sub-datasets by using a dynamic data flow graph, as shown in Fig. 4. The 11 blocks with pre-trained weights could be considered as the trunk of GraftNet. The second step is to separately fine-tune and graft branches onto the trunk for each attribute. By training trunk and branches in a two-step way, GraftNet could save time and labor for both annotation and training. Sub-datasets of different attributes could be maintained separately and incrementally, i.e. new attributes or samples could be added without any re-work on the existing data set. Besides, training task of one-branch-for-one-attribute (the iteration of samples re-collecting and model fine-tuning) is more manageable in practice for a team-work. So to speak, the very basic consideration of the design of GraftNet is that the requirement of recognizing a new attribute could come at any time and we don't want any re-work because of that (Fig. 5).

Since GraftNet is deployed on cloud but not embedded devices in our system, we focus more on extendability rather than efficiency. From some perspectives, our work is quite like an inverse process compared to network pruning or weights compression [35]. Rather than to reduce the redundancy of neural networks for a fixed task, what we do is to leverage the over-parameterization and maximum its usage to recognize new attributes with a few extra branches.

3.4 Power Lines Communication (PLC)

In circumstances of elevator, it may be too expensive and not convenient for a cable or telephone company to install the infrastructure necessary with

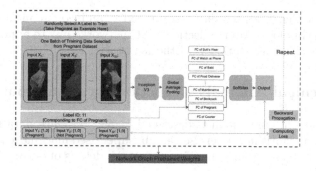

Fig. 5. GraftNet: process of training with dynamic data flow graph.

broadband Internet access. One potential solution for this problem is power line communication, since it can use existing infrastructure to deliver broadband Internet access. Meanwhile, the wireless routers have drawbacks such as signal interference from walls, floors, and other objects. Power line communication (PLC) is a technology that can allow data to be transmitted by an existing electricity infrastructure and can be used the existing wiring in a home or elevator. These systems typically involve an adapter that allows a modem to be connected to a power outlet via an Ethernet cable. Additional adapters can then be plugged into outlets around the elevator, allowing computers or other devices access to the network. PLC technology has the following advantages: low implementation cost, large reach, low running cost and indoor high speed. These advantages lead to more implementations of PLC networks in various industries.

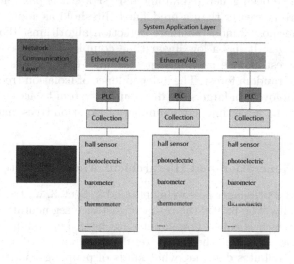

Fig. 6. PLC for elevator system.

As show in Fig. 6, sensor data are uploaded and communicated with the help of PLC technology. After collection, PLC networks link to application layer which contains the work station via Ethernet or 4G/5G.

4   Hierarchical Anomaly Detection for Abnormal Activity

The architecture of our system is described in Sect. 2. Once data is collected, computer vision algorithm, supervised and unsupervised machine learning model can be used for the anomalies. In this section, the details of our model deployed on cloud will discussed.

4.1   Isolation Forest: Anomaly Detection of Unsupervised Learning

Isolation forest (IForest) is an unsupervised learning algorithm dealing with anomaly detection problem. Instead of building a model of normal instance like common techniques use, the principle of Isolation Forest is isolating anomalous points which means the tendency of anomalous instances can be easier to be split from the rest samples in a data set, compared with normal points, because anomalous data points has two quantitative properties: different and fewer than normal data points.

Anomaly detection with Isolation Forest is a process composed of two main stages. In the first stage, a training data set is used to build isolation trees (iTrees). In the second stage, each instance in test set is passed through the iTrees build in the previous stage, and a proper 'anomaly score' is assigned to the instance according to the average path length of iTrees. Once all the instances in the test set have been generated an anomaly score, it is possible to mark the point whose score is greater than a predefined threshold as anomaly.

As one of the most famous anomaly detection algorithms, IForest has outstanding advantages: It has a low linear time complexity and a small memory requirement. IForest can be used in huge amounts of data sets because of its basic approach of random forest. The independence of Isolation trees ensures this model can be employed on large scale distributed system to accelerate Computing Platform. At the same time, large number of Isolation trees makes algorithm more stable.

4.2   Feature Generation and Hierarchical Anomaly Detection

For the generalized passenger flow we mentioned in Sect. 3, we treat them as two parts hierarchically. The first is the result of instance segmentation, embedding and clustering, which is called flow-count data here, i.e. how many people get in/out of elevator. And the other is the result of human attributes recognition, which is called attributes data, i.e. what kinds of people get in/out of elevator. The hierarchy is defined here because the flow-count data is actually byproduct of our system in commercial use but attributes data is not. Since our IoT system is deployed in more than 100000 elevators which transport tens of millions people daily, to additionally recognize attributes for all these passengers is computationally not affordable for us. Besides, the original requirement from our customer at the very beginning is to find out over crowded residence (e.g. more than 20 illegal migrants live in one small apartment), it's reasonable that we put more consideration on flow-count data. Therefore we decide to perform anomaly detection hierarchically, first on flow-count data then on attributes data.

Flow-count data is used for the first round of anomaly detection. For the weekdays in the last 15 days, we calculate the mean $m1$ and standard deviation $s1$ of passenger flow per floor per elevator, $m2$ and $s2$ of the flow per elevator, and $m3$ and $s3$ of the flow of all elevators in the same residential estate. Considering citizens are highly civilized and socialized, $m4 - m6$ and $s4 - s6$ are calculated for the weekends in the last 15 days, the same as $m1 - m3$ and $s1 - s3$ on weekdays. Including the floor number, we get feature vectors of length 13 per floor per elevator.

The contamination parameter of isolation forest during training procedure prescribes the proportion of outliers in the data set. We set it as 0.2 to output as many records as possible for the next second round anomaly detection.

Attributes recognition is only performed on the output of the first round anomaly detection to reduce computation. Besides the $l2$ values of mean and standard deviation generated in first round (floor number excluded), the attribute features are adopted by calculating the mean of attribute recognition result per floor per elevator. In detail, for passengers who get in/out elevator of certain floor, attributes recognition with GraftNet is performed to get feature vectors (22 classification results and 22 corresponding scores), then mean of these attribute feature vectors are calculated. The head count and distribution of time of appearance in 24-h are also included.

The contamination parameter of isolation forest is set as 0.01 for the second round detection. There are around 1 million records for each floor from 100000 elevators. In our experiment, after two rounds of anomaly detection, we finally get 643 outliers output.

4.3 Manual Review and Analysis

One fact that we have to admit is that sometimes the outliers obtained from anomaly detection of unsupervised learning might not be activities with public safety hazard. The anomaly of such outliers could be caused by malfunction of IoT system (e.g. malfunction of sensors, camera, network), or misentries in our database. For example, most of the elevators in our system are from residence buildings, and very few are from non-residence buildings, such as office building, hospital, school, and shopping mall. The activities of people in such non-residence buildings are obviously different from residence buildings. Our abnormal activity capture is supposed to perform on residence buildings only. However, some non-residence buildings are misentried as residence ones in our system, which could probably make them captured as anomaly. Similarly malfunction of IoT system could also cause exception data which might be captured.

Fig. 7. Interface of inspection tool.

To verify the outliers and keep improving the result, we build inspection tools to review and analyze the output manually. Corresponding to each output, the image-pairs successively captured will be reviewed, together with the statistical data such as distribution of attributes and time of appearance in 24 h, as shown in Fig. 7. All data exceptions caused by malfunction/misentries and abnormal activities clearly without any public safety hazard (e.g. running company in home office, decorators getting in/out, etc.) will be logged and excluded from next round of anomaly detection. Meantime confirmed records with suspicions of safety hazard will be reported to our customer.

Out of the 643 records output in our experiment we randomly pick 412 and review them one by one with the inspection tool. The result is shown in Table 1.

Table 1. Results after reviewed

Review result	Safety hazard	Comments	Number
Positive	Probably yes/unsure	Something different is there. Need to be checked by property manager	289
Positive	No	Caused by malfunction of sensors	13
Positive	No	Apartment under decoration	32
Positive	No	Dormitory/hotel	27
Positive	No	Shopping mall/entertainment venue	2
Positive	No	Office building	40
Positive	Yes	Catering service running in apartment	3
Positive	Yes	Over crowded residence	6

4.4 Anomaly Multi-classification

Based on manual review and analysis data, supervised machine learning can be used to distinguish the anomaly. A data set containing 15440 samples (floors) is built whose features come from 1286 lifts, and affiliated to 13 categories including normal residence, group rental, apartment, office, decoration, dormitory, system abnormality, shopping mall, entertainment place, unable to judge, hotel, restaurant and educational institution. The ratio of different categories, which is unbalanced, can be seen in Fig. 8. In details, the normal residence takes up 57.2% while educational institution holds only 0.19%. Meanwhile, as show in Subsect. 4.3, the feature contains both numerical and category type[1]. Catboost [36] is used for multi-classification task under this situation.

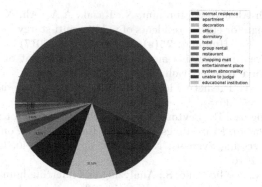

Fig. 8. Data distribution of different classifications

The data set is split-ted into training and test set, which account 80% and 20% respectively. Catboost model achieves 85.6% accuracy and 84.7% recall for the test stage. A plot of the ROC curve is also created in Fig. 9.

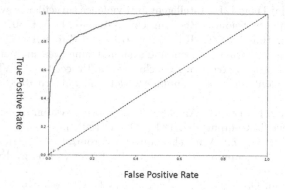

Fig. 9. ROC curve

---

[1] https://pan.baidu.com/s/10Cty8nJcpbp9B0_oGXjPww, extraction code: llqi.

5   Conclusion

As for now, a work flow is proposed which helps to detect the anomalies of floor. The proposed model is different from traditional ones which make the conclusion merely based on the results of computer vision with the help of deep machine learning. Our work flow is comprehensive system which has been deployed more than 100 thousands elevators in different places of China. By collecting pictures and some other data of sensors, supervised and unsupervised model are combined to make the discussion.

References

1. Hanapi, N.L., Sh Ahmad, S., Ibrahim, N., Razak, A.A., Ali, N.M.: Suitability of escape route design for elderly residents of public multi-storey residential building. Pertanika J. Soc. Sci. Humanit. **25(s)**(2017), 251–258 (2017)
2. Yan-Bin, W.: Creating effective mechanism of management of urban residential community. J. Yuxi Teachers Coll. 40–43 (2002)
3. Aitor, A., Gorka, A.: Predicting human behaviour with recurrent neural networks. Appl. Sci. **8**(2), 305 (2018)
4. Hartford, J., Wright, J.R., Leyton-Brown, K.: Deep learning for predicting human strategic behavior. In: Proceedings of the 30th International Conference on Neural Information Processing Systems, NIPS 2016, pp. 2432–2440. Curran Associates Inc., Red Hook (2016)
5. Luceri, L., Braun, T., Giordano, S.: Analyzing and inferring human real-life behavior through online social networks with social influence deep learning. Appl. Netw. Sci. **4**(1), 1–25 (2019). https://doi.org/10.1007/s41109-019-0134-3
6. Phan, N., Dou, D., Wang, H., Kil, D., Piniewski, B.: Ontology-based deep learning for human behavior prediction with explanations in health social networks. Inf. Sci. **384**, 298–313 (2017)
7. Zihan, M., Shaoyi, H., Zhanbin, Z., Shuang, X.: Elevator safety monitoring system based on internet of things. Int. J. Online Eng. (iJOE) **14**(08), 121 (2018)
8. Yi-Ping, T., Hai-Feng, L.U.: Intelligent anti-violence surveillance system in elevator based on computer vision. J. Zhejiang Univ. Technol. **6**, 591–597 (2009)
9. Gui-Xiong, L., Hai-Bing, Z., Ruo-Quan, H.E., Yu-Hui, K.E.: Design of elevator real-time energy efficiency recorder and system. China Measurement & Test (2012)
10. Dollar, P.: Pedestrian detection: a benchmark. In: Proceedings/CVPR, IEEE Computer Society Conference on Computer Vision and Pattern Recognition, pp. 304–311 (2009)
11. Zhou, Y., Wang, K., Liu, H.: An elevator monitoring system based on the internet of things. Procedia Comput. Sci. **131**, 541–544 (2018)
12. Li, J., Luo, C., Xu, Z.: A novel timing synchronization metric for low-voltage OFDM powerline communication system. In: Power & Energy Engineering Conference (2012)
13. Bolya, D., Zhou, C., Xiao, F., Yong, J.L.: YOLACT: real-time instance segmentation. In: Proceedings of the IEEE/CVF International Conference on Computer Vision (ICCV 2019) (2020)
14. Kaiming, H., Georgia, G., Piotr, D., Ross, G.: Mask R-CNN. IEEE Trans. Pattern Anal. Mach. Intell. **PP**, 1 (2017)

15. White, T.: Hadoop: The Definitive Guide. O'reilly Media Inc., Sebastopol (2012). 215(11): 1–4
16. Acuña, P.: Kubernetes (2016)
17. Duong, T.V.: Activity recognition and abnormality detection with the switching hidden semi-Markov models. In: Proceedings of the 2005 IEEE Computer Society Conference on Computer (2005)
18. Hu, W., Tan, T., Wang, L., Maybank, S.: A survey on visual surveillance of object motion and behaviors. IEEE Trans. Syst. Man Cybern. **34**(3), 334–352 (1986)
19. Räty, T.D.: Survey on contemporary remote surveillance systems for public safety. IEEE Trans. Syst. Man Cybern. Part C **40**(5), 493–515 (2010)
20. Xiang, T., Gong, S.: Video behavior profiling for anomaly detection. IEEE Trans. Pattern Anal. Mach. Intell. **30**(5), 893–908 (2008)
21. Oliver, N.M., Rosario, B., Pentland, A.P.: A Bayesian computer vision system for modeling human interactions. IEEE Trans. Pattern Anal. Mach. Intell. **22**(8), 255–272 (2000)
22. Loy, C.C., Gong, X.S.: Time-delayed correlation analysis for multi-camera activity understanding. Int. J. Comput. Vision **90**, 106–129 (2010)
23. Gong, S., Xiang, T.: Recognition of group activities using dynamic probabilistic networks. In: Proceedings of the Ninth IEEE International Conference on Computer Vision (2003)
24. Davis, J.W., Sharma, V., Tyagi, A., Keck, M.: Human detection and tracking. In: Li, S.Z., Jain, A. (eds.) Encyclopedia of Biometrics, pp. 882–887. Springer, Boston (2009). https://doi.org/10.1007/978-0-387-73003-5_35
25. Sodemann, A.A., Ross, M.P., Borghetti, B.J.: A review of anomaly detection in automated surveillance. IEEE Trans. Syst. Man Cybern. Part C **42**(6), 1257–1272 (2012)
26. Kalinichenko, L.A., Shanin, I., Taraban, I.: Methods for anomaly detection: a survey. In: Proceedings of the 16th Russian Conference on Digital Libraries RCDL 2014, CEUR Workshop Proceedings (CEUR-WS.org), vol. 1297, pp. 20–25. ceur-ws.org (2014)
27. Angiulli, F., Basta, S., Pizzuti, C.: Distance-based detection and prediction of outliers. IEEE Trans. Knowl. Data Eng. **18**(2), 145–160 (2005)
28. Idé, T., Lozano, A.C., Abe, N., Liu, Y.: Proximity-based anomaly detection using sparse structure learning. In: Proceedings of the SIAM International Conference on Data Mining, SDM, 30 April 2009–2 May 2009, Sparks, Nevada, USA, p. 2009 (2009)
29. Akouemo, H.N., Povinelli, R.J.: Probabilistic anomaly detection in natural gas time series data. Int. J. Forecast. **32**(3), 948–956 (2016)
30. Xiong, L., Póczos, B., Schneider, J.G., Connolly, A., Vanderplas, J.: Hierarchical probabilistic models for group anomaly detection. J. Mach. Learn. Res. **15**, 789–797 (2011)
31. Niu, Z., Yu, K., Wu, X.: LSTM-based VAE-GAN for time-series anomaly detection. Sensors **20**(13), 3738 (2020)
32. Liu, F.T., Ting, K.M., Zhou, Z.H.: Isolation-based anomaly detection. Acm Trans. Knowl. Discovery Data **6**(1), 1–39 (2012)
33. Zhao, Y., Nasrullah, Z., Li, Z.: PyOD: a python toolbox for scalable outlier detection. J. Mach. Learn. Res. **20**(96), 1–7 (2019)
34. Schroff, F., Kalenichenko, D., Philbin, J.: FaceNet: a unified embedding for face recognition and clustering (2015)
35. Song, H., Mao, H., Dally, W.J.: Deep compression: compressing deep neural networks with pruning, trained quantization and Huffman coding. In: ICLR (2016)
36. Prokhorenkova, L., Gusev, G., Vorobev, A., Dorogush, A.V., Gulin, A.: CatBoost: unbiased boosting with categorical features (2017)

Real-Time Task Scheduling in Smart Factories Employing Fog Computing

Ming-Tuo Zhou[1]([⊠]), Tian-Feng Ren[1,2], Zhi-Ming Dai[1,2], and Xin-Yu Feng[1,2]

[1] Shanghai Institute of Microsystem and Information Technology,
Chinese Academy of Sciences, Shanghai, China
mingtuo.zhou@mail.sim.ac.cn
[2] University of Chinese Academy of Sciences, Beijing, China

Abstract. With the development of the new generation of information technology, traditional factories are gradually transforming into smart factories. How to meet the low-latency requirements of task processing in smart factories so as to improve factory production efficiency is still a problem to be studied. For real-time tasks in smart factories, this paper proposes a resource scheduling architecture combined with cloud and fog computing, and establishes a real-time task delay optimization model in smart factories based on the ARQ (Automatic Repeat-request) protocol. For the solution of the optimization model, this paper proposes the GSA-P (Genetic Scheduling Arithmetic With Penalty Function) algorithm to solve the model based on the GSA (Genetic Scheduling Arithmetic) algorithm. Simulation experiments show that when the penalty factor of the GSA-P algorithm is set to 6, the total task processing delay of the GSA-P algorithm is about 80% lower than that of the GSA-R(Genetic Scheduling Arithmetic Reasonable) algorithm, and 66% lower than that of the Joines & Houck method algorithm; In addition, the simulation results show that the combined cloud and fog computing method used in this paper reduces the total task delay by 18% and 7% compared with the traditional cloud computing and pure fog computing methods, respectively.

Keywords: Smart factory · Fog computing · ARQ protocol · Genetic algorithm · Resource scheduling

1 Introduction

The new generation of information technology such as the Internet, Internet of Things, cloud computing, fog computing, artificial intelligence, big data, etc. has brought valuable development opportunities for many industries [1, 2]. Traditional industries are undergoing technological changes caused by the development of information technology. Smart factory was born under such a background [3, 4]. Compared with traditional factories, smart factories need to process massive amounts of data. At present, there are two mainstream processing methods. One is to use remote cloud computing for processing and return the results. However, this method has many drawbacks [5], such as:

© ICST Institute for Computer Sciences, Social Informatics and Telecommunications Engineering 2021
Published by Springer Nature Switzerland AG 2021. All Rights Reserved
L. Peñalver and L. Parra (Eds.): Industrial IoT 2020, LNICST 365, pp. 18–33, 2021.
https://doi.org/10.1007/978-3-030-71061-3_2

relatively large delay and high bandwidth requirements. And there is no guarantee of security and privacy.

In order to alleviate this problem, another method, fog computing is proposed [6], which transfers computing, storage, control, and network functions from the end to the fog, thereby reducing data transmission delay and the required bandwidth. It allows a group of adjacent end users, network edge devices, and access devices to collaborate to complete tasks that require resources. Therefore, many computing tasks that originally required cloud computing can be effectively completed at the edge of the network through the distributed computing resources around the data generating device.

The rest of this paper is as follows: Sect. 2 is related works, Sect. 3 analyzes the task scheduling framework, Sect. 4 establishes the mathematical model of the system, and discusses the GSA-P algorithm. Section 5 shows and analyzes the simulation results, and we summarize and draws the conclusion in Sect. 6.

2 Related Works

There have been some related studies on this issue. Olena Skarlat et al. optimized the resource allocation problem of the cloud and fog [7], reduced the task delay by 39%, and provided a fog resource allocation scheme for delay-sensitive applications. Luxiu Yin et al. replaced virtual machines with containers to execute tasks in smart factories [8], and proposed a container-based task scheduling algorithm. The task execution is divided into two steps: first consider whether the task is accepted or rejected, and then consider whether to run on the local fog node or upload to the cloud. Experimental verification shows that the task scheduling algorithm reduces the task execution time by 10%. Hend Gedawy et al. used a group of heterogeneous mobile and Internet devices to form an edge micro cloud [9], under the condition of ensuring that the energy consumption is below the threshold, maximize the computing throughput and minimize the delay. In order to solve this non-linear problem, they used heuristic algorithms. The simulation results show that the computational throughput is increased by 30% and the delay is reduced by 10% to 40%.

However, the existing research still has some shortcomings: First, the current task scheduling of smart factories is basically based on fog computing or cloud computing, but when the task volume is large, blindly handing over tasks to fog resource computing will lead to The calculation pressure of the fog node is too high, and once the task is completely delivered to the cloud resource for calculation, it will cause the problem of excessive delay; Second, in the actual production environment, network packet loss will have some impact on communication, but in the current research on resource scheduling analysis, the impact of network packet loss on task processing is not considered.

Compared with other research, this article has made overall improvements in system models and algorithms based on the characteristics of today's smart factories. First, we improve the fog computing framework, and then model the problem based on the improved framework, and finally use the improved genetic algorithm to solve the fog computing resource scheduling model. The work and main contributions of this paper are as follows:

1) Framework improvement: In order to further reduce the delay of real-time tasks in smart factories, this article adds cloud computing resources to the traditional fog computing architecture, so that the current fog computing architecture can disassemble a part of the task when the computing pressure is high. And deliver it to the cloud for processing. At the same time, considering the impact of network packet loss on task delay during actual task transmission, and based on this impact, a time delay optimization model for smart factory real-time tasks under constraint conditions is established.

2) Algorithm improvement: the real-time task delay model based on the improved framework is a NP (Nondeterministic Polynomially) problem with constraints. For this problem, we usually use heuristic algorithm to solve it [10], such as genetic algorithm [11], but the traditional genetic algorithm has some shortcomings that are difficult to solve the constraint problem. Therefore, this paper proposes GSA-P algorithm, which transforms the original constraint problem into unconstrained problem by constructing penalty function.

3) Simulation verification: The real-time data simulated in this paper adopts the industrial Internet of Things data of real-time path planning of industrial robots [12], and 4 fog nodes and a cloud server are set up. In the simulation, the difference of approximate optimal solution under different penalty factors is compared. Meanwhile, the differences of optimization results of GSA-P, GSA-R, Joines&Houck method are compared. Finally, the performance improvement of cloud collaborative processing compared with cloud computing and pure fog computing is demonstrated.

3 Scheduling Frameworks in Smart Factories

3.1 Task Classification

In a smart factory, there are multiple tasks with different requirements for delay and storage. In order to improve the production efficiency of the smart factory, it is necessary to effectively classify the different tasks in the smart manufacturing factory. According to the task's tolerance to delay and the size of task data, tasks can be divided into the following categories.

1) Real-time tasks with low load: tasks with small data volume and low latency requirements, such as: judgment of the operating status of key smart devices and faults.

2) Real-time tasks with high load: tasks with large data volume and low latency requirements, such as: monitoring the quality of products in the entire manufacturing process, processing video information in the factory, and production materials in smart factories registration.

3) Storage tasks: tasks that can accept low latency, such as: data analysis for each production line and analysis of the energy consumption of the entire factory, and other intelligent calculations and processing that can improve the efficiency of the factory.

In the case of 1), due to the small size of data and less requirements for computing resources, the task can be allocated to fog resources for processing.

In the case of 2), due to the large size of data for this type of task, if the data is only deployed on the fog node for calculation, it will cause excessive pressure on the fog node calculation, therefore, cloud computing is needed to reduce the computational pressure of fog nodes.

In the case of 3), regardless of the size of the task's data, it can be directly transferred to the cloud server for processing, and the result will be returned at an appropriate time. Therefore, for the entire smart factory system, the task scheduling framework can be seen in Fig. 1.

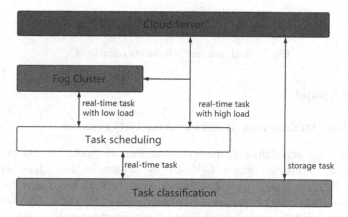

Fig. 1. Task scheduling framework

3.2 Scheduling Framework for Real-Time Tasks

We refer to 1) and 2) in Sect. 2.1 collectively as real-time tasks. For real-time tasks, we need to consider how to divide tasks. For low-load real-time problems, we need to appropriately allocate tasks to the fog node cluster. For high-load real-time tasks, we have to consider allocating tasks on cloud servers and fog node clusters at the same time.

Therefore, we consider adding a fog management node to assign tasks to fog nodes and cloud servers. When a real-time task is delivered, the fog management node determines the task distribution. The scheduling framework of real-time tasks can be seen in Fig. 2.

This paper mainly studies the resource scheduling of real-time tasks in smart factories under this framework.

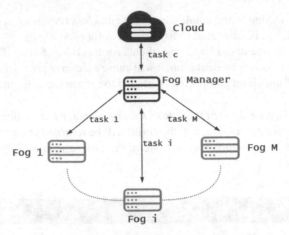

Fig. 2. Real time task scheduling framework

4 System Model

4.1 Time Delay Optimization Model Based on ARQ Protocol

The real-time task scheduling framework described in Sect. 2.2 can be regarded as a weighted undirected graph $G(V, E)$ as shown in Fig. 3, where $V = \{F_1, F_2, \ldots, F_i, F_M, \ldots, F_m, C\}$ is a vertex set, F_i is the fog node, F_M is the fog manager, C is cloud server $E = \{e_{F_M F_1}, \ldots, e_{F_M F_i}, \ldots, e_{F_M C}\}$ is the edge set, $e_{F_M F_i}$ a communication link between fog node F_i and fog manager, weight on edge is $W_{F_M F_i}$. The fog manager only allocates tasks and does not perform specific tasks. The computing power of F_i is denoted as A_{F_i}, the computing power of C is denoted as A_C. For m fog nodes and 1 cloud server, Task D can be divided into m subtasks of different sizes, which is denoted as $D = \{d_1, d_2, \ldots, d_j, \ldots, d_C, \ldots, d_m\}$, where d_C is the subtask that is assigned to the cloud server.

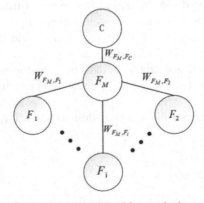

Fig. 3. Undirected graph of fog exclusive node

The total delay of F_i processing task d_j can be expressed as:

$$T_a(F_i, d_j) = \frac{d_j}{A_{F_i}} + T_t(F_i, d_j) \tag{1}$$

where $\frac{d_j}{A_{F_i}}$ is the computing delay of the F_i processing task d_j, $T_t(F_i, d_j)$ is the communication delay between F_i and F_M by transfer d_j.

Similarly, the total delay of cloud server C processing task d_j is:

$$T_a(C, d_C) = \frac{d_c}{A_C} + T_t(C, d_c) \tag{2}$$

where $\frac{d_c}{A_C}$ is the computing delay of C processing task d_C, $T_t(C, d_c)$ is the communication delay between C and F_M by transfer d_C.

When the network transmits task d_j, d_j is divided into several packets. Suppose a packet length is L_p and the data transmission rate between F_i and F_M is v_i, when there is no network packet loss between communication links, the delay of a data packet's successful transmission is calculated as follows:

$$T_{S_i} = \frac{L_p}{v_i} \tag{3}$$

In the actual transmission process, there must be a packet loss rate between links. When packet loss occurs on the network, the stop-and-wait ARQ protocol is often used to retransmit data packets. The principle of the stop-and-equal ARQ protocol [13] is: after the data message is sent, the sender waits for the status report of the receiver, if the status report message is sent successfully, the subsequent data message is sent, otherwise the message is retransmitted.

Let T_L represent the time required for data packet transmission between F_i and F_M when there is a packet loss rate, ignoring the queue delay. Suppose n is the number of times of transmissions required to successfully send a data packet, and E_i is the packet loss rate between F_i and F_M. When the m-th data packet is transmitted incorrectly, the probability of its n-th transmission success is:

$$P(m = n) = (1 - E_i)E_i^{(n-1)} \forall n = 1, 2, 3 \ldots \tag{4}$$

According to the TCP protocol, the waiting time before retransmission is generally: $T_{out} = 2 \times T_{S_i}$, the size of a single packet is $L_p = 1448B$, Therefore, the packet transmission time between F_i and F_M can be expressed as:

$$T_L = T_{S_i} + T_{out} \sum_{n=1}^{\infty} (n - 1)P(m = n) \tag{5}$$

Combining Eq. (4), we can finally get the average transmission time of a single data packet when the packet loss rate is E_i:

$$T_L = T_{S_i} \frac{1 + E_i}{1 - E_i} \tag{6}$$

Therefore, the communication delay $T_t(F_i, d_j)$ caused by the transmission of d_j between F_i and F_M is:

$$T_t(F_i, d_j) = \frac{d_j}{L_p} \times T_L = \frac{d_j}{v_i} \times \frac{1 + E_i}{1 - E_i} \tag{7}$$

Similarly, we can get the delay between F_i and C:

$$T_t(C, d_C) = \frac{d_C}{v_C} \times \frac{1 + E_C}{1 - E_C} \tag{8}$$

In summary, when the fog node and cloud server are not faulty, the total time delay $T(d_j, d_C)$ spent by the task can be expressed as:

$$T(d_j, d_C) = max\{T_a(F_i, d_j), T_a(C, d_C)\} \, j = 1, 2, 3, \ldots \tag{9}$$

When processing real-time tasks, in order to reduce the processing delay of tasks, it is necessary to integrate the computing power of all fog nodes and the computing power of cloud server to find a task D allocation method $D = \{d_1, d_2, \ldots, d_j, \ldots, d_C, \ldots, d_m\}$ to minimize formula (10). Therefore, we finally get the constrained optimization problem:

$$minT(d_j, d_C) \, j = 1, 2, 3, \ldots$$
$$s.t. \, 0 \le d_j, d_C \le D \tag{10}$$

$$\sum_{j=1}^{m-1} d_j + d_C = D$$

4.2 GSA-P Algorithm

In Sect. 3.1, the real-time task delay optimization problem belongs to NP problem with constraints. GSA algorithm can not effectively deal with the optimization problem with constraints, so it needs some additional skills to deal with constraints. When using genetic algorithm to do constrained optimization, the following two ways are generally used:

1) A penalty function is used to transform a constrained problem into an unconstrained one.
2) Reasonable crossover and mutation operators are designed so that only chromosomes satisfying constraint conditions can be generated in each iteration.

In this section, we discuss the first method.

Construct Penalty Function

For the NP problem with constraints, this paper uses the method of constructing penalty function to solve it. The penalty method generally divides the solution space into feasible region and infeasible region, and the solution that does not meet the constraint conditions belongs to the infeasible region. If the current solution is close to the constraint boundary, the penalty function value is very small, otherwise the penalty function value is very large. When the penalty method is used to solve the problem, an excellent penalty function $\psi(x)$ is very important because it can guide the iterative results to the feasible region, and at the same time, it transforms the constrained optimization problem into unconstrained optimization problem by punishing the infeasible solution.

When the penalty function is used to punish the infeasible solution, the idea can be taken as follows:

1) Death penalty: For an infeasible solution, directly adjust its fitness to a size that is very easy to be eliminated, and let it be eliminated directly.
2) Static penalty: Static penalty will reduce the fitness value of the individual who violates the constraint in the fitness function, but the penalty coefficient will not change with the iteration of the algorithm.
3) Dynamic penalty: The penalty coefficient will change with the iteration times, in order to ensure convergence, the penalty coefficient will gradually become larger.
4) Adaptive penalty: the idea of adaptive penalty is to get feedback from the iterative process of genetic algorithm, and automatically change the penalty function according to the solution.

In order to ensure that the greater the degree of deviation of the solution from the feasible region, the greater the penalty, this paper designs an adaptive penalty function based on the concept of offset. First construct the chromosome of genetic algorithm: $x_i = \{\delta_1, \delta_2, \ldots, \delta_j, \ldots, \delta_m, \delta_C\}$, where δ_j is scale factor, it is defined as:

$$\delta_j = \frac{d_j}{D} j = 1, 2, 3, \ldots \tag{11}$$

Then, the original constraint can be converted to:

$$s.t. \, 0 \leq g_j(x_i) \leq 1 j = 1, 2, 3 \ldots \tag{12}$$

$$h(x_i) - 1 = 0$$

where $g_j(x_i)$ and $h(x_i)$ is:

$$g_j(x_i) = \delta_j j = 1, 2, 3 \ldots \tag{13}$$

$$h(x_i) = \sum_{j-1,}^{m-1} \delta_j + \delta_C \tag{14}$$

Suppose that $g_z(x_j)$, $g_f(x_j)$ is the positive and negative offset value of the solution x_i to the inequality constraint function in the problem, respectively. Then we can use (15)–(16) to express it:

$$g_z(x_i) = max\{0, g_j(x_i) - 1\} j = 1, 2, 3 \ldots \tag{15}$$

$$g_f(x_i) = min\{0, g_j(x_i)\} \, j = 1, 2, 3 \ldots \tag{16}$$

Similarly, we have the positive and negative offset value of $h(x_j)$:

$$h_z(x_i) = max\{0, h(x_i) - 1\} \tag{17}$$

$$h_f(x_i) = min\{0, h(x_i) - 1\} \tag{18}$$

In the chromosome set $\{x_i\}$, we can find the infeasible solution set according to (15)–(18), it is denote as $\left\{x_j^{reject}\right\}$, thus, the positive and negative offset degrees constrained in Eq. (12) are introduced:

$$G_z(x_i) = \frac{g_z(x_i)}{max\left\{g_z\left(x_j^{reject}\right)\right\} - g_z(x_i)} \tag{19}$$

$$G_f(x_i) = g_f(x_i) \vee \frac{}{min\left\{g_f\left(x_j^{reject}\right)\right\} \vee -g_f(x_i)\vee} \tag{20}$$

$$H_z(x_i) = \frac{h_z(x_i)}{max\left\{h_z\left(x_j^{reject}\right)\right\} - h_z(x_i)} \tag{21}$$

$$H_f(x_i) = h_f(x_i) \vee \frac{}{min\{h_f\left(x_j^{reject}\right) \vee -h_f(x_i)\vee} \tag{22}$$

Based on (19)–(22) we can define $\phi(x_i), \xi(x_i)$ as the offset degree of the current solution x_i to the inequality constraint function, its expression is:

$$\phi_j(x_i) = \begin{cases} 1 & 0 \leq g_j(x_i) \leq 1 \\ e^{-G_z(x_i)} & g_j(x_i) > 1 \\ e^{-G_f(x_i)} & g_j(x_i) < 1 \end{cases} \tag{23}$$

$$\xi(x_i) = \begin{cases} 1 & h(x_i) = 1 \\ e^{-H_z(x_i)} & h(x_i) > 1 \\ e^{-H_f(x_i)} & h(x_i) < 1 \end{cases} \tag{24}$$

Finally, according to (23)–(24), we set the dynamic penalty function in the genetic algorithm as:

$$\psi(x_i) = \left(2 - \frac{1}{2}\left(\xi(x_i) + \frac{1}{m}\sum_{j=1}^{m}\phi_j(x_i)\right)\right)^{\beta} \tag{25}$$

where β is penalty factor. If x_i is a feasible solution, the value of the penalty function $\psi(x_i) = 1$. When x_i is not a feasible solution, $1 < \psi(x_i) < 2^{\beta}$, so as to ensure that the penalty function $\psi(x_i)$ can appropriately penalize the infeasible solution according to the constraints, and the greater the β is, the greater the penalty is.

By introducing a penalty function, the original constrained optimization problem is finally transformed into an unconstrained optimization problem:

$$minT\left(d_j, d_c\right) \times \psi(x_i)\, j = 1, 2, 3, \ldots \tag{26}$$

GSA-P algorithm Flow

In summary, the algorithm flow of GSA-P is as follows, and the flowchart is shown in Fig. 4:

1) Initialization: Define the scale of chromosomes as Y, the number of fog nodes as k, and the number of cloud servers as 1, so the length of each chromosome is equal to the number of fog nodes without fog manager plus the number of cloud servers, that is, $k - 1 + 1 = k$. Chromosomes are as defined in Sect. 3.2.1: $x_i = \{\delta_1, \delta_2, ..\delta_k\}$.
2) Use the penalty function as the fitness function in the genetic algorithm to calculate the fitness value of each chromosome x_i. The fitness function is expressed by:

$$f(x_i) = T\left(d_j, d_c\right) \times \psi(x_i) \tag{27}$$

3) Calculate the fitness value. Because there is no need to ensure the feasibility of the solution during the cross-mutation process, the chromosome can be cross-mutated by the random method.
4) Keep individuals with large fitness function values to ensure that the genes of outstanding individuals can be preserved.

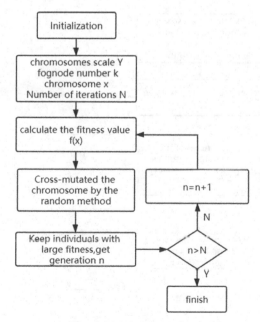

Fig. 4. GSA-P flow chart

4.3 GSA-R Algorithm

As mentioned in Sect. 3.2, in addition to the penalty function, a reasonable cross-mutation operator can be designed to ensure that the solution during the iteration is a feasible solution, in order to compare the GSA-P and the GSA-R.

This paper combines the GSA algorithm with the reasonable cross-mutation operator in reference [14], and obtains an algorithm GSA-R that solves the constrained optimization delay problem, which can ensure that the offspring generated after cross-mutation does not violate the constraint condition. The GSA-R algorithm flow is, and the flowchart is shown in Fig. 5:

1) Initialization: same as GSA-P
2) According to 10, calculate the fitness value of each chromosome x_i:

$$f(x_i) = T(d_j, d_C) \tag{28}$$

3) Select two parent individuals from individuals with appropriate fitness values, and then perform crossover operations. The relationship between offspring and parents in crossover operations is as follows:

$$x_1^s = \lambda \times x_1 + (1 - \lambda) \times x_2 \tag{29}$$

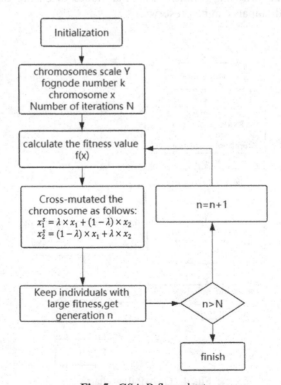

Fig. 5. GSA-R flow chart

$$x_2^s = (1 - \lambda) \times x_1 + \lambda \times x_2 \tag{30}$$

The above formula can ensure that the feasible solutions are still feasible solutions in the process of crossover.

4) According to the method proposed in reference [14] during mutation operation, boundary mutation and non-uniform mutation are used for feasible and infeasible solutions respectively.

5 Simulation Experiment

5.1 Simulation Environment

In the simulation, the number of fog nodes is set to 4, and a cloud server is added at the same time. The computing power of each fog node and cloud server is different. The data transmission capabilities of fog nodes, cloud servers, and management nodes are different. The packet loss rates are also independent of each other. The computing power and data transmission rate of fog nodes and cloud servers are set in reference [15]. The relevant parameters of the fog nodes and servers that handle real-time tasks are shown in Table 1.

Table 1. Parameters related to fog exclusive node and cloud server

Parameter type	F_1	F_2	F_3	F_4	C
CPU frequency (GHz)	4	4.5	5	3	10
Bandwidth (Mbps)	100	350	200	250	50
Packet loss rate	0.0232	0.014	0.0154	0.0175	0.02

In the simulation, the real-time task data uses the industrial Internet of Things data of the real-time path planning of industrial robots [53]. The amount of data transmitted for each path planning task is 125 KB, and the CPU cycles required to calculate the path planning task is 200M. The basic parameters of the GSA-P and GSA-R algorithms: the population size is 100, and the maximum number of iterations is 3000.

5.2 Results and Analysis

Comparison of Penalty Factors
When using the penalty function, the main problem is how to choose an appropriate penalty factor β. In order to verify whether the solution with the lowest delay obtained by the GSA-P algorithm is a feasible solution when the penalty factor β is different, this paper changes the β Range to simulate and analyze the GSA-P algorithm.

In the simulation, the value of β is set to {20, 15, 10, 8, 6, 4}, the GSA-P algorithm iterates 3000 times to obtain the lowest delay, and then when different values of β are

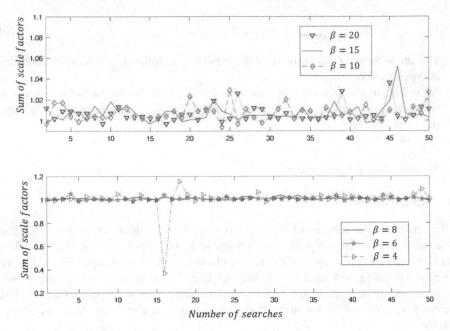

Fig. 6. Simulation diagram of GSA-P when different penalty factors

calculated, the GSA-P algorithm is calculated whether the solution with the lowest time delay meets the constraint conditions, count 50 results for comparison.

It can be seen from Fig. 6 that the greater the β is, the greater the probability that the solution is a feasible solution.

For example, when the penalty factor $\beta = 20$, due to the large penalty factor, the penalty for the infeasible solution is large, so the chromosome population will be more concentrated in the feasible region.

When β is a small value, for example, $\beta = 4$, the ethnic group will search in the infeasible region more actively, but because the penalty is small, the solution may be an infeasible solution.

We can also see from the line that when the value is 20, 15, 10, 8, the final solution in most cases is a feasible solution or an approximate feasible solution, but when the value is less than 6, due to the penalty is small, the result is very different from the feasible solution. Therefore, in order to ensure that the results are feasible, β should be set as larger than 6 as possible when solving.

Comparison of GSA-R and GSA-P Algorithms

According to Sect. 4.2.1, it is better that $\beta \geq 6$. But the value of β is not the bigger the better. This simulation compares GSA-P algorithm with GSA-R algorithm, and obtains a value upper limit of β. At the same time, the performance of GSA-P algorithm is compared with that of Joines&Houck method [16]. The simulation result is shown in Fig. 7.

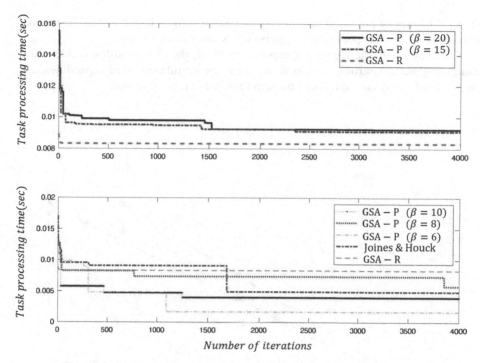

Fig. 7. Performance simulation diagram of GSA-R and GSA-P algorithms

It can be seen from Fig. 7 that when β is large, searching for the optimal solution to the infeasible region is discouraged, and it is more likely to converge to a local optimal solution.

As shown in Fig. 7, when the β of the GSA-P is set to 20 and 15, the final optimal delay obtained by GSA-P is larger than that of the GSA-R.

When β is small, the population will actively search for the optimal solution in the infeasible region, so it can find the global approximate optimal solution.

When the β of the GSA-P is set to 10, 8, and 6, the final optimal delay obtained is smaller than that of the GSA-R. When the penalty factor is set to 6, the total task processing delay of GSA-P algorithm is about 80% lower than that of GSA-R algorithm, and about 66% lower than that of Joines&Houck method.

Comparison of Different Computing Scenarios

This section compares the difference between cloud and fog calculation methods and other calculation methods. In the simulation, the number of iterations is 3000, the GSA-P algorithm is used, and the penalty factor $\beta = 6$.

It can be seen from Fig. 8 that the calculation method of cloud-fog collaboration is better than pure cloud or pure fog computing.

Although the cloud computing capability is powerful and can reduce the calculation delay of the task, the cloud server is generally far away from the smart factory, the network link bandwidth is limited, and there is a large communication delay. Therefore, the total latency of pure cloud computing task processing is larger, and as the number of tasks increases, the performance gap becomes more and more obvious.

Compared with the pure fog computing method, the cloud-and-fog collaborative computing method introduces a cloud server with powerful computing capabilities, and the total task delay can be reduced through reasonable task allocation.

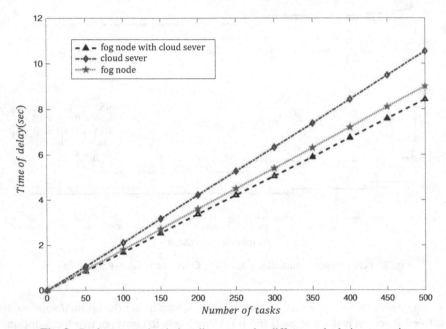

Fig. 8. Performance simulation diagram under different calculation scenarios

Compared with the traditional cloud computing method and fog computing method, the method adopted in this paper can reduce the total task delay by 18% and 7% when the number of users is 500, thereby ensuring the improvement of the efficiency of the smart factory.

6   Conclusion

For real-time tasks in a smart factory, this paper first establishes a time delay optimization model for real-time tasks in a smart factory based on the ARQ protocol. But this model is an NP problem with constraints, ordinary genetic algorithms cannot solve it. In this paper, the GSA-P algorithm is proposed on the basis of the GSA algorithm, which transforms the constraint problem into a non-constraint problem by designing a penalty function.

Simulation experiments show that when the penalty factor of the GSA-P is 6, the delay is reduced by 80% compared with the GSA-R, and 66% lower than the Joines& Houck method algorithm. When the number of users is 500, cloud and fog collaboration computing method used in this paper reduces the task delay by 18% compared with the traditional cloud computing method, and reduces the total task delay by 7% compared with the fog computing method.

In the future work, we will further discuss the resource scheduling problem in the intelligent factory. We will not only consider the processing of real-time tasks, but also study the processing methods of storage tasks.

Acknowledgement. This work was supported by the Science and Technology Commission of Shanghai Municipality under Grant 18511106500.

References

1. Yang, Y., Luo, X., Chu, X., et al.: Fog-Enabled Intelligent IoT Systems, pp. 29–31. Springer, Cham, Switzerland (2019). https://doi.org/10.1007/978-3-030-23185-9
2. Chiang, M., Zhang, T.: Fog and IoT: an overview of research opportunities. IEEE Internet Things J. **3**(6), 854–864 (2016)
3. Mourtzis, D., Vlachou, E., Milas, N.: Industrial big data as a result of IoT adoption in manufacturing. In: ES, pp. 290–295 (2016)
4. Gazis, V., Leonardi, A., Mathioudakis, K., et al.: Components of fog computing in an industrial internet of things context. In: 2015 12th Annual IEEE International Conference on Sensing, Communication, and Networking - Workshops (SECON Workshops). IEEE (2015)
5. Fazio, M., Celesti, A., Ranjan, R., et al.: Open issues in scheduling microservices in the cloud. IEEE Cloud Comput. **3**(5), 81–88 (2016)
6. Chen, N., Yang, Y., Zhang, T., et al.: Fog as a service technology. IEEE Commun. Mag. 1–7 (2018)
7. Skarlat, O., Nardelli, M., Schulte, S., et al.: Resource provisioning for IoT services in the fog. SOCA **11**(4), 427–443 (2016)
8. Luxiu, Y., Juan, L., Haibo, L.: Tasks scheduling and resource allocation in fog computing based on containers for smart manufacture. IEEE Trans. Industr. Inform. 1–1 (2018)
9. Gedawy, H., Habak, K., Harras, K., et al.: [IEEE 2018 IEEE International Conference on Edge Computing (EDGE) - San Francisco, CA (2018.7.2–2018.7.7)] 2018 IEEE International Conference on Edge Computing (EDGE) - An Energy-Aware IoT Femtocloud System, pp. 58–65 (2018)
10. Wei, G., Vasilakos, A.V., Zheng, Y., et al.: A game-theoretic method of fair resource allocation for cloud computing services. J. Supercomputing **54**(2), 252–269 (2010)
11. Zhan, Z.H., Liu, X.F., Gong, Y.J., et al.: Cloud computing resource scheduling and a survey of its evolutionary approaches. ACM Comput. Surv. **47**(4), 1–33 (2015)
12. Miettinen, A.P., Nurminen, J.K.: Energy efficiency of mobile clients in cloud computing. In: Usenix Conference on Hot Topics in Cloud Computing USENIX Association (2010)
13. Li, Y., Li, J., et al.: The research on ARP protocol based authentication mechanism. In: International Conference on Applied Mathematics, Simulation and Modelling (AMSM) (2016)
14. Ximing, I., Haoyu, Q., Wen, L.: Genetic algorithm for solving constrained optimization problem. Comput. Eng. **36**(014), 147–149 (2010)
15. Xiao, M., Hassan, M.A., Wei, Q., Chen S.: Help your mobile applications with fogcomputing. In: Seattle, WA, USA : 2015 12th Annual IEEE International Conference on Sensing, Communication, and Networking - Workshops (SECON Workshops), pp. 1–6 (2015)
16. Ichalewicz, Z.: A survey of constraint handling techniques in evolutionary computation methods. In: Proceedings of the 4th Annual Conference on Evolutionary Programming, pp. 135–155. MIT Press, Cambridge (1995)

An Efficient Network-Wide Reliable Broadcast Protocol for Medical Sensor Networks

Xinguo Wang, Run Hu[✉], Lutao Wang, Dongrui Gao, Yuyuan Su, and Bin Yang

Chengdu University of Information Technology, Chengdu 610225, People's Republic of China
{wxg,wanglt,gdr1987}@cuit.edu.cn, seeinghr@163.com,
774816068@qq.com, 763215080@qq.com

Abstract. Medical sensor networks provide rich contextual information and alerting mechanisms with continuous monitoring. Broadcast is an important communication mode for medical sensor networks. Most existing broadcast protocols for wireless sensor networks use a minimal virtual backbone subnetwork to broadcast packets, which can minimize the total number of transmissions. However, since the unreliability of wireless link is not considered, the broadcast efficiency of these protocols is not high in factual networks. This paper proposes an efficient networkwide reliable broadcast protocol (ENWRB), which adopts network coding scheme to reduce the retransmissions in single-hop broadcast and a link quality-aware virtual backbone election algorithm to generate the more efficient broadcast backbone. Simulation results show that, under the same premise of ensuring all nodes receive broadcast packets successfully, the efficiency of ENWRB is higher than that of Hierarchical CDS-based Algorithm (HCA) greatly.

Keywords: Network-wide reliable broadcast · Medical sensor networks · Virtual backbone · Network coding

1 Introduction

The combination of wireless sensors and sensor networks with computing and artificial intelligence research has built a cross-disciplinary concept of ambient intelligence in order to overcome the challenges we face in everyday life. Wearable and implantable body sensor network systems [1] allow people to be monitored during all their everyday activities. Medical sensor networks [2] can help people by providing healthcare services such as medical monitoring, memory enhancement, control of home appliances, medical data access, and communication in emergency situations. Constant monitoring will increase early detection of emergency conditions and diseases for at risk patients and also provide wide range of healthcare services for people with various degrees of cognitive and physical disabilities. Network-wide broadcasting, is an important communication mode in medical sensor networks, where the packets originate from any node need to be delivered to the other nodes. It can be widely utilized by various of network services, such as notification, paging, routing discovery and etc. A network-wide broadcast protocol must ensure that all nodes can receive broadcast packets correctly, which means

© ICST Institute for Computer Sciences, Social Informatics and Telecommunications Engineering 2021
Published by Springer Nature Switzerland AG 2021. All Rights Reserved
L. Peñalver and L. Parra (Eds.): Industrial IoT 2020, LNICST 365, pp. 34–44, 2021.
https://doi.org/10.1007/978-3-030-71061-3_3

that the whole network needs to be covered fully, and the total number of transmissions should be reduced as much as possible to improve the broadcasting efficiency.

At this stage, there is a rich body of researches on network-wide broadcasting protocols [3−9], these can be roughly divided into the following three categories, namely network flooding, probability-based forwarding, backbone-based forwarding and so on [10]. In network flooding protocols, all nodes participate in forwarding broadcast packets, which can achieve full network coverage with very high probability at the cost of introducing too many redundant transmissions. In probability-based forwarding, each node is assigned a probability of participating in packet forwarding. Although it can reduce the number of transmissions, it is difficult to guarantee the full coverage by selecting an appropriate forwarding probability. In backbone-based forwarding, a connected subnetwork is established, where each node is either a backbone node, or has at least one back-bone neighbor. When the nodes in the backbone subnetwork participate in forwarding broadcast packets, all the other nodes can be covered fully.

Obviously, the smaller the size of such a virtual backbone network, the fewer the total transmissions and so the higher the broadcast efficiency. Therefore, the existing studies mainly focus on how to generate the smallest virtual backbone network. In [11], the authors have already proved that generating the smallest virtual backbone even with the global topology information is a NP (Non-deterministic Polynomial) - hard problem. The subsequent studies are committed to approximate optimal algorithms instead. Moreover, it is costly to obtain the global topology knowledge in large-scale medical sensor networks. In [12], the authors proposed a distributed backbone election algorithm only based on the local topology information.

However, these works all assume that the wireless links are reliable. In factual networks, due to the ubiquitous link errors, there will be a large of retransmissions in order to achieve really full coverage. We argue that broadcast forwarding based on the smallest virtual backbone cannot minimize the total number of transmissions any more. In this paper, our contributions are twofold. Firstly, we introduce the network coding technique into the retransmitting procedure and reduce the transmissions of single-hop broadcasting greatly through a greedy coding scheme. Secondly, we analyze how many transmissions are needed for each node to deliver the broadcasting packet to all of its neighbors successfully. Finally, this new metric is used in a distributed backbone election algorithm, where the node with a small metric value is preferred to be elected as a backbone node. Extensive simulation results show that the proposed network-wide broadcasting protocol can reduce the total number of transmissions greatly.

The rest of this paper is organized as follows. Section 2 studies how to use network-coding to reduce the retransmissions of the single-hop reliable broadcasting. Section 3 analyzes the performance gain achieved by network-coding. Section 4 proposes the backbone-based network-wide broadcasting protocol formally. Section 5 presents the simulation results. In final, Sect. 6 concludes this paper and discusses the future research direction.

2 Single-Hop Broadcast

In this section, we consider the single-hop reliable broadcast problem for medical sensor networks, where a sender s needs to reliably deliver M pieces of packets to N direct neighbors, which are denoted by $R = \{R_1, R_2, \ldots, R_N\}$. In traditional protocols, sender s has to retransmit each packet until all neighbors have acknowledged that they have received it successfully. It is costly to complete reliable broadcast delivery through such a stupid retransmission mechanism.

Since the link states are independent of each other, different neighbors may request sender s to retransmit the different packets, resulting in too many retransmissions. If these packets have the same length, sender s can encode multiple packets asked by different neighbors into one packet and only retransmit the coded one. Combined with the previously received packets, each neighbor can recover one original packet from the coded packet. By utilizing this gain, network coding can reduce the number of retransmissions and improve the broadcast efficiency greatly. The more packets encoded, the more gain achieved [13].

Specifically, each sender uses an acknowledgement matrix $A_{N \times M}$, to record the reception status of N neighbors about M packets. If neighbor i has acknowledged the successful reception of packet j, $a_{i,j}$ is equal to 1. Otherwise, $a_{i,j}$ is equal to 0. Senders uses XOR coding to encode $m(m \leq M)$ packets $P_1, P_2, \ldots, P_m$ into one packet $\oplus(P_1, P_2, \ldots, P_m)$, which is equal to $P_1 \oplus P_2 \cdots \oplus P_m$. A neighbor can recover the missing packet by using $\oplus(P_1, P_2, \ldots, P_m)$ to execute XOR operation with the previously received $m - 1$ packets serially.

As shown in Fig. 1, five packets need to be delivered to all three neighbors. For the convenience of analysis, we assume that there is no retransmission error. If no coding is applied, five transmissions are needed since all five packets are asked by at least one neighbor. If coding is applied, sender s needs to retransmit $\oplus(P_1, P_2)$, $\oplus(P_3, P_4)$, and P_5, sum to three transmissions. Thus, network coding can reduce the total transmissions of a reliable single-hop broadcasting.

	P1	P2	P3	P4	P5
R1	1	0	1	0	1
R2	1	1	0	1	1
R3	0	1	1	1	0

Fig. 1. Reception status matrix for reliable broadcast

In fact, there is a better coding solution for the scenario in Fig. 1. Sender s only needs to retransmit $\oplus(P_1, P_2, P_3)$ and $\oplus(P_4, P_5)$, where two transmissions are enough. The authors in [14] have already proved that finding the best coding solution based on reception matrix is also a NP-hard problem. Due to the limitation of XOR coding, sender s cannot encode multiple original packets that are requested by the same neighbor into one packet. Otherwise, this neighbor cannot decode it. In addition, an original packet that is requested by more neighbors helps to obtain a larger coding gain. Here, we propose the following heuristic coding algorithm based on greedy strategy.

Algorithm 1 The coding algorithm based on greedy strategy

1: Step1: $S \leftarrow \Phi$, $C \leftarrow \Phi$

2: Step2: Execute the following sub-operations circularly until (1) can't find any eligible packet

　3: (1) find the packet p_i based on the following rules:

　4: 　a) exclude the packets asked by any neighbor in S

　5: 　b) maximize the number of neighbors that needs p_i

　6: 　c) minimize i, the index of p_i, based on a) and b)

　7: (2) add p_i into set C

　8: (3) add all the neighbors that request to retransmit p_i into set S

　9: (4) set column i of matrix A to be all-one

10: Step3: encode all the packets in C into a new packet p_j

Algorithm 1 describes the process of encoding multiple original packets into the one packet. C denotes the set of original packets to be encoded and S denotes the set of neighbors that can decode the packet successfully. In line 1, these two sets are both initialized to be empty. From line 3 to line 6, picks out the packet that is not requested by any neighbor already in S and has the largest coding gain by far. In line 7 and line 8, p_i and the neighbors that request retransmit p_i are added into C and S, respectively. Then, the reception matrix is updated. These operations are executed circularly until there is no longer any eligible packet. Finally, all the packets in C are encoded into one packet. This packet becomes a new original packet and only needs to be delivered to a subset of N neighbors.

3　Network Coding Gain

In this section, we analyze the gain brought by network coding. We assume that the packet error ratios between sender s and N neighbors are $e_1, e_2, \ldots, e_N$, respectively. Without network coding, sender s needs to retransmit an original packet once any neighbor fails to receive it. For a generic link, if sender s transmits k packets, the probability that neighbor i can receive one or more packets is equal to $1 - e_i^k$. Due to the independency of link states, the probability that N neighbors all receive at least one packet from k packets are given by $\prod_{i=1}^{N}(1 - e_i^k)$. Next, the probability that sender s needs to transmit k packets to ensure that all N neighbors receive at least one packet can be calculated as $\prod_{i=1}^{N}(1 - e_i^k) - \prod_{i=1}^{N}(1 - e_i^{k-1})$. In final, we can get the expected value of the total number of transmissions to guarantee all N neighbors to receive M original packets, which is given by the following expression,

$$T_x(N, M) = M \sum_{k=1}^{\infty} k \left(\prod_{i=1}^{N}\left(1 - e_i^k\right) - \prod_{i=1}^{N}\left(1 - e_i^{k-1}\right) \right) \tag{1}$$

$$= M \sum_{l_1, l_2, \ldots, l_N} \frac{(-1)^{\left(\sum_{i=1}^{N} l_i\right) - 1}}{1 - \prod_{i=1}^{N}\left(e_i^{l_i}\right)} \tag{2}$$

where l_i is a binary variable and $\sum_{i=1}^{N} l_i > 0$.

Next, we analyze how many transmissions needed by a single-hop reliable broadcast when applying network coding mechanism. Without loss of generality, we assume that $e_1 \leq e_2 \cdots \leq e_N$ and $\sum_{i=1}^{N} e_i \leq 1$.

Theorem 1. The minimal number of coded packets needed by delivering M original packets to N neighbors successfully is equal to M_{e_N}.

Proof. The proof is straightforward. Since each neighbor can recover only one original packet from a coded packet, the neighbor whose link error ratio is e_N needs to at least receive M_{e_N} coded packets to recover all M original packets.

Theorem 2. If the condition $\sum_{i=1}^{N} e_i < 1$ is satisfied, N neighbors all can recover M original packets after receiving M_{e_N} coded packets successfully.

Proof. If $\sum_{i=1}^{N} a_{i,j} \geq N - 1$ for $\forall j$ the coding algorithm will select one original packet for all the neighbors in $R - \{r_i | \sum_{j=1}^{M} a_{i,j} = M\}$. Then, N neighbors can recover all M original packets after receiving M_{e_N} coded packets. Otherwise, without loss of generality, assume $\exists j', \sum_{i=1}^{N} a_{i,j'} < N - 1$ and $\forall j \neq j', \sum_{i=1}^{N} a_{i,j} \geq N - 1$. Since $\sum_{i=1}^{N} e_i \leq 1$, $A_{N \times M}$ has $N - 1 - \sum_{i=1}^{N} a_{i,j}$ all-one columns so far. Therefore, N neighbors all can recover M original packets after receiving M_{e_N} coded packets successfully.

Sender s first broadcasts M original packets. Then, Algorithm 1 will select one missing packet for each neighbor who have not received all M packets at each round. All M_{e_N} coded packets can be divided into N batches according to the number of e_N that can recover some packet. The numbers of these batches are $M_{e_1}, M_{(e_2 - e_1)}, \ldots, M_{(e_N - e_{N-1})}$. Since the first M_{e_1} coded packets are delivered to N neighbors, the expected number of transmissions is $T_x(N, M_{e_1})$. The second $M_{(e_1 - e_2)}$ coded packets are only delivered to $N - 1$ neighbors, and the expected number of transmissions is $T_x(N - 1, M_{(e_2 - e_1)})$. Likewise, the final $M_{(e_N - e_{N-1})}$ coded packets are only delivered to 1 neighbor and the expected number of transmissions is $T_x(1, M_{(e_N - e_{N-1})})$. Therefore, the total number of transmissions of a single-hop broadcast using network coding can be estimated as the following expressions,

$$T_X^{NC}(N, M) = M + \sum_{i=1}^{N} T_X(i, M(e_{N+1-i} - e_{N-i})) \tag{3}$$

4 Network-Wide Broadcast

In network-wide broadcast, packet needs to be delivered to all the nodes of the whole network. When taking transmission errors into account, the optimization goal of back-bone based network-wide broadcast is no longer to minimize the number of virtual back-bone nodes, but to minimize the total number of transmissions. In this section, we will propose an efficient network-wide reliable broadcast (ENWRB) protocol based on network coding and backbone network, which can reduce the total number of transmissions greatly.

Like the other distributed backbone election algorithms [15], ENWRB protocol is divided into an initial phase and a pruning phase. In the initial phase, a backbone network with high connectivity is constructed according to the 2-hop neighbor information. In the pruning phase, unnecessary nodes with low broadcast efficiency will be deleted from the initial backbone network. For description convenience, we denote the set of 1-hop neighbor nodes of node u by $N(u)$.

In the initial phase, each node broadcasts *HELLO* packets, which includes *ID* information of itself and its 1-hop neighbors. If node u has two neighbors, for nodes v and w example, which are not adjacent to each other, it indicates that v and w may need to forward packets through u. Thus, node u becomes the initial backbone node. It is obvious that this mechanism can generate a backbone subnetwork. As shown in Fig. 2, nodes b, c, f and h form the initial backbone. However, there are many redundant backbone nodes, which will reduce the efficiency of network-wide broadcast.

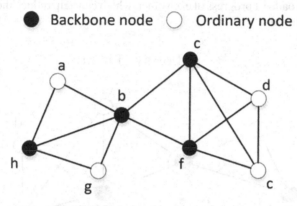

Fig. 2. Initial virtual backbone network

In the second phase, each backbone node elected in the initial phase will decide to whether be a final backbone node or not according to 2-hop topology information and the efficiency as a broadcast backbone, which is defined by the following expression,

$$\eta = \frac{N \times M}{T_X^{NC}(N.M)} \tag{4}$$

The larger the η value, the higher the priority of being a final backbone node. Thus, ENWRB protocol prefers to choose the nodes with high node degrees and good links. The packet error ratios can be obtained through counting the correct reception ratio or signal strength of the periodical *HELLO* packets. A generic backbone node u decides to whether be a final backbone node according to the following rules,

a. If there is another initial backbone node v, which can cover all the 1-hop neighbors of node u, (namely $N(u) - \{v\} \subset N(v)$), and the priority of node v is higher than u, then u will quit the election of backbone node.

b. If there are another two initial backbone nodes v and w, which are adjacent to each other and they can cover all the 1-hop neighbors of node u cooperatively, (namely $N(u) - \{v; w\} \subset N(v) \cup N(w)$), and the priorities of nodes v and w are higher than u, then u will quit the election of backbone node.

As shown in Fig. 3, the high packet error ratio between node c and d leads to a low broadcast efficiency of node c, and so node c will not become the final backbone node. In the protocol proposed in [15], node h will not become a backbone node, but h will become a backbone node in our protocol, which can avoid a large number of retransmissions due to the worse link between node b to g. Therefore, nodes b, f, and h constitute the final virtual backbone subnetwork. The link layer protocol usually sends *HELLO* packets and contains the information needed by generating the virtual backbone network, so the proposed mechanism does not introduce an extra overhead. In fact, multiple backbone nodes that cover the same ordinary node redundantly can cooperate with each other by overhearing the broadcast progress of each other, which can help reduce the total number of transmissions further.

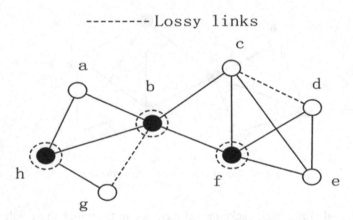

Fig. 3. Final virtual backbone network

5 Simulation Results

In this section, we evaluate the performance of proposed protocol. Firstly, we compare the number of transmissions of reliable single-hop broadcast with or without network coding on the MATLAB platform. The number of neighbors is set as 20 and 10, while the number of original packets is set as 100 and 50, respectively. The packet error ratio of each wire-less link is randomly generated [16, 17], where the minimal ratio is equal to 0 and the maximal ratio ranges from 0.01 to 0.05. The results shown in Fig. 4 are the average values of 100 simulations. In general, the total transmissions increase with the number of neighbors and the number of original packets, and the results with network coding is much less than without network coding. For example, when $N = 20, M = 100$, and the maximal packet error ratio is equal to 0.05, the total number of transmissions

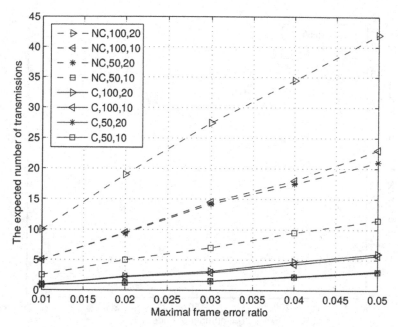

Fig. 4. Expected number of transmissions for single-hop broadcast

without network coding is approximately equal to 42.7, meanwhile the total number with network coding is approximately equal to 7.3.

Next, we compare the performance of ENWRB protocol with HCA (Hierarchical CDS-based Algorithm) proposed in [12], in terms of the size of backbone subnetwork and the total number of transmissions of network-wide broadcast. We implement these two protocols based on NS (Network Simulation) platform. For the sake of fairness, it is assumed that HCA also adopts the single-hop broadcast mechanism based on network coding to reduce the number of transmissions of single-hop broadcast. All nodes are distributed randomly within a square area, where the length is 200 m. The communication radius of each node is equal to 50 m. The maximum packet error ratio of the link is 0.05, and M is set to 100. The source nodes of broadcasting packets are randomly generated and all the original packets have the same length. The forwarding nodes can distinguish these packets according to the ID of source node and the unique sequence number of packets.

The numbers of backbone nodes are given in Fig. 5. We can see that ENWRB generates a slightly larger backbone sub-network than HCA generally in order to achieve higher broadcast efficiency. This phenomenon is more obvious in networks with lower node densities. The total numbers of transmissions of broadcasting an original packet to all nodes in the entire network are shown in Fig. 6, where each point is the average value of 10000 original packets. In general, the efficiency of ENWRB is higher than HCA, since its total number of transmissions is less than HCA. Such an advantage increases with the network density. When the number of network nodes increases to 200, the total number of transmissions of ENWRB is only about 72% of HCA.

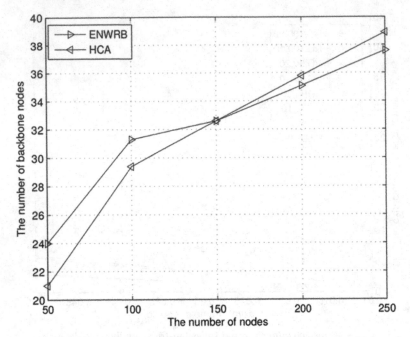

Fig. 5. Number of backbone nodes for network-wide broadcast

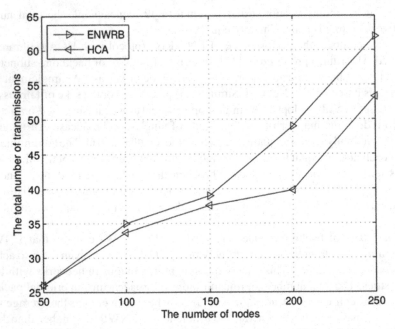

Fig. 6. Total number of transmissions for network-wide broadcast

6 Conclusion

In this paper, we study the network-wide reliable broadcast problem. Firstly, network coding is used in the single-hop broadcast to reduce the number of retransmissions. Meanwhile, the corresponding gain brought by network coding is analyzed. Then, based on the single-hop broadcast mechanism, a network-wide reliable broadcast protocol based on virtual backbone network is proposed to reduce the total number of transmissions across the network. The simulation results show that ENWRB has higher broadcasting efficiency than HCA, under the premise that all nodes in the whole network should receive broadcast packets correctly. Due to the network coding mechanism may increase the time of completing the broadcast of the whole network, so in our future works, we will take some measures to decrease the delay of ENWRB effectively and efficiently.

Acknowledgments. This paper is supported by Sichuan Science and Technology Program under 2019YFG0196 and 2020YFG0442.

References

1. Movassaghi, S., Abolhasan, M., Lipman, J., Smith, D., Jamalipour, A.: Wireless body area networks: a survey. IEEE Commun. Surv. Tutorials **16**(3), 1658–1686 (2014) Third Quarter
2. Ko, J., Lu, C., Srivastava, M.B., Stankovic, J.A., Terzis, A., Welsh, M.: Wireless sensor networks for healthcare. In: Proceedings of the IEEE, vol. 98, no. 11, pp. 1947–1960, November 2010
3. Tavli, B., Heinzelman, W.B.: Energy and spatial reuse efficient network-wide real-time data broadcasting in mobile ad hoc networks. IEEE Trans. Mobile Comput. **5**(10), 1297–1312 (2006)
4. Hurni, P., Braun, T.: An energy-efficient broadcasting scheme for unsynchronized wireless sensor MAC protocols. In: 2010 Seventh International Conference on Wireless On-demand Network Systems and Services (WONS), Kranjska Gora, pp. 39–46 (2010)
5. Lichtblau, B., Redlich, J.: Network-wide broadcasts for wireless mesh networks with regard to reliability. In: 2012 19th IEEE Symposium on Communications and Vehicular Technology in the Benelux (SCVT), Eindhoven, pp. 1–6 (2012)
6. Lichtblau, B., Dittrich, A.: Probabilistic breadth-first search - a method for evaluation of network-wide broadcast protocols. In: 2014 6th International Conference on New Technologies, Mobility and Security (NTMS), Dubai, pp. 1–6 (2014)
7. Zhang, X., Yan, F., Li, C., Ding, Q.: Coverage efficiency-based broadcast protocol for asynchronous wireless sensor networks. IEEE Wirel. Commun. Lett. **5**(1), 76–79 (2016)
8. Zhang, X., Jia, X., Yan, F.: Dynamic delegation-based efficient broadcast protocol for asynchronous wireless sensor networks. IEEE Commun. Lett. **20**(6), 1195–1198 (2016)
9. Wang, X., Wu, X., Zhang, X., Liang, Y.: An energy-efficient network-wide broadcast protocol for asynchronous wireless sensor networks. IEEE Wirel. Commun. Lett. **7**(6), 918–921 (2018)
10. Wisitpongphan, N., Tonguz, O.K., Parikh, J.S., Mudalige, P., Bai, F., Sadekar, V.: Broadcast storm mitigation techniques in vehicular ad hoc networks. IEEE Wirel. Commun. **14**(6), 84–96 (2007)
11. Hong, J., Cao, J., Li, W., Lu, S., Chen, D.: Minimum-transmission broadcast in uncoordinated duty-cycled wireless ad hoc networks. IEEE Trans. Veh. Technol. **59**(1), 307–318 (2010)

12. Tang, B., Ye, B., Hong, J., You, K., Lu, S.: Distributed low redundancy broadcast for unco-ordinated duty-cycled WANETs. In: 2011 IEEE Global Telecommunications Conference, pp. 1–5. IEEE (2011)
13. Nguyen, D., Tran, T., Nguyen, T., Bose, B.: Wireless broadcast using network coding. IEEE Trans. Veh. Technol. **58**(2), 914–925 (2009)
14. Chi, K., Jiang, X., Ye, B., Horiguchi, S.: Efficient network coding-based loss recovery for reliable multicast in wireless networks. IEICE Trans. Commun. **E93.B**(4), 971–981 (2010)
15. Dai, F., Wu, J.: An extended localized algorithm for connected dominating set formation in ad hoc wireless networks. IEEE Trans. Parallel Distrib. Syst. **15**(10), 908–920 (2004)
16. Basagni, S., Mastrogiovanni, M., Panconesi, A., Petrioli, C.: Localized protocols for ad hoc clustering and backbone formation: a performance comparison. IEEE Trans. Parallel Distrib. Syst. **17**(4), 292–306 (2006)
17. Kumar, G., Kumar Rai, M.: An energy efficient and optimized load balanced localization method using CDS with one-hop neighbourhood and genetic algorithm in WSNs. J. Network Comput. Appl. **78**, 73–82 (2017)

Session 2

Session 2

Beyond Anchors: Optimal Equality Constraints in Cooperative Localization

Ping Zhang[1,2(✉)], Fei Cheng[1,2], and Jian Lu[1,2]

[1] The Key Laboratory of Computer Application Technology,
Anhui Polytechnic University, Wuhu 241000, China
{pingzhang,feicheng}@ahpu.edu.cn
[2] The School of Information Science and Engineering, Southeast University,
Nanjing 210096, China
lujian1980@seu.edu.cn

Abstract. Although anchors are the most common in cooperative localizations, they are not the optimal in the class of equality constraints which provide the global reference information for deriving absolute locations. Using Cramér-Rao lower bound (CRLB) to evaluate the localization accuracy, this paper derives the optimal equality constraints that achieve the lowest CRLB trace under given constraint number, and analyzes the feasibility of constructing the optimal constraints before knowing the node ground truth locations. Simulations compare the performance between the anchor-type constraints and the optimal ones, and suggest a cooperative localization algorithm by using the optimal equality constraints.

Keywords: Cramér-Rao Lower Bound (CRLB) · Equality constraints · Maximum Likelihood Estimate (MLE) · Singular Value Decomposition (SVD) · Wireless Sensor Networks (WSN)

1 Introduction

Knowing the locations of a large number of nodes is essential to performing location based service (LBS) in wireless sensor networks (WSN), 5G, and Internet of things (IoT) [1,2]. Compared with the traditional localization approaches such as global positioning system (GPS), cooperative localization introduces the measurements between the unknown nodes to construct a lowcost localization strategy, which can be implemented during internode communications [3,4]. But internode measurements provide only the node location information relative to each other. To get the absolution locations, global constrains, *e.g.*, anchor locations, should be introduced to fix the relative locations onto a coordinate system [5].

Restricted to the anchor-type constraints, where to deploy the anchors is critical for ensuring the localizability and improving localization accuracy, which is

L. Peñalver and L. Parra (Eds.): Industrial IoT 2020, LNICST 365, pp. 47–59, 2021.
https://doi.org/10.1007/978-3-030-71061-3_4

known as anchor selection problem. Based on the exhaustive search of all possible anchor locations, some empirical results are derived to offer some guidance on anchor deployment [6]. Despite the difficulty in finding the optimal anchors, whether introducing anchors is the optimal for constructing global constraints is questionable.

This paper extends the anchor-type constraints to general equality constraints, and derives the optimal ones that can provide the most accurate location estimate. The accuracy of the location estimate is quantified by performing Cramér-Rao lower bound (CRLB) analysis [7] under given internode measurements and global constraints, which offers the lower bound of the variance of any unbiased estimate and is independent of specific localization algorithms. From the CRLB analysis, it can be found that anchor-type constraints are far from the optimal in terms of localization accuracy.

The practicability of constructing optimal equality constraints is also considered in this paper. Compared with the anchor-type constraints which are constructing by locating a small portion of the nodes, constructing the optimal equality constraints needs the ground truth node locations apriori. Actually, it is proved in this paper that no global constraints can be taken as the optimal for all possible node locations. Therefore, it is suggested that the rough prior locations of the nodes can be used to derive suboptimal equality constraints. In our prior work [8], a specific case under minimally constraint number has been investigated for calibrating rough GPS locations, which is extended to general equality constraints in this paper.

The following of this paper is organized as follows. Section 3 reviews the literature related to the problem. Section 3 introduces the internode measurement model, and provides the CRLB under general equality constraints. Section 4 derives the optimal equality constraints and discuss how to use the optimal equality constraints in practice. Simulations in Sect. 5 compare the anchor-type constraints with the optimal ones, and exhibit the performance of the maximum likelihood estimates of the node locations under the optimal equality constraints.

2   Related Work

In cooperative localization, the measurements between the nodes can be used to aid the location estimate [9], so that the nodes at unknowns locations can be located in a multi-hop manner under the existence of a small portion of anchors/references (*i.e.*, nodes at known absolute locations) [9,10]. This greatly alleviates the burden on the task of node localization as opposed to manual calibrations, or reduces the cost on the devices as opposed to being equipped with global positioning system (GPS) modules.

The above process is conventionally called anchor-based localization, where abundant algorithms are built by fusing the relative location information contained in internode measurements and absolute location information embodied in anchor positions [11–17]. These algorithms provide the absolute location estimates for unknown nodes, but it is somewhat complicated to answer the question that which information dominates the localization accuracy. Conventionally, one may fix the anchors and investigate the influence from the internode measurements, where the Cramér-Rao lower bound (CRLB) analysis serves as a convenient tool [9]. Or on the contrary, one can also fix the internode measurements to investigate how the number and positions of anchors affect the localization accuracy, which is the well-known anchor selection problem [18–21]. Although these approaches help to answer that question in some extent, the relatively high cost in producing/deploying the anchors and the difficulty in finding the optimal anchor deployment pose challenges in the design of efficient and applicable anchor-based localization system.

On the other hand, anchor-free Localization uses only internode measurements, where no anchors are involved [22]. Since the internode measurements involve merely relative location information, only the network's *relative configuration* [23], or called *relative map* [24], can be estimated, while the network's transformation uncertainty, including global translation, rotation, reflection and in some cases scaling, can not be specified yet. To investigate the relative configuration, statistical shape analysis methods are introduced to explore the "shape" of the network [5], where the optimal minimally constraint system is derived to specify the location, orientation and sometimes scaling of the network [8]. However, in existing work, the optimality is restricted to the minimally constraint systems, which usually 3 for 2-dimensional rigid network. For other equality numbers, the optimality has not been explored.

3   Problem Formation

3.1   Internode Measurements

Let us consider n nodes, whose locations are $\mathbf{s}_i = [s_{i,x}, s_{i,y}]^T$, $i = 1, 2, \ldots, n$, distributed on a two-dimensional plane. Each node, say the ith node, emits wireless signal with a preset strength P_i (dBm), and any other node, say the jth node, receives the signal and records the received signal strength (RSS) P_j (dBm). When both the emission strength P_i and the received strength P_j are available, the signal attenuation $r_{i,j} = P_i - P_j$ can be measured, which follows the signal attenuation model

$$r_{i,j} = 10\alpha \log_{10} \|\mathbf{s}_i - \mathbf{s}_j\| + \epsilon_{i,j}, \ (i,j) \in \mathcal{E} \tag{1}$$

where $\alpha > 2$ is a path-loss exponent, $\| \cdot \|$ denotes Euclidean norm, and $\epsilon_{i,j}$, $(i,j) \in \mathcal{E}$, are independent and identically distributed Gaussian noises with mean 0 and variance σ^2. $\mathcal{E}$ is the set of the connected edges, where $(i,j) \in \mathcal{E}$ means the signal emitted from the ith signal can be received by the jth node. Here, the measurements are assumed to be symmetrical, so that any $(i,j) \in \mathcal{E}$ is required to fulfill $i < j$ for simplicity.

3.2   Global Constraints

The internode measurement model (1) specifies only the relative location information between the nodes. To get the absolute locations, global constraints, or named global reference information are needed. In this letter, the global constraints are restricted to equality constants

$$g(s) = 0 \qquad (2)$$

where the location vector $s = [s_1^T, s_2^T, \ldots, s_n^T]^T$, and the constraint number is k. For example, when anchor-type constraints are chosen, the equality constraints can be represented as

$$g(s) = [s_j - a_j]_{j \in \mathcal{A}} = 0 \qquad (3)$$

where a_j, $j \in \mathcal{A}$, are known anchor locations, $\mathcal{A}$ is the index set of the anchors, and the constraints number is twice of the number of the anchors.

The introduction of global constraints contributes both the network localizability and localization accuracy. For a two-dimensional localization problem, when the internode (distance) measurements are sufficient to make the network globally rigid, e.g., fully connected, only 3 equality constraints are required to specify the two-dimensional location and orientation (up to a global reflection) of the network. When the internode measurements are not sufficient, more equality constraints are required. The minimum number of the equality constraints (2) to make the network rigid, named minimally constrained system (MCS) [23], depends on the spatial dimension and network connectivity, where the performance has been explored in [8]. But due to the internode measurements noise, introducing more global constraints might be required to improve the localization accuracy, where the optimal ones are explored in this letter. Notably, we do not use the equality constraints to identify the local/global reflections, where the latter can identified by some inequality constraints or proper initials in iterative localization algorithms.

3.3   CRLB

Constrained CRLB analysis is performed on the measurement model (1) under the constraints (2). In statistics, CRLB serves as a lower bound for the variance of any unbiased estimate, and can be asymptotically achieved by the maximum likelihood estimate (MLE). To avoid the discussion of specific localization algorithms, the performance metric in this paper is set as the CRLB trace, which serves as a benchmark for the performance of most localization algorithms [3, 15, 25].

Under the measurement model (1), the log-likelihood function of s is

$$l(s) = \frac{1}{2\sigma^2} \sum_{(i,j) \in \mathcal{E}} \left(10\alpha \log_{10} \|s_i - s_j\| - r_{i,j} \right)^2 + c \qquad (4)$$

where the constant c is independent of s. This log-likelihood function leads to the (Fisher information matrix) FIM of s as

$$\mathbf{J} = \mathrm{E}\left[\frac{\partial l(\mathbf{s})}{\partial \mathbf{s}}\frac{\partial l(\mathbf{s})}{\partial \mathbf{s}^T}\right] = \sigma^{-2}\mathbf{F}^T\mathbf{F} \tag{5}$$

where $\mathrm{E}[\cdot]$ denotes the expectation operation and $\mathbf{F}$ is stacked in row by

$$\left[\mathbf{0}_{1\times 2(i-1)}, \mathbf{a}_{i,j}^T, \mathbf{0}_{1\times 2(j-i-1)}, \mathbf{a}_{j,i}^T, \mathbf{0}_{1\times 2(n-j)}\right] \tag{6}$$

where

$$\mathbf{a}_{i,j} = -\mathbf{a}_{j,i} = \frac{10\alpha}{\log_e 10}\frac{\mathbf{s}_i - \mathbf{s}_j}{\|\mathbf{s}_i - \mathbf{s}_j\|^2}. \tag{7}$$

The FIM $\mathbf{J}$ is rank deficient. It requires the global constraints (2) as a regularization condition to obtain the CRLB. By implementing the constrained CRLB theory [26, 27], the CRLB of $\mathbf{s}$ can be represented as

$$\mathbf{C} = \mathbf{U}\left(\mathbf{U}^T\mathbf{J}\mathbf{U}\right)^{-1}\mathbf{U}^T \tag{8}$$

where $\mathbf{U}$ is a $2n$-by-$(2n - k)$ matrix whose columns form an orthonormal basis of the null space of $\mathbf{G}^T = \frac{\partial \mathbf{g}(\mathbf{s})}{\partial \mathbf{s}^T}$, and $\mathbf{g}(\mathbf{s})$ is properly designed so that $\mathbf{U}^T\mathbf{J}\mathbf{U}$ is invertible.

Throughout the following of this paper, finding the optimal equality constraints is formulated as constructing $\mathbf{g}(\mathbf{s}) = \mathbf{0}$ to minimizing the CRLB trace $\mathrm{tr}(\mathbf{C})$.

4   Optimal Equality Constraints

The optimal equality constraints refer to the equality constraints $\mathbf{g}(\mathbf{s}) = \mathbf{0}$ that minimizes the trace of the constrained CRLB (8). These equality constraints can be constructed by corresponding global measurements, which produce the most accurate location estimates together with the internode measurements.

4.1   Construction

We first derive the lower bound of the trace of (8), and provide a method to construct the equality constraints to achieve this bound, seen in Proposition 1.

Proposition 1. *The trace of the CRLB (8) is lower bounded by $\sum_{i=1}^{2n-k}\lambda_i^{-1}$, where λ_i is the ith largest eigenvalue of the FIM (5).*

Proof 1. We first represent the CRLB trace $\mathrm{tr}(\mathbf{C})$ *by the eigenvalues of* $\mathbf{U}^T\mathbf{J}\mathbf{U}$ *as*

$$\mathrm{tr}(\mathbf{C}) = \mathrm{tr}\left(\mathbf{U}\left(\mathbf{U}^T\mathbf{J}\mathbf{U}\right)^{-1}\mathbf{U}^T\right)$$

$$= \mathrm{tr}\left(\left(\mathbf{U}^T\mathbf{J}\mathbf{U}\right)^{-1}\right)$$

$$= \sum_{i=1}^{2n-k}\lambda_i^{-1}\left(\mathbf{U}^T\mathbf{J}\mathbf{U}\right) \tag{9}$$

where $\lambda_i\left(\mathbf{U}^T\mathbf{J}\mathbf{U}\right)$ *denotes the ith largest eigenvalue of* $\mathbf{U}^T\mathbf{J}\mathbf{U}$.

Note that $\mathbf{U}^T \mathbf{J} \mathbf{U} = \sigma^{-2} \mathbf{U}^T \mathbf{F}^T \mathbf{F} \mathbf{U}$, *it owns the same non-zero eigenvalues as* $\sigma^{-2} \mathbf{F} \mathbf{U} \mathbf{U}^T \mathbf{F}^T$. *Since*

$$\sigma^{-2} \mathbf{F} \mathbf{U} \mathbf{U}^T \mathbf{F}^T \le \sigma^{-2} \mathbf{F} \mathbf{F}^T = \mathbf{J} \tag{10}$$

we have

$$\lambda_i \left(\mathbf{U}^T \mathbf{J} \mathbf{U} \right) \le \lambda_i \tag{11}$$

where λ_i *denotes the ith largest eigenvalue of the FIM* $\mathbf{J}$.

Substituting (11) into (9), we get a lower bound of the CRLB trace as

$$\mathrm{tr}(\mathbf{C}) \ge \sum_{i=1}^{2n-k} \lambda_i^{-1}. \tag{12}$$

$\square$

The lower bound $\sum_{i=1}^{2n-k} \lambda_i^{-1}$ is achieved when the columns of $\mathbf{U}$ are the eigenvectors corresponding to the $2n-k$ largest eigenvalues of $\mathbf{J}$. In other words, the lower bound $\sum_{i=1}^{2n-k} \lambda_i^{-1}$ is achieved when the columns of $\mathbf{G} = \frac{\partial \mathbf{g}^T(\mathbf{s})}{\partial \mathbf{s}}$ span the subspace related to the k smallest eigenvalues of $\mathbf{J}$. For example, the following constraints

$$\mathbf{G}^T \mathbf{s} - \mathbf{b} = \mathbf{0} \tag{13}$$

are optimal constraints, where the columns are $\mathbf{G}$ the eigenvectors refers to the k smallest eigenvalues of $\mathbf{J}$.

But constructing (13) needs the node locations, which is possible only in simulations or experiments where the ground truth locations of the nodes are known. In practice, no ground truth locations are available, so we should find other approach to construct the equality constraints which are the optimal for all possible node locations. Do these constraints exist?

4.2   Feasibility

Unfortunately, no equality constraints keep the optimal for all possible node locations, as proved in Proposition 2.

Proposition 2. *There is no* $\mathbf{g}(\mathbf{s}) = \mathbf{0}$ *whose CRLB trace achieves the lower bound* $\sum_{i=1}^{2n-k} \lambda_i^{-1}$ *for all* $\mathbf{s} \in \mathbb{R}^{2n}$.

Proof 2. It is easy to verify from the proof of Proposition 1 that the trace of the CRLB (8) achieves its lower bound $\sum_{i=1}^{2n-k} \lambda_i^{-1}$ *if and only if the columns of* $\mathbf{U}$ *span the eigenspace corresponding to the* $2n-k$ *largest eigenvalue of* $\mathbf{J}$, *and thus the columns of* $\mathbf{G} = \frac{\partial \mathbf{g}^T(\mathbf{s})}{\partial \mathbf{s}}$ *span the eigenspace corresponding to the* k *smallest eigenvalues of* $\mathbf{J}$.

Note that the null space of $\mathbf{J}$ *involves the vectors* $\mathbf{1}_x = [1, 0, \ldots, 1, 0]^T \in \mathbb{R}^{2n}$, $\mathbf{1}_y = [0, 1, \ldots, 0, 1]^T \in \mathbb{R}^{2n}$, *and* $\mathbf{v_s} = [s_{1,y}, -s_{1,x}, \ldots s_{n,y}, , -s_{n,x}]^T \in \mathbb{R}^{2n}$, *there should exist a 3-by-k matrix* $\mathbf{T}(\mathbf{s})$ *which makes the equalities*

$$[\mathbf{1}_x, \mathbf{1}_y, \mathbf{v_s}]^T = \mathbf{T}(\mathbf{s}) \frac{\partial \mathbf{g}(\mathbf{s})}{\partial \mathbf{s}^T} \tag{14}$$

hold.

Since $\mathbf{g}(\mathbf{s}) = \mathbf{0}$, *we have*

$$[\mathbf{1}_x, \mathbf{1}_y, \mathbf{v_s}]^T = \mathbf{T}(\mathbf{s})\frac{\partial \mathbf{g}(\mathbf{s})}{\partial \mathbf{s}^T} = \frac{\partial \mathbf{T}(\mathbf{s})\mathbf{g}(\mathbf{s})}{\partial \mathbf{s}^T}. \tag{15}$$

Therefore, there must exist a function $\tilde{g}(\mathbf{s})$, *which is the last element of* $\mathbf{T}(\mathbf{s})\mathbf{g}(\mathbf{s})$, *satisfying* $\frac{\partial \tilde{g}(\mathbf{s})}{\partial \mathbf{s}} = \mathbf{v_s}$ *to make the last equality in (15) hold. But such* $\tilde{g}(\mathbf{s})$ *does not exist since* $\frac{\partial \tilde{g}(\mathbf{s})}{\partial s_{1,x}} = s_{1,y}$ *and* $\frac{\partial \tilde{g}(\mathbf{s})}{\partial s_{1,y}} = -s_{1,x}$ *lead to two contradictory expressions of* $\tilde{g}(\mathbf{s})$ *as*

$$\begin{aligned} \tilde{g}(\mathbf{s}) &= s_{1,x}s_{1,y} + c_1 \\ &= -s_{1,x}s_{1,y} + c_2, \end{aligned} \tag{16}$$

where c_1 *and* c_2 *are independent of* $s_{1,x}$ *and* $s_{1,y}$, *respectively. Therefore, there exists no* $\mathbf{g}(\mathbf{s}) = \mathbf{0}$ *whose CRLB trace achieves the lower bound* $\sum_{i=1}^{2n-k} \lambda_i^{-1}$ *uniformly across all* $\mathbf{s} \in \mathbb{R}^{2n}$.   □

Although constructing the optimal equality constraints is unfeasible in practice, one can still construct suboptimal constraints to fulfil practical requirement. For example, if the nodes' rough locations are available, (13) can be constructed and its performance can be evaluated through biased CRLB analysis similar to Proposition 6 in [5], where the constraint number k can be selected according to the quality and the quantity of the internode measurements. Anchor-type constraints are also admissible, where anchor selection problem can also be viewed as a sparse construction of $\mathbf{G}$ (13).

When the internode measurements are sufficient to make the network rigid, at least $k = 3$ global constraints, named minimally constrained system [5], are required to locate the nodes up to local reflections. In this case, one can maximize the log-likelihood (4) directly, then superimpose the results onto the node ground truth locations through global translations and rotations/reflections. This superimposing operation produces an MLE under the optimal equality constraints. It achieves the lower bound of the CRLB (8) asymptotically as the measurement noise decreases to zero, seen in [28].

5 Simulations

Anchor selection in cooperative localization refers to providing absolute locations of a small portion of the nodes to ensure the localizability and increase the localization accuracy. In previous work, although some empirical strategies are suggested, finding the optimal anchor set actually requires the exhaustive search of all possible anchor sets [6]. Viewed the optimal selection of the anchors as some equality constraints, we use the optimal equality constraints as a benchmark for anchor selection problem, and investigate its relationship with the optimal anchor set.

Table 1. Sensor locations

Sensor no. i	$s_{i,x}$	$s_{i,y}$	Sensor no. i	$s_{i,x}$	$s_{i,y}$
1	6.5574	2.7603	16	8.2346	9.5929
2	0.3571	6.7970	17	6.9483	5.4722
3	8.4913	6.5510	18	3.1710	1.3862
4	9.3399	1.6261	19	9.5022	1.4929
5	6.7874	1.1900	20	0.3445	2.5751
6	7.5774	4.9836	21	4.3874	8.4072
7	7.4313	9.5974	22	3.8156	2.5428
8	3.9223	3.4039	23	7.6552	8.1428
9	6.5548	5.8527	24	7.9520	2.4352
10	1.7119	2.2381	25	1.8687	9.2926
11	7.0605	7.5127	26	4.8976	3.4998
12	0.3183	2.5510	27	4.4559	1.9660
13	2.7692	5.0596	28	6.4631	2.5108
14	0.4617	6.9908	29	7.0936	6.1604
15	0.9713	8.9090	30	7.5469	4.7329

We randomly generate 30 nodes on a 10-by-10 plane, whose locations are given in Table 1. Under the assumption that network is full-connected and the measurement variance is 1, we can derive the FIM (5) and get the CRLB (8) under the anchor-type constraints for a given anchor set. In simulations, the exhaustive search of all possible anchor set is performed under given anchor number respectively.

Figure 1 shows the boxplot of the logarithm of the CRLB traces where the anchor number varies from 3 to 8, with the comparison of the corresponding optimal equality constraints. Similar trends can be found between the optimal anchor set and the optimal equality constraints, which hints the use of the optimal equality constraints as a benchmark for anchor selection. In fact, the CRLB trace under the optimal equality constraints evaluates the quality of the internode measurements, which can be used to determine the refinement of the localization accuracy should be achieve by improving internode measurement accuracy or introducing more global constraints.

We also investigate the constrained MLE of the node locations, which maximizes the likelihood (4) under the optimal equality constraints (13). In our simulations, the nodes deployed at the locations Table 1, and the variance of the measurement error ranges from -30 dB to 30 dB. To construct equality constraints, we introduce three types of reference, $i.e.$, ground truth reference, low error reference obtained by disturbing the ground truth locations using zero mean Gaussian noise with variance 0.01, and high error reference obtained by disturbing the ground truth locations using zero mean Gaussian noise with variance 1. 1000 simulations are performed to get the mean squared error of the estimates.

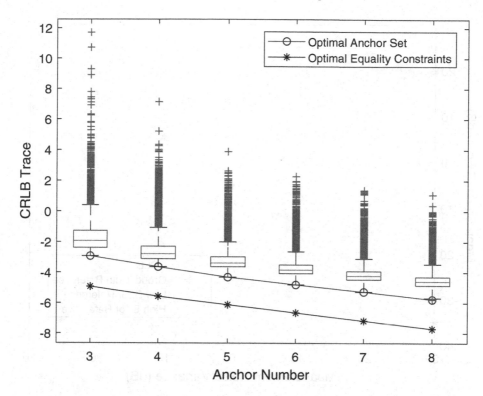

Fig. 1. Boxplot of CRLB traces: Under given anchor number, the CRLB trace of the optimal anchor selection (blue circles: ∘) from all possible anchor sets is compared with the CRLB trace of corresponding optimal equality constraints (black asterisk: ∗). (Color figure online)

Just as the theoretical result that the mean squared error of the MLE approaches the CRLB asymptotically when measurement noise approaches zero, the mean squared error of constrained MLE derived through 1000 simulations approaches the CRLB under the optimal equality constraints constructed by using the node ground truth locations, seen in Fig. 2. In practice, suboptimal equality constraints constructed by using the reference locations, which can be viewed as the rough estimates of the node locations, can be used to derive the constrained MLE. Compared with the mean squared error of the reference locations, which are −2.4772 for the low error reference and 18.3801 for the high error reference, the location estimates under both the case are refined under moderate internode measurement noise. However, unlike using the ground truth reference, using the error reference introduce some bias which cannot be eliminated by improving internode measurement accuracy.

How to choose the suitable number of the equality is also investigated in simulations, seen in Fig. 3. Similar as the simulations in Fig. 2, we fix the variance

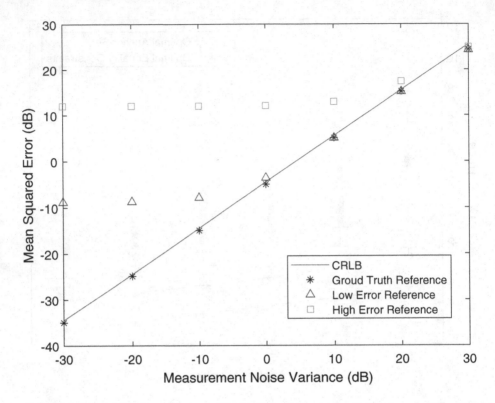

Fig. 2. Mean squared error of constrained MLE: Under given the variance of the measurement noise, the mean squared error of constrained MLE under ground truth reference (black asterisk: ∗)), low error reference (blue triangles: △), and high error reference (green square: ☐) are compared with the CRLB trace (red line: −). (Color figure online)

of the measurement noise at 1, and ranges the constraint number from 3 to 30. Other settings are the same as the ones in Fig. 2.

Using the ground truth reference, it is obvious that introducing more equality constraints can reduce the location estimate error asymptotically to zero. But taken the reference error into consideration, more equality constraints may cause large bias that can not be eliminated by improving the internode measurement accuracy. Therefore, there exists a trade-off between the contribution of equality constraints and the fault caused by reference error, which should be balanced by choosing suitable number of the equality constraints. In Fig. 3, it is preferred to choice only 3 equality constraints in high error reference case and 13 equality constraints low error reference case.

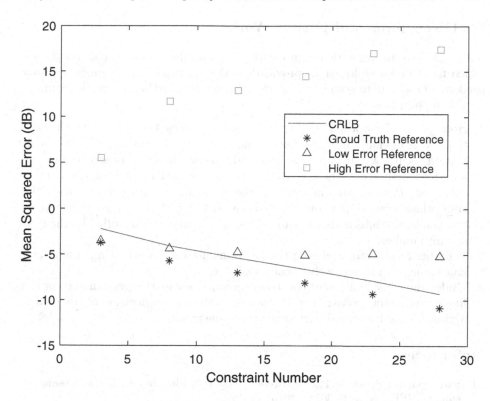

Fig. 3. Mean squared error of constrained MLE: Under given constraint number, the mean squared error of constrained MLE under ground truth reference (black asterisk: *)), low error reference (blue triangles: △), and high error reference (green square: □) are compared with the CRLB trace (red line: −). (Color figure online)

6 Conclusions

The optimal equality constraints for the internode RSS measurements are derived by constrained CRLB analysis, which outperform the anchor-type constraints in terms of localization accuracy. Compared with the exhaustive search of the optimal anchor sets, the optimal equality constraints can be directly derived from the eigen subspace of the FIM of the internode measurements, which serve as a bench mark for the anchor selections. In practice, although the optimal equality constraints cannot be derived because of the unknown ground truth locations, the references with locations error can be introduced to construct suboptimal constraints to provide relatively accurately location estimated by exploring the internode measurements. The results are not restricted to the internode RSS measurements. It can be directly derived from other range based measurements such as distances or time-of-arrivals (ToAs), and extended to angle-of-arrivals (AoAs) with some modifications.

7   Discussions and Future Work

Although introducing node rough locations can produce suboptimal constraints which fix the relative locations provided by the internode measurements onto a predefined coordinate system, the performance needs further study. Some directions are given below.

1. How to set the optimal constraint number? Using the ground truth locations, it is obvious that introducing more constraints can improve the localization accuracy. But in practice, since the constraints are constructed by the locations with error, the relative locations provided by the internode measurements may be contaminated by the constraints. Therefore, we hope the suboptimal constraints contribute more on the node locations that cannot provide by the internode measurements, which may be controlled by the constraint number.
2. Whether recursively updating the locations used in constructing suboptimal constraints can improve the localization accuracy?
3. Under the consideration of constraint error, whether the performance of the linear constraints constructed by the eigenvalue decomposition of the FIM is a good choice compared with other type constraints.

References

1. Sadowski, S., Spachos, P.: RSSI-based indoor localization with the internet of things. IEEE Access **6**, 30149–30161 (2018)
2. Kim, H., Granström, K., Gao, L., Battistelli, G., Kim, S., Wymeersch, H.: 5G mmWave cooperative positioning and mapping using multi-model PHD filter and map fusion. IEEE Trans. Wirel. Commun. **19**(6), 3782–3795 (2020)
3. Patwari, N., Ash, J.N., Kyperountas, S., Hero III, A.O., Moses, R.L., Correal, N.S.: Locating the nodes: cooperative localization in wireless sensor networks. IEEE Signal Process. Mag. **22**(4), 54–69 (2005)
4. Jawad, M., Azam, H., Siddiqi, S.J., Imtiaz-Ul-Haq, M., Ahmad, T.: Comparative analysis of localization schemes in conventional vs. next generation cellular networks. In: Proceedings of the 15th International Conference on Emerging Technologies (ICET 2019), pp. 1–6 (2019)
5. Zhang, P., Wang, Q.: On using the relative configuration to explore cooperative localization. IEEE Trans. Signal Process. **62**(4), 968–980 (2014)
6. Zhang, P., Cao, A., Liu, T.: Bound analysis for anchor selection in cooperative localization. In: Chen, F., Luo, Y. (eds.) Industrial IoT 2017. LNICST, vol. 202, pp. 1–10. Springer, Cham (2017). https://doi.org/10.1007/978-3-319-60753-5_1
7. Huang, J., Liang, J., Luo, S.: Method and analysis of TOA-based localization in 5G ultra-dense networks with randomly distributed nodes. IEEE Access **7**, 174986–175002 (2019)
8. Zhang, P., Yan, N., Zhang, J., Yuen, C.: Optimal minimally constrained system in cooperative localization. In: International Conference on Wireless Communications Signal Processing (WCSP 2015), pp. 1–5 (2015)
9. Patwari, N., Hero III, A.O., Perkins, M., Correal, N.S., O'Dea, R.J.: Relative location estimation in wireless sensor networks. IEEE Trans. Signal Process. **51**(8), 2137–2148 (2003)

10. Savvides, A., Garber, W., Adlakha, S., Moses, R., Srivastava, M.B.: On the error characteristics of multihop node localization in ad-hoc sensor networks. In: Zhao, F., Guibas, L. (eds.) IPSN 2003. LNCS, vol. 2634, pp. 317–332. Springer, Heidelberg (2003). https://doi.org/10.1007/3-540-36978-3_21
11. Niculescu, D., Nath, B.: Ad hoc positioning system (APS). In: Proceedings of the IEEE Global Communication Conference, vol. 5, pp. 2926–2931 (2001)
12. Langendoen, K., Reijers, N.: Distributed localization in wireless sensor networks: a quantitative comparison. Comput. Netw. 43(4), 499–518 (2003)
13. Biswas, P., Lian, T.C., Wang, T.C., Ye, Y.: Semidefinite programming based algorithms for sensor network localization. ACM Trans. Sen. Netw. 2(2), 188–220 (2006)
14. Chan, F.K.W., So, H.C.: Accurate distributed range-based positioning algorithm for wireless sensor networks. IEEE Trans. Signal Process. 57(10), 4101–4105 (2009)
15. Sun, M., Ho, K.C.: Successive and asymptotically efficient localization of sensor nodes in closed-form. IEEE Trans. Signal Process. 57(11), 4522–4537 (2009)
16. Vemula, M., Bugallo, M.F., Djuric, P.M.: Sensor self-localization with beacon position uncertainty. Signal Process. 89(6), 1144–1154 (2009)
17. Garcia, M., Martinez, C., Tomas, J., Lloret, J.: Wireless sensors self-location in an indoor WLAN environment. In: Proceedings of the 2007 International Conference on Sensor Technologies and Applications (SENSORCOMM 2007), pp. 146–151 (2007)
18. Eren, T., et al.: Rigidity, computation, and randomization in network localization. In: Proceedings of the IEEE Conference on Computer Communication, vol. 4, pp. 2673–2684 (2004)
19. Bishop, A.N., Fidan, B.I., Anderson, B., Dogançay, K.I., Pathirana, P.N.: Optimality analysis of sensor-target localization geometries. Automatica 46, 479–492 (2010)
20. Huang, M., Chen, S., Wang, Y.: Minimum cost localization problem in wireless sensor networks. Ad Hoc Netw. 9(3), 387–399 (2011)
21. Zhang, P., Wang, Q.: Anchor selection with anchor location uncertainty in wireless sensor network localization. In: Proceedings of the IEEE International Conference on Acoustics, Speech, Signal Processing, pp. 4172–4175 (2011)
22. Priyantha, N.B., Balakrishnan, H., Demaine, E., Teller, S.: Anchor-free distributed localization in sensor networks. Technical report 892, MIT Laboratory for Computer Science (2003)
23. Ash, J.N., Moses, R.L.: On the relative and absolute positioning errors in self-localization systems. IEEE Trans. Signal Process. 56(11), 5668–5679 (2008)
24. Shang, Y., Rumi, W., Zhang, Y., Fromherz, M.: Localization from connectivity in sensor networks. IEEE Trans. Parallel Distrib. Syst. 15(11), 961–974 (2004)
25. Yang, L., Ho, K.C.: On using multiple calibration emitters and their geometric effects for removing sensor position errors in TDOA localization. In: Proceedings of the IEEE International Conference on Acoustics, Speech, Signal Processing, pp. 2702–2705 (2010)
26. Gorman, J.D., Hero, A.O.: Lower bounds for parametric estimation with constraints. IEEE Trans. Inform. Theory 36(6), 1285–1301 (1990)
27. Stoica, P., Ng, B.C.: On the Cramér-Rao bound under parametric constraints. IEEE Signal Process. Lett. 5(7), 177–179 (1998)
28. Zhang, P., Lu, J., Wang, Q.: Performance bounds for relative configuration and global transformation in cooperative localization. ICT Express 2(1), 14–18 (2016). Special Issue on Positioning Techniques and Applications

End-to-End Error Control Coding Capability of NB-IoT Transmissions in a GEO Satellite System with Time-Packed Optical Feeder Link

Joan Bas[1]([✉]) and Alexis A. Dowhuszko[2]

[1] Department of Array & Multi-Sensor Processing, Centre Tecnològic de Telecomunicacions de Catalunya (CTTC), Castellefels, Spain
joan.bas@cttc.es
[2] Department of Communications and Networking, Aalto University, Espoo, Finland
alexis.dowhuszko@aalto.fi

Abstract. This paper focuses on the return link of a GEO satellite system that collects information from a large number of sparsely distributed IoT devices in a large geographical area. Narrow-Band (NB) IoT transmissions, with suitable Modulation and Coding Scheme (MCS), are Detected-and-Forwarded onboard the satellite, mapping each QAM symbol of the radio access link (uplink) into another PAM symbol that modulates optical feeder link's intensity (downlink). Given the massive number of IoT devices that is expected to be served by the GEO satellite system, the feeder link (downlink) of the return channel is expected to be the bottleneck. To tackle this limitation, time-packing signaling is used in the waveform that modulates the intensity of the optical feeder link (downlink); this way, the symbol time is reduced, and the number of IoT devices that can be simultaneously served in the radio access link (uplink) can augment without increasing the signal bandwidth in the optical feeder link. The Inter-Symbol Interference (ISI) that the time-packed feeder link generates is partially mitigated in the satellite gateway, using for this purpose an adaptive linear equalizer. After optical-to-electrical conversion, the NB-IoT codewords that are received in the gateway are decoded, correcting simultaneously errors introduced in both radio access and optical feeder links. The aim of this paper is to evaluate the error correction capability that MCS of NB-IoT standard has when used to protect end-to-end the hybrid radio/optical return link that results, particularly when using large overlapping factors in the optical feeder link to increase its achievable data rate.

Keywords: High-Throughput Satellite · Optical feeder link · Narrow-Band IoT · Return channel · Time-packing · Modulation and coding

This work has received funding from the Spanish Ministry of Science, Innovation and Universities under project TERESA-TEC2017-90093-C3-1-R (AEI/FEDER, UE) and from the Catalan Government under grants 2017-SGR-891 and 2017-SGR-1479.

L. Peñalver and L. Parra (Eds.): Industrial IoT 2020, LNICST 365, pp. 60–79, 2021.
https://doi.org/10.1007/978-3-030-71061-3_5

1   Introduction

The improvement of spectral efficiency is key for achieving higher data rate links in the next generation of wireless communication systems. This fact becomes critical in Satellite Communications (SatCom) and IoT systems, where the link propagation delay is large and the orders of the modulation schemes that are available for communication are low. In this regard, the Faster-Than-Nyquist (FTN) technique [12], so-called *time-packing*, has been recently reconsidered as a good candidate solution for increasing the spectral efficiency of Beyond 5G [14]. As a side-benefit, time-packing can also provide some additional PHY-layer security feature by adjusting the temporal separation between consecutive pulse-shapes, such that only the authorized user(s) is(are) able to detect the transmitted symbol stream with low enough Bit Error Rate (BER) [6].

The increased spectral efficiency that time-packing provides, as well as the additional PHY-layer security feature that enables, represents an interesting combination that would fuel the commercial success Satellite-based IoT services. According to Northern Sky Research reports, telemetry applications have the largest share (28%) when measuring the services with highest economic impact in IoT technology nowadays, followed by Telematics/Analytics applications (13%) and Asset Tracking services (11%), respectively [11,15]. It is important to highlight that the three previously listed IoT applications usually demand Narrow-Band (NB) communications and high levels of security. Therefore, time-packing is a good candidate solution to fulfill these two IoT requirements, particularly when relying on SatCom systems with extremely large coverage areas.

The use of time-packing reduces the temporal duration of the IoT frames, which is beneficial for increasing the amount of traffic that can be simultaneously collected in the radio access links – enabled by multiple spot-beams, which is then aggregated in the point-to-point optical feeder link toward the satellite gateway. However, the use of time-packing in optical feeder links has also some implementation challenges. For example, when adjacent data-carrying pulses are more densely packed in time, the Peak-to-Average Power Ratio (PAPR) of the resulting time-domain signal increases, reducing the end-to-end spectral efficiency as certain blocks of the transmission chain – such as the radio power amplifiers and the external optical Match-Zehnder Modulators (MZM) – have a linear response only on a limited input signal range. It is important to highlight that the PAPR of the time-packed waveform does not depend only on the selected overlapping factor, but also on the roll-off factor of the pulse-shaping filter that is used, which could be *e.g.* a Square-Root Raised-Cosine (SRRC) filter [5].

Finally, when focusing on the received signal processing in the satellite gateway, we note that the use of large overlapping factors and/or low roll-off factors on the time-packed waveform introduces notable Inter-Symbol Interference (ISI). This means that it is very difficult to implement a Maximum Likelihood Sequence Detector (MLSD) or Viterbi Equalizer, particularly when the modulation order of the data-carrying signal is large. Therefore, sub-optimal adaptive linear equalizers can be used to remove most of the ISI that time-packing introduces and,

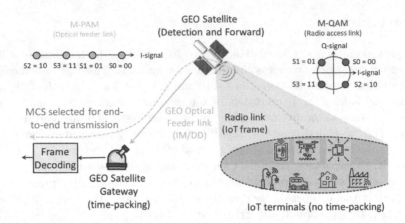

Fig. 1. Block diagram of a GEO satellite system that implements time-packing in the optical feeder link to augment the number of connected NB-IoT devices that can be simultaneously served. The GEO satellite implements a Detection-and-Forward strategy, mapping the M-QAM symbols of the radio access link to M-PAM symbols to modulate the intensity of the laser diode. The coding scheme that the NB-IoT devices select is used to correct errors introduced in both radio access and optical feeder parts of the return link.

after that, a low-complexity symbol-by-symbol detectors can be implemented. In this paper, we aim at characterizing the end-to-end error control correction capabilities that Modulation and Coding Schemes (MCS) of NB-IoT standard can provide when concatenating the radio access link with the optical feeder link in a GEO SatCom system. Note that the use of end-to-end error control coding makes sense in low-complexity satellite systems, as no additional decoding/encoding processing is needed onboard the satellite to protect the end-to-end transmission against the error in the optical part. This is the reason why the Detection-and-Forward architecture has been proposed, where only the hard-detection of the M-QAM symbols (access link) and its mapping into M-PAM symbols (feeder link) should be performed onboard the satellite.

This paper has been structured as follows: Sect. 2 presents the system model, including details of the NB-IoT transmission on the radio access link, as well as the generation of the time-packed signal that modulates the intensity of the optical feeder link. Section 3 explains the adaptive linear equalization approach that is used to mitigate the ISI that time-packing generates, whereas Sect. 4 presents the simulation setup and the performance evaluation when different MCS of NB-IoT standard are used to control the errors introduced end-to-end in the reverse. Finally, Sect. 5 summarizes the main outcomes.

2   System Model

The block diagram of the proposed High-Throughput Satellite (HTS) system model is shown in Fig. 1. It consists of a large number of sparsely deployed

Table 1. Details of the Resource Units and Uplink slots for each NPUSCH format, including separations between different subcarriers (see Table 10.1.2.3-1 of [2]).

NPUSCH format	Δf	N_{sc}^{RU}	N_{slots}^{UL}	N_{symb}^{UL}
1	3.75 kHz	1	16	7
	15 kHz	1	16	
		3	8	
		6	4	
		12	2	
2	3.75 kHz	1	4	
	15 kHz	1	4	

IoT devices, which use the Geosynchronous Equatorial Orbit (GEO) satellite as Detect-and-Forward relaying node to reach the remote satellite gateway. Different wireless communication technologies are used for the access link (uplink) and feeder link (downlink), namely radio and optical wireless, respectively.

The radio waveform that the IoT terminals generate for the uplink transmission follows the NB-IoT standard. In the satellite, the M-QAM symbols that are received in uplink are first detected and then mapped into points of an M-PAM constellation, to make them suitable to modulate in intensity the light beam that the laser diode on-board the satellite emits in downlink. When performing this electrical-to-optical conversion, the time-packing feature is introduced in the M-PAM downlink transmission to reduce the symbol time and increase the number of IoT terminals that can be simultaneously served in the satellite spot-beams. In the next sections, the signal model for both radio access link and optical feeder link are explained in further detail.

2.1   NB-IoT Transmission in Radio Access (Uplink of Reverse Link)

The reverse NB-IoT communication, which starts in the IoT device(s) and ends in the satellite gateway, consist of the following physical channels [1–3]:

- Narrowband Physical Uplink Shared Channel (NPUSCH), which is used to transmit uplink transport block on the orthogonal Resource Units (RUs) that have been scheduled for the target IoT device.
- Narrow Band Physical Random Access Channels (NPRACH), which enables the random access procedure among the IoT devices that have information to transmit in the shared radio access link.

From both channels, this paper focused on the NPUSCH, and assumes that the random access procedure has been successfully performed, such that the IoT devices known the orthogonal RUs that have been reserved for its uplink communication. The NPUSCH is based on the following parts: 24 bits of Cyclic Redundancy Check (CRC), Turbo channel encoding with a mother code of 1/3, rate matching, physical-layer Hybrid Automatic Repeat Request (HARQ), scrambling, modulations of $\pi/2$-BPSK and $\pi/4$-QPSK for single-tone transmissions, and QPSK for multi-tone transmissions.

Table 2. Supported modulation formats in NPUSCH (see Table 10.1.3.2-1 of [2]).

NPUSCH format	N_{sc}^{RU}	Modulation scheme
1	1	BPSK, QPSK
	>1	QPSK
2	1	BPSK

Table 3. Relation/mapping between Modulation order, Transport Block Size index, and Modulation and Coding Scheme index (see Table 16.5.1.2-1 of [3]).

MCS Index I_{MCS}	Modulation Order Q_m	TBS Index I_{TBS}
0	1	0
1	1	2
2	2	1
3	2	3
4	2	4
5	2	5
6	2	6
7	2	7
8	2	8
9	2	9
10	2	10

Moreover, the NPUSCH has two formats: Format 1 is used for data transmissions on the Uplink Shared Channel (UL-SCH), whereas Format 2 is used for Uplink Control Information (UCI), such as ACK/NACK transmissions of the HARQ mechanism. The uplink transmission can support two different sub-carrier separations (Δf). When $\Delta f = 15$ kHz, 12 consecutive sub-carriers are allocated for uplink transmission using time slots of duration 0.5 ms. On the other hand, when $\Delta f = 3.75$ kHz, 48 consecutive sub-carriers are allocated for uplink transmission in time slots of duration 2 ms. The distribution of the number of resource units (N_{sc}^{RU}) and number of slots (N_{slots}^{UL}) for the different formats of the NPUSCH is provided in Table 1 (See Table 10.1.2.3-1 of [2]). The modulation scheme that is used depends on the value that N_{sc}^{RU} takes, as illustrated in Table 2 (See Table 10.1.3.2-1 of [2]). From this table, we will focus on Format 1 and single-subcarrier transmissions (i.e., $N_{sc}^{RU} = 1$), since it enables the use of both BPSK and QPSK modulation schemes.

The following step consists in associating the modulation format with the error control coding scheme, which will define the Transport Block Size (TBS) and the corresponding code rate. More precisely, the NPUSCH can support up to 11 different MCS, whose relation with the modulation and TBS index is shown in Table 3 (See Table 16.5.1.2-1 of [3]). From these values, we observe that BPSK modulation is used only in the first two possible MCS indexes (i.e., $I_{MSC} = 0, 1$), whereas the other MCS indexes rely on QPSK modulation (i.e., $I_{MSC} = 2, \ldots, 10$). Table 3 also relates the index of the MCS (I_{MSC}) with the index of the TBS (I_{TBS}). NB-IoT has multiple possible TBS values, which depend on the modulation and the code rate that is used in each case. Thus, from the I_{TBS} point of view, the first and third MCS indexes utilize BPSK, whereas the others utilize QPSK. Then, in order to identify the transport block size, Table 4 associates each TBS index (I_{TBS}) with the Resource Unit index (I_{RU}).

From Table 4, it is possible to observe that the minimum and maximum TBS for the NPUSCH is 16 bits and 2536 bits, respectively. We note that the different TBS may be associated with different modulation formats. For example, when BPSK modulation is used, the minimum and maximum TBS that is possible is 16 bits and 424 bits, respectively. On the other hand, when using QPSK modulation, the minimum and maximum TBS is 24 bits and 2536 bits, respectively. Nonetheless, the code rate that is associated to each TBS is fixed, and depends on the values that I_{TBS} and I_{RU} take. More precisely, the code rate that correspond to a given NB-IoT transmission in uplink is given by

$$R_{\text{c}}^{\text{UL}} = \frac{\text{TBS}}{N_{\text{RE}}\, N_{\text{RU}}\, N_{\text{b}}},$$

(1)

where N_{RE} is the number of Resource Elements (RE) allocated per RU, N_{RU} is the number of RUs utilized in each NB-IoT information block, and N_{b} is the number of bits that is transmitted in each resource element. Note that $N_{\text{RE}} = 96$ (144) for single-tone (multi-tone) transmission, whereas $N_{\text{b}} = 1$ (2) for BPSK (QPSK) modulation, respectively. In addition, Table 5 shows the number of RUs that fit in each information block as function of the RU index that is selected.

Table 4. Number of bits per information block as function of the Transport Block Size index and the Resource Unit index (see Table 16.5.1.2-2 of [3]).

I_{TBS}	I_{RU}							
	0	1	2	3	4	5	6	7
0	16	32	56	88	120	152	208	256
1	24	56	88	144	176	208	256	344
2	32	72	144	176	208	256	328	424
3	40	104	176	208	256	328	440	568
4	56	120	208	256	328	408	552	680
5	72	144	224	328	424	504	680	872
6	88	176	256	392	504	600	808	1000
7	104	224	328	472	584	712	1000	1224
8	120	256	392	536	680	808	1096	1384
9	136	296	456	616	776	936	1256	1544
10	144	328	504	680	872	1000	1384	1736
11	176	376	584	776	1000	1192	1608	2024
12	208	440	680	1000	1128	1352	1800	2280
13	224	488	744	1032	1256	1544	2024	2536

In our simulation setting, the value of TBS was fixed. Then, from Table 4, we obtained the different I_{TBS} and I_{RU} combinations that can be supported with the selected TBS. Each I_{RU} can be associated with the required number of resource units (N_{RU}) taking advantage of Table 5. Note that when $N_{\text{RU}} = 1$, then we are in presence of a single-tone transmission, where the number of resource elements

Table 5. Number of Resource Units that corresponds to the different Resource Unit indexes of the NPUSCH (see Table 16.5.1.1-2 of [3]).

I_{RU}	N_{RU}
0	1
1	2
2	3
3	4
4	5
5	6
6	8
7	10

Table 6. Code rates for NPUSCH Format 1 in terms of the Transport Block Size and Resource Unit indexes for a single-tone transmission. Code rates are obtained from (1).

Modulation Order	I_{TBS}	Index of Resource Units I_{RU} (Single-Tone case)							
		0	1	2	3	4	5	6	7
1	0	0.17	0.17	0.19	0.23	0.25	0.26	0.27	0.27
1	2	0.33	0.38	0.50	0.46	0.43	0.44	0.43	0.44
2	1	0.13	0.15	0.15	0.19	0.18	0.18	0.17	0.18
2	3	0.21	0.27	0.31	0.27	0.27	0.28	0.29	0.30
2	4	0.29	0.31	0.36	0.33	0.34	0.35	0.36	0.35
2	5	0.38	0.38	0.39	0.43	0.44	0.44	0.44	0.45
2	6	0.46	0.46	0.44	0.51	0.53	0.52	0.53	0.52
2	7	0.54	0.58	0.57	0.61	0.61	0.62	0.65	0.64
2	8	0.63	0.67	0.68	0.70	0.71	0.70	0.71	0.72
2	9	0.71	0.77	0.79	0.80	0.81	0.81	0.82	0.80
2	10	0.75	0.85	0.88	0.89	0.91	0.87	0.90	0.90

is $N_{RE} = 96$. Otherwise, the transmission is multi-tone, and the number of resource elements is $N_{RE} = 144$. Assuming that the value of I_{TBS} is known, the associated modulation order of the transmission (N_b) can be found in Table 3. Finally, Table 6 shows the code rates supported in a single-tone transmission.

For instance, if we set TBS equal to 256 bits, then Table 6 shows the code rates that the NPUSCH Format 1 can support when BPSK and QPSK modulation for different Resource Unit indexes (I_{RU}). Therefore, from Table 7, we observe that if

Table 7. Code rates for NPUSCH Format 1 in terms of Resource Unit index for a single-tone transmission when the Transport Block Size is set to 256 bits.

Modulation	Index of Resource Units I_{RU} (Single-Tone case)							
	0	1	2	3	4	5	6	7
BPSK	-	-	-	-	-	0.44	-	0.27
QPSK	-	0.67	0.44	0.33	0.27	-	0.17	-

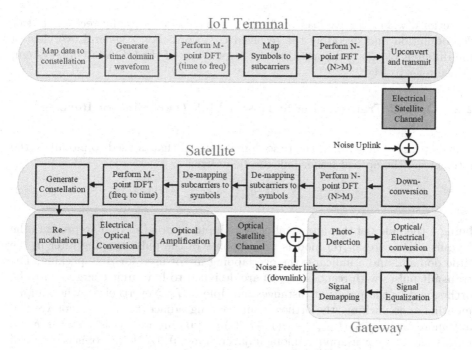

Fig. 2. Block diagram of the hybrid radio/optical reverse link of the IoT satellite system. The radio access link starts in the IoT terminal (green blocks) and ends in the GEO satellite (blue blocks). The M-QAM symbols detected onboard the satellite are forwarded in the optical feeder link using a M-PAM constellation. Finally, the IoT payload bits are finally recovered in the satellite gateway after error control decoding (orange blocks). (Color figure online)

the value of TBS is set to 256 bits and $N_b = 1$ (BPSK modulation), then it is only possible to use two different code rates: $R_c^{UL} = 0.27$ (with $I_{RU} = 9$) and $R_c^{UL} = 0.44$ (with $I_{RU} = 5$). On the contrary, for a TBS of 256 bits and $N_b = 2$ (QPSK modulation), there are five possible code rates: $R_c^{UL} = 0.17, 0.27, 0.33, 0.44, 0.67$ (with $I_{RU} = 1, 2, 3, 4, 6$, respectively). Note that when $I_{RU} = 0$, there is no MCS that can be supported for a TBS of 256 bits.

After the encoding and modulation is performed, the uplink NB-IoT symbols are accommodated into a Single-Carrier Frequency Division Multiplex Access (SC-FDMA) waveform, which can be efficiently implemented with the aid of a Discrete Fourier Transform (DFT) pre-processing, just before the Inverse Fast Fourier Transform (IFFT) block. After that, the signal is upconverted and transmitted to the satellite on a suitable Radio Frequency (RF) band. The SC-FDMA signal that is received in the satellite is then demodulated and re-mapped into a single-carrier M-PAM waveform, which is suitable to vary the intensity of light beam that the laser diode emits in a proportional way to signal's amplitude in downlink. On the other side of optical feeder link, the satellite gateway performs the optical-to-electrical conversion with the aid of a photodetector (direct detection), where the payload of the IoT transmission is finally recovered after demodulation and decoding the received codeword. For a general overview of the different blocks that constitute the reverse link of the GEO satellite system, please refer to Fig. 2.

2.2 Optical Transmission in Feeder Link (Downlink of Reverse Link)

Without loss of generality, the time-domain signal that is used to modulate the intensity of the optical feeder link can be written as

$$s(t) = \sum_k s[k]\, g_{\text{tx}}\big(t - k(1-\delta)T_{\text{s}}\big), \tag{2}$$

being k the index of the data symbol in its input vector $\{s[k]\}$, T_{s} represents the Nyquist data rate, $g_{\text{tx}}(t)$ models the response of the pulse-shaping filter in the time domain, and δ indicates the overlapping factor used for time-packing. The transmit pulses with response $g_{\text{tx}}(t)$ are designed to have unit energy and to be orthogonal to the pulses at distances multiple of T_{s}. Nevertheless, when implementing time-packing, the orthogonality among adjacent pulses is not verified any more, as $\int_{-\infty}^{\infty} g_{\text{tx}}(t)g_{\text{tx}}\big(t - n(1-\delta)T_{\text{s}}\big)dt = 0$ only it is satisfied when $\delta = 0$ (*i.e.*, there is no overlapping among adjacent pulses). By doing so, it is obtained a higher data rate at expenses of introducing ISI. Specifically, the obtained data rate is *i.e.*,

$$R_{\text{s}}' = \frac{R_{\text{s}}}{(1-\delta)} \geq R_{\text{s}} = \frac{1}{T_{\text{s}}}. \tag{3}$$

Note that the new R_{s}' can be attained without enlarging the transmission bandwidth. Thanks to this approach, it can be concluded that time-packing is able to use the communication bandwidth in a more efficient way. The price to pay is the addition of ISI in the transmitted signal, which must be mitigated in reception.

The driving voltage of the external MZM that is placed onboard the satellite for Electrical-to-Optical (E/O) conversion is given by

$$v_{\text{mzm}}(t) = V_{\text{B}} + \beta\, \tilde{s}(t)\, (V_\pi/\pi), \tag{4}$$

where V_{B} and V_π are the bias and half-wavelength voltages of the MZM, β is the intensity modulation index, and

$$\tilde{s}(t) = s(t)/\sqrt{\mathbb{E}\{|s(t)|^2\}} \tag{5}$$

is the constellation with unity energy. In the latter formula, $\mathbb{E}\{\cdot\}$ represents the mathematical expectation of the corresponding time-domain signal. There the parameter β determines the MZM's working range. Large β) augment the transmitted optical power but also the non-linear distortion the output of the Photodetector (PD) in the satellite gateway. The relationship between the electrical voltage and optical field that provides the MZM is given by [10]

$$E_{\text{o}}(t) = \cos\left(\frac{\pi}{2}\frac{v_{\text{mzm}}(t)}{V_\pi}\right)\sqrt{2\,P_{\text{o,ld}}}\cos\left(\omega_{\text{o}}t\right), \tag{6}$$

where $P_{\mathrm{o,ld}}$ is the average optical power of the Laser Diode (LD) that feeds the MZM whereas ω_{o} represents the angular frequency of the transmitted *unmodulated optical carrier* in the *optical sidebands*. Thus, the temporal optical intensity modulated signal at the output of the MZM is

$$p_{\mathrm{o}}(t) = E_{\mathrm{o}}^2(t) = \cos^2\left(\frac{\pi}{2}\frac{v_{\mathrm{mzm}}(t)}{V_{\pi}}\right) 2P_{\mathrm{o,ld}}\cos^2\left(\omega_{\mathrm{o}}t\right)$$

$$= \left[1 + \cos\left(\frac{\pi V_{\mathrm{B}}}{V_{\pi}} + \beta\,\tilde{s}(t)\right)\right]P_{\mathrm{o,ld}}\cos^2\left(\omega_{\mathrm{o}}t\right). \qquad (7)$$

considering that the quadrature bias point is $V_{\mathrm{B}} = (3V_{\pi})/2$, then,

$$p_{\mathrm{o}}(t) = \left[1 + \sin\left(\beta\,\tilde{s}(t)\right)\right]P_{\mathrm{o,ld}}\cos^2\left(\omega_{\mathrm{o}}t\right) \approx \underbrace{\left[1 + \beta\,\tilde{s}(t)\right]}_{\text{modulating signal}}\underbrace{P_{\mathrm{o,ld}}\cos^2\left(\omega_{\mathrm{o}}t\right)}_{\text{optical carrier}} \quad \beta \ll 1, \quad (8)$$

where in previous expression it has been the following approach $\sin(x) \approx x$ for $x \ll 1$. Thus, the impact of the MZM's non-linear effects can be neglected. Next, the optical Free Space Loss (FSL) is

$$L_{\mathrm{o,fsl}} = \lambda^2/\left(4\pi d_{\mathrm{fso}}\right)^2, \qquad (9)$$

where d_{fso} is the link range and λ is the wavelength that the optical feeder link utilizes. Besides the FSL, it is required to take the atmospheric losses, loss $L_{\mathrm{o,atm}}$, into account. Specially, when there are bad weather conditions.

The optical signal that reaches the PD generates an electrical current, *i.e.*,

$$i_{\mathrm{D}}(t) = I_{\mathrm{D}} + i_{\mathrm{d}}(t) = \mu\,\frac{G_{\mathrm{o,tx}}\,G_{\mathrm{o,rx}}\,G_{\mathrm{o,edfa}}}{L_{\mathrm{o,fsl}}\,L_{\mathrm{o,atm}}\,L_{\mathrm{o,sys}}}\int_{t}^{t+T_{\mathrm{o}}} p_{\mathrm{o}}(\tau)\,d\tau, \qquad (10)$$

$$\int_{t}^{t+T_{\mathrm{o}}} p_{\mathrm{o}}(\tau)\,d\tau = \frac{P_{\mathrm{o,ld}}}{2}\left[1 + \sin\left(\beta\,\tilde{s}(t)\right)\right], \qquad (11)$$

being $T_{\mathrm{o}} = 2\pi/\omega_{\mathrm{o}}$ the optical's carrier period, μ [A/W] is the PD responsivity, $G_{\mathrm{o,tx}}$ and $G_{\mathrm{o,rx}}$ represent the optical gains of the transmit and receive telescopes, $G_{\mathrm{o,edfa}}$ identifies the gain of the Erbium-Doped Fiber Amplifier (EDFA) sited before the satellite gateway's PD, and $L_{\mathrm{o,sys}}$ symbolizes the system losses in the optical feeder link. At this point, it is necessary to remark that the current in (10) is decomposed in two components, where the DC component is given by

$$I_{\mathrm{D}} = \mu\,\frac{G_{\mathrm{o,tx}}\,G_{\mathrm{o,rx}}\,G_{\mathrm{o,edfa}}}{L_{\mathrm{o,fsl}}\,L_{\mathrm{o,atm}}\,L_{\mathrm{o,sys}}}\,\frac{P_{\mathrm{o,ld}}}{2}, \qquad (12)$$

and it is independent of β, whereas the AC component depends on it, and can be equated as

$$i_{\mathrm{d}}(t) = i_{\mathrm{D}}(t) - I_{\mathrm{D}} = I_{\mathrm{D}}\sin\left(\beta\tilde{s}(t)\right) \approx I_{\mathrm{D}}\,\beta\,\tilde{s}(t) \quad \beta \ll 1. \qquad (13)$$

The direct-detected electrical's signal SNR by the satellite gateway's PD is

$$\mathrm{SNR}_{\mathrm{e,pd}} = \frac{\mathbb{E}\{|i_{\mathrm{d}}(t)|^2\}}{\mathbb{E}\{|n_{\mathrm{o}}(t)|^2\}} \approx \frac{I_D^2\,\beta^2}{\mathbb{E}\{|n_{\mathrm{o}}(t)|^2\}} \quad \beta \ll 1, \qquad (14)$$

where

$$\mathbb{E}\{|n_o(t)|^2\} = \mathbb{E}\{|i_{\mathrm{shot}}(t)|^2\} + \mathbb{E}\{|i_{\mathrm{thermal}}(t)|^2\} + \mathbb{E}\{|i_{\mathrm{rin}}(t)|^2\} + \mathbb{E}\{|i_{\mathrm{beat}}(t)|^2\} \tag{15}$$

includes the contribution of all noise sources in the optical feeder link, namely the *shot noise* sources, *thermal noise*, *Relative Intensity Noise* (RIN) of LD, and *beat noise* [7]. Note that shot noise term includes the contribution of the received optical signal, the Amplified Spontaneous Emission (ASE) noise, the background optical noise and the dark current noise, whereas the beat noise term accounts the effect of combining the received optical signal with the ASE noise.

If the received optical power is ranged between -90 and $-20\,\mathrm{dBW}$, the beat noise is the dominant one in the optical's feeder link SNR [13]. In this situation,

$$\mathbb{E}\{|n_o(t)|^2\} \approx \mathbb{E}\{|i_{\mathrm{beat}}(t)|^2\} = 4\,I_D\,I_{\mathrm{ase}}\big(B_e/B_o\big), \tag{16}$$

where B_o is the bandwidth of the optical signal at the PD input, B_e is the bandwidth of the electrical signal at the PD output, and $I_{\mathrm{ase}} = \mu\,G_{o,\mathrm{edfa}}\,P_{\mathrm{ase}}$ is the DC component generated by the ASE noise, whose equivalent noise power at the input of the EDFA (*i.e.*, before amplification) is given by $P_{\mathrm{ase}} = \rho_{\mathrm{ase}}\,B_o$.

Let $r(t) = s(t) + n(t)$ be the continuous-time received signal, being $n(t)$ the Additive White Gaussian Noise (AWGN). Then, after applying Matched Filtering (MF) [8], the received signal samples can be written as

$$r[n] = \int_{-\infty}^{\infty} r(t)\,g_{\mathrm{rx}}\Big(t - n(1-\delta)T_s\Big)\,dt = \sum_k s[k]\,c[k-n] + \eta[n]. \tag{17}$$

Taking into account that $g_{\mathrm{rx}}(t) = g_{\mathrm{tx}}(-t)^*$, it is possible to show that

$$c[k-n] = \int_{-\infty}^{\infty} g_{\mathrm{tx}}\Big(t - k(1-\delta)T_s\Big)\,g_{\mathrm{tx}}\Big(-t + n(1-\delta)T_s\Big)^*\,dt, \tag{18}$$

$$\eta[n] = \int_{-\infty}^{\infty} n(t)\,g_{\mathrm{tx}}\Big(-t + n(1-\delta)T_s\Big)^*\,dt. \tag{19}$$

We note that this is the observation model of Ungerboeck [17]. Unfortunately, the ISI in (17) is non-causal and the noise samples $\eta[n]$ are correlated. To circumvent these drawbacks, it has been whitened the signal after the MF block [16]. By doing so, we obtain

$$r'[n] = \sum_k s[k]\,c'[k-n] + \eta'[n], \tag{20}$$

where $c'[k]$ for $k \neq n$ is the causal ISI, verifying $c'[k]*c'[-k]^* = c[k]$, and $\eta'[n]$ are AWGN samples. The duration and value of ISI depends on the selected roll-off ρ, the modulation order M, and overlapping δ.

We now focus on re-writing the received signal samples in (20) in a vector-matrix form. For this, we define $\mathbf{r}' \in \mathbb{R}^{(N+L_c)\times 1}$ as the vector that stacks the received time-packed samples, *i.e.*,

$$\mathbf{r}' = \left[r'\!\left[\frac{(-L_c+1)}{2}\right] \cdots r'[n] \cdots r'\!\left[N + \frac{(L_c-1)}{2}\right] \right]^{\mathrm{T}}, \tag{21}$$

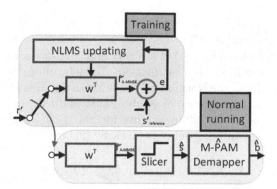

Fig. 3. Equalization process using Normalized Least Mean Squares algorithm. Green (orange) blocks illustrate the training (normal) operation phase of the equalizer.

where L_c is the number of delayed signal samples after the MF, and N is the number of modulated symbols to-be-transmitted. Then, we can show that

$$\mathbf{r}' = \mathbf{H}\mathbf{s} + \eta', \tag{22}$$

where $\mathbf{s} \in \mathbb{R}^{(N+(L_c-1)/2)\times 1}$ and $\eta' \in \mathbb{R}^{(N+L_c)\times 1}$ are the vectors containing the transmitted symbols and the received noise samples, respectively, while $\mathbf{H} \in \mathbb{R}^{(N+L_c)\times(N+(L_c-1)/2)}$ is the so-called convolution channel matrix. After explaining the key concepts behind time-packing transmission, we are now ready to study the detection strategies to recover the transmitted symbol stream.

3 Adaptive Equalization

The most convenient strategy to remove the interference in a multi-path communication channel consist in using the Maximum Likelihood Sequence Estimator (MLSE), whose practical implementation can be notably simplified in a recursive way via the Viterbi Algorithm (VA) [8,18]. Unfortunately, the trellis diagram that results when implementing the VA in the received sequence of symbol samples has an exponential relationship with the constellation size (M) and the channel memory. Note that the channel memory parameter for time-packed signals depends on the pulse-shapping's overlapping (δ) and the roll-off (ρ). Thus, the larger is the overlapping factor and/or the lower is the roll-off of factor, the higher is the ISI from time-packing signalling. Unfortunately, using large overlapping factors and low roll-off factors are of high interest, since they permit to increase the throughput of the communication link. Therefore, for these cases, it is not recommended to use VA. Alternatively, we use an adaptive transversal filter that performs linear equalization, as suggested in [4]. By doing so, the received signal sample before performing a symbol-by-symbol detection becomes

$$\hat{s}[n] = \mathbf{w}^T \mathbf{y}[n], \tag{23}$$

where $\mathbf{w} = \begin{bmatrix} w[0] & \cdots & w[L_w - 1] \end{bmatrix}^T$ is the vector that stacks the L_w weights of the transversal filter, and $\mathbf{y}[n] = \begin{bmatrix} r'[n-(L_w-1)/2] & \cdots & r'[n] & \cdots & r'[n+(L_w-1)/2] \end{bmatrix}^T$ is the vector that stacks the $(L_w - 1)/2$ *a priori* and *a posteriori* received samples to perform the transmit symbol estimation. To determine the weights of the adaptive linear equalizer, the Normalized Least Mean Squares (NLMS) algorithm is used with the training sequence of symbols that is illustrated in Fig. 3. Then, the updating process of the filter weights for the j-th Monte-Carlo training sequence at the n-th training symbol is given by [9]

$$\mathbf{w}_j[n] = \mathbf{w}_j[n-1] + \frac{\mu}{P_y} e_j[n]\mathbf{y}_j[n], \tag{24}$$

where $\mathbf{w}_j[n] \in \mathbb{R}^{L_w \times 1}$ and $\mathbf{w}_j[n-1] \in \mathbb{R}^{L_w \times 1}$ represent the vector of L_w coefficients of the transversal filter at the current and previous training iteration, respectively, μ is the forgetting factor of the NLMS algorithm, P_y represents the power of the received signal, $e_j[n] = s_j[n] - \hat{s}_j[n]$ equates the error from the current estimated symbol and the training one, which are equated as $\hat{s}_j[n]$ and $s_j[n]$.

4 Performance Evaluation

The error correction capabilities that the MCS of the NB-IoT standard has on the *end-to-end* reverse link of the GEO satellite system (*i.e.*, from the IoT devices to the satellite gateway) is now evaluated. For this purpose, we first present the simulation setup and, after that, we show the different computed figures of merit that are relevant to characterize the end-to-end error correction performance.

4.1 Simulation Setup

The NB-IoT transmitted signal corresponds to the NPUSCH Format 1, assuming that TBS $= 256$ bits in all cases. The corresponding simulated code rates are:

– $R_c^{UL} = 0.27, 0.44$ for BPSK (2-PAM) in the radio access (optical feeder) link.
– $R_c^{UL} = 0.17, 0.67$ for QPSK (4-PAM) in the radio access (optical feeder) link.

The BPSK (QPSK) modulation symbols that the satellite receives in uplink from the IoT terminal are first detected and then re-modulated, using for this purpose a 2-PAM (4-PAM) constellation with a SRRC pulse shaping filter with roll-off factor $\rho = 0.25$ and overlapping factor $\delta = \{0, 25, 40\}\%$. The resulting time-domain signal is used to modulate in intensity the light beam that the LD onboard the satellite generates, using for this purpose an external MZM that works in its linear region. Finally, the optical signal that the satellite gateway receives in downlink is amplified, converted into an electrical signal using a PIN-diode Photodetector (Direct Detection), matched-filtered with the transmit SRRC pulse shape, equalized using an adaptive linear MMSE filter, and turbo decoded.

Table 8. Parameters of the optical feeder link used in the NB-IoT satellite system.

Symbol	Optical Link Parameter	Value	Unit
$P_{o,ld}$	Optical power of LD (incl. EDFA booster)	23.0	dBm
$G_{o,tx}$	Optical gain of transmitter (satellite telescope)	114.3	dBi
$G_{o,rx}$	Optical gain of receiver (ground telescope)	125.8	dBi
$L_{o,fsl}$	FSL of optical link (1550 nm, 39000 km)	290.0	dB
$L_{o,atm}$	Atmospheric attenuation	1.7	dB
$L_{o,sys}$	System losses in the optical feeder link	6.5	dB
G_{edfa}	Gain of the optical amplifier (EDFA)	50.0	dB
μ	Responsivity of photodetector (PIN diode)	0.5	A/W
B_e	Bandwidth of electrical filter (PD output)	1.5	GHz
B_o	Bandwidth of optical channel (1550 nm)	12.5	GHz
ρ_{ase}	PSD of amplified spontaneous emissions	2.0×10^{-19}	W/Hz
ρ_{rin}	PSD of RIN process (normalized)	-160	dBc/Hz
ρ_{back}	PSD of background noise at EDFA input	7.6×10^{-25}	W/Hz
i_n	Electrical noise current spectral density	1.0×10^{-11}	A
i_{dark}	Dark current at the PIN diode output	1.0×10^{-10}	A

Table 8 shows the optical feeder link parameters, taking both the optical gains and losses, and the sources of optical noise [13] into account. The effect of any other parameter not listed in this table is considered negligible. From Table 8 it is observed that the average received optical power is formulated as

$$P_{o,rx}[\text{dBm}] = P_{o,ld}[\text{dBm}] + G_{o,tx}[\text{dB}] + G_{o,rx}[\text{dB}] - L_{o,fsl}[\text{dB}]$$
$$- L_{o,sys}[\text{dB}] - L_{o,atm}[\text{dB}] = -33.4[\text{dBm}] - L_{o,atm}[\text{dB}]. \quad (25)$$

When $L_{o,atm} = 0\,\text{dB}$ (*i.e.*, clear-sky conditions), the DC current at the PD output is $I_D = 11.43\,\text{mA}$, whereas the DC current from the ASE noise is $I_{ase} = 0.125\,\text{mA}$ regardless of the weather. Thus, if $\beta = 0.5$, the PD's output electrical SNR becomes

$$\text{SNR}_{e,pd}[\text{dB}] = 16.75[\text{dB}] - L_{o,atm}[\text{dB}]. \quad (26)$$

The larger is the intensity modulation index β, the more notable becomes the non-linear distortion introduced by the MZM. In this situation, Digital Pre-Distortion (DPD) is needed to keep non-linear distortion under control [7].

The minimum and maximum E_b/N_0 values that were tested in the access link were $E_b/N_{0_{min}} = 0\,\text{dB}$ and $E_b/N_{0_{max}} = 11\,\text{dB}$, respectively, with a fixed step size of 0.1 dB. Finally, the SNR for the feeder link was set to $\text{SNR}_{fl} = 15\,\text{dB}$ for all performance evaluations, according to the parameters listed in Table 8.

Table 9. Maximum throughput in the hybrid radio/optical NB-IoT satellite link.

Modulation	Rc=0.27	Rc=0.44	Rc=0.17	Rc=0.67
BPSK	δ=0%=> γ=0.216	δ=0%=> γ=0.352	-	-
	δ=25%=> γ=0.288	δ=25%=> γ=0.469		
	δ=40%=> γ=0.36	δ=40%=> γ=0.58		
QPSK	-	-	δ=0%=> γ=0.17	δ=0%=> γ=1.072
			δ=25%=> γ=0.362	δ=25%=> γ=1.4293
			δ=40%=> γ=0.4533	δ=40%=> γ=1.7867

Thus, we can now show the effect that the optical feeder link transmission (downlink) has in the end-to-end BER, Packet Error Rate (PER) and normalized Throughput. Furthermore, for the uncoded case ($R_c = 1$), we also visualize the upper bound performance for the end-to-end BER, PER and Throughput, which would be achievable in case of an ideal optical feeder link (SNR$_{e,pd} \gg 1$), $i.e.$,

$$P_{b,\text{BPSK}} = \frac{1}{2}\text{erfc}\left(\sqrt{\frac{E_b}{N_0}}\right), \tag{27}$$

$$P_{b,\text{QPSK}} = \frac{1}{2}\text{erfc}\left(\sqrt{\frac{E_b}{N_0}}\right)\left[1 - \frac{1}{4}\text{erfc}\left(\sqrt{\frac{E_b}{N_0}}\right)\right] \tag{28}$$

Then, PER $= 1 - (1 - P_b)^N$, where N is the length of the data sequence to transmit, and P_b is the BER of the access link in case of BPSK/QPSK (here, good enough SNR in the optical feeder link was assumed). Regarding the normalized throughput, it is equal to

$$\text{TP} = \frac{(1 - \text{PER})\, N_b\, R_c}{(1 + \rho)(1 - \delta)}, \tag{29}$$

where N_b is the number of bits per modulated symbol. Note that the roll-off factor (ρ) of the optical feeder link and the code rate R_c of the NB-IoT transmission penalize the throughput of the end-to-end link, whereas the overlapping factor (δ) and the modulation order (N_b) increase it.

The use of time-packing compensates in part the reduction in the data rate that the use of error control coding and finite-duration SRRC pulses introduce. Moreover, the selection of suitable MCS in the end-to-end NB-IoT transmission controls the errors that are added either in the radio access and optical feeder links of the reverse GEO satellite channel. In this regards, Table 9 shows the maximum throughput that is achievable when $R_c = 0.27, 0.44$ ($R_c = 0.17, 0.67$) with BPSK/2-PAM (QPSK/4-PAM) are used in the access/feeder link, with overlapping factors $\delta = 0, 25, 40\%$. This maximum throughput attains the form $\gamma = \frac{N_b R_c}{(1+\rho)(1-\delta)}$. Finally, the receive equalizer relies on an adaptive linear MMSE filter, as described in Sect. 3, with a 100 000-symbol training, $L_w = 13$ coefficients to estimate the current symbol, and forgetting factor $\mu = 0.05$.

4.2   Simulation Results

Figure 4 shows the BER of the reverse link (end-to-end) in terms of the E_b/N_0. It is composed of three sub-figures, each of them for a different overlapping factor: $\delta = 0\%$ (Fig. 4a), $\delta = 25\%$ (Fig. 4b), and $\delta = 40\%$ (Fig. 4c). In these figures, the modulation is not the essential parameter, but rather the code rate, as the Energy-per-Bit is kept constant for all tested schemes. Consequently, we should expect that the lower is the code rate, the better is the BER. However, this conclusions is valid at high E_b/N_0, since the redundancy that introduces the channel coding may increase the number of erroneous bits after its iterative decoding process at lower values of E_b/N_0. As a result, we are able to distinguish three regions in Fig. 4: i) low E_b/N_0 values ($E_b/N_0 \leq 5\,\mathrm{dB}$), ii) Medium E_b/N_0 values ($5\,\mathrm{dB} \leq E_b/N_0 \leq 7.5\,\mathrm{dB}$), and iii) High E_b/N_0 values ($E_b/N_0 \geq 7.5\,\mathrm{dB}$). In the first region, the scheme with best BER uses QPSK/4-PAM in the access/feeder link with $R_c = 1$. This means that the best option at low SNR is an uncoded transmission, since the turbo decoding process augments the number of errors when it is used at lower code rates (i.e., diverges). Next, in the Medium SNR

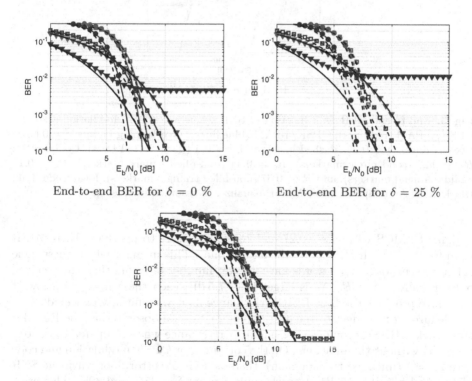

End-to-end BER for $\delta = 0\ \%$ End-to-end BER for $\delta = 25\ \%$

Fig. 4. End-to-end BER as a function of E_b/N_0 when $\rho = 0.25$. Modulation schemes: BPSK/2-PAM (red lines), QPSK/4-PAM (blue lines). Coded rates: $R_c = 0.27$ (solid circle markers), $R_c = 0.44$ (non-filled square markers), $R_c = 0.17$ (solid diamond markers), and $R_c = 0.67$ (non-filled triangle markers). Ideal feeder link: Black lines. An adaptive linear MMSE equalizer is used in reception at the satellite gateway.

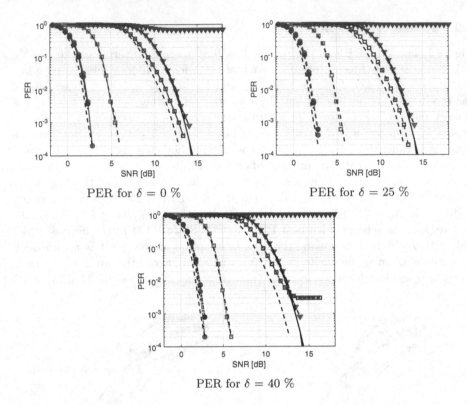

PER for $\delta = 0$ %   PER for $\delta = 25$ %

PER for $\delta = 40$ %

Fig. 5. End-to-end PER as a function of SNR when $\rho = 0.25$. Modulation schemes: BPSK/2-PAM (red lines), QPSK/4-PAM (blue lines). Overlapping factors: $\delta = 0$ (continuous lines), $\delta = 0.25$ (dashed lines), and $\delta = 0.4$ (dash-dotted lines). Coded rates: $R_c = 0.27$ (solid circle markers), $R_c = 0.44$ (non-filled square markers), $R_c = 0.17$ (solid diamond markers), and $R_c = 0.67$ (non-filled triangle markers). Ideal feeder link: Black lines. An adaptive linear MMSE equalizer is assumed in reception.

region, the MCS with $R_c = 0.27$ and $R_c = 0.44$ start to provide a better BER than the MCS with $R_c = 0.67$ (the largest one). This means that for these code rates, the turbo-decoded words have a lower number of errors than the received ones. Finally, if the E_b/N_0 is larger than 7.5 dB, then the scheme with lowest code rate provides the best BER performance as it was initially expected.

Regarding the effect of the overlapping factor, we observe that the BER for time-packed BPSK provides very similar performance when compared to the one of BPSK without time-packing. On the contrary, for QPSK modulation and code rate $R_c = 1$ (uncoded transmission), there is a visible error floor when the SNR of the feeder link is 15 dB at overlapping factors $\delta = 25\%$ and 40%. This error floor disappears when the SNR of the feeder link increases. So, the turbo-code permits to reduce/remove the time-packed ISI that the equalizer cannot remove.

Next, Fig. 5 shows the end-to-end PER of the reverse link as function of the SNR of the access link. Similarly, it contains three subfigures, each of them with

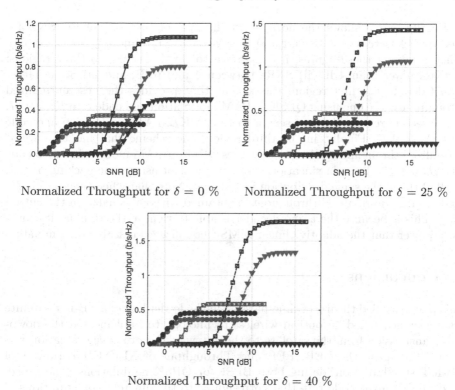

Normalized Throughput for $\delta = 0$ %   Normalized Throughput for $\delta = 25$ %

Normalized Throughput for $\delta = 40$ %

Fig. 6. Normalized throughput as a function of SNR when roll-off factor is $\rho = 0.25$. Modulation schemes: BPSK/2-PAM (red lines), QPSK/4-PAM (blue lines). Overlapping factors: $\delta = 0$ (continuous lines), $\delta = 0.25$ (dashed lines), and $\delta = 0.4$ (dashed-dotted lines). Code Rates: BPSK/2-PAM $R_c = 0.27$ (solid circle markers) and $R_c = 0.44$ (non-filled square markers); QPSK/4-PAM $R_c = 0.17$ (solid diamond markers) and $R_c = 0.67$ (non-filled triangle markers). Equalizer used in detection: adaptive MMSE.

a different overlapping factor: $\delta = 0\%$ (Fig. 5a), $\delta = 25\%$ (Fig. 5b), and $\delta = 40\%$ (Fig. 5c). In this case, the distribution of the plotted curves is quite different from Fig. 4, and we observe the lower is the code rate for the given modulation, the better is the PER performance. In this case, it is possible to check that QPSK with $R_c = 0.17$ and BPSK with $R_c = 0.27$ provide the best results. Next, it comes the BPSK with $R_c = 0.44$ and QPSK with $R_c = 0.67$. In both cases, PER performance with and without time-packing shows similar performance results. Finally, the uncoded transmissions ($R_c = 1$) provide the worst PER. In fact, all cases with and without time-packing show an error floor. Moreover, the theoretical PER is close to the optimal one for BPSK/QPSK in part of this bound. On the contrary, coded transmissions with(out) time-packing do not show any error floor when the SNR of the feeder link is 15 dB. Furthermore, their performance is close to the one when the feeder link SNR is good enough.

Finally, Fig. 6 shows the normalized throughput in terms of the SNR for overlapping factors $\delta = 0\%$ (Fig. 6a), $\delta = 25\%$ (Fig. 6b) and $\delta = 40\%$ (Fig. 6c). When studying these figures, it is possible to divide them into three regions: i) SNRs lower than 4 dB, ii) SNRs between 4 and 6 dB, and iii) SNRs larger than 6 dB. In the first region, the scheme that provides the best normalized throughput is the one using QPSK/4-PAM modulation and code rate $R_c = 0.17$. In the second region, the best scheme uses BPSK/2-PAM modulation and code rate $R_c = 0.27$. Finally, in the third region, the scheme that has the largest normalized throughput is the one that uses QPSK/4-PAM modulation with code rate $R_c = 0.67$. This classification is independent of using time-packing or not. In all of them, the same distribution is observed. Note that when time-packing is used, a larger normalized throughput is obtained without penalty on the cut-off SNR. This is because the turbo-decoder is able to remove the residual ISI-plus-noise power that the adaptive linear MMSE equalizer is not able to eliminate.

5   Conclusions

This paper studied the use of time-packing in the feeder link of a NB-IoT satellite system, which relied on optical wireless technology to implemented the down-link transmission from the satellite to the gateway. Performance evaluation was carried out using the BER, PER and Throughput of NPUSCH Format 1 of NB-IoT standard, considering both BPSK or QPSK modulations. The procedure to obtain the code rate that corresponds to the different configurations of the NPUSCH of NB-IoT standard was described, assuming that the Transport Block Size was 256 bits regardless the modulation. It was also assumed that the GEO satellite implemented a Detect-and-Forward strategy, performing a symbol-by-symbol detection, QAM-to-PAM symbol-mapping, time-packing processing, electrical-to-optical conversion, and downlink transmission to the satellite gateway. Finally, an adaptive-MMSE equalizer was assumed in reception at the gateway, in order to mitigate the ISI introduced by time-packing. Simulation results showed that this adaptive-MMSE equalizer was able to remove most of the ISI, leaving aside just a minimal residual part. It was also possible to see that the lower is the SNR of the optical feeder link and/or the higher is the modulation order of the NB-IoT transmission, the worse is the capability of the adaptive-MMSE equalizer to remove the ISI. It was also observed that uncoded BPSK/2-PAM transmissions did not present any error floor at practical optical feeder link SNR values ($SNR_{fl} = 15$ dB) and medium/large overlapping factors ($\delta = 25$ and 40%). However, this is not the case for uncoded QPSK/4-PAM modulation, which showed an error floor in the same SNR range. To remove this residual ISI, this paper took advantage of the turbo-decoding process that NB-IoT receivers perform. Simulation results showed that most residual ISI power can be eliminated in reception, even for moderate SNR values in the optical feeder link and large overlapping factors. Consequently, it is possible to conclude that wireless optical links assisted by time-packed waveforms represent an interesting solution for extending the data rates Beyond 5G, particularly in integrated terrestrial-satellite networks. This claim becomes more relevant in IoT services, whose traffic demand will notably increase in the next few years.

References

1. 3GPP: LTE; Evolved universal terrestrial radio access (E-UTRA); Multiplexing and channel coding. 3GPP tech. specification, TS 36.212, Ver. 15.9 Rel. 15 (2018)
2. 3GPP: LTE; Evolved universal terrestrial radio access (E-UTRA); Physical channels and modulation. 3GPP tech. specification, TS 36.211, Ver. 15.2 Rel. 15 (2018)
3. 3GPP: LTE; Evolved universal terrestrial radio access (E-UTRA); Physical layer procedures. 3GPP tech. specification, TS 36.213, Ver. 15.9 Rel. 15 (2018)
4. Bas, J., Dowhuszko, A.: Linear time-packing detectors for optical feeder link in high throughput satellite systems. In: Proceedings of 1st Mosharaka International Conference on Emerging Applications of Electrical Engineering, pp. 1–6, September 2020
5. Bas, J., Dowhuszko, A.: Time-packing as enabler of optical feeder link adaptation in high throughput satellite systems. In: Proceedings of 5G World Forum, pp. 1–7, September 2020
6. Bas, J., Pérez-Neira, A.: On the physical layer security of IoT devices over satellite. In: Proceedings of European Signal Processing Conference, pp. 1–5, September 2019
7. Dowhuszko, A., Mengali, A., Arapoglou, P., Pérez-Neira, A.: Total degradation of a DVB-S2 satellite system with analog transparent optical feeder link. In: Proceedings of IEEE Global Communications Conference, pp. 1–6, December 2019
8. Forney, G.: Maximum-likelihood sequence estimation of digital sequences in the presence of intersymbol interference. IEEE Trans. Inform. Theory $18(3)$, 363–378 (1972)
9. Haykin, S.: Adaptive Filter Theory: International Edition. Pearson Education Limited, London (2014)
10. Leibrich, J., Ali, A., Paul, H., Rosenkranz, W., Kammeyer, K.: Impact of modulator bias on the OSNR requirement of direct-detection optical OFDM. IEEE Photonics Technol. Lett. $21(15)$, 1033–1035 (2009)
11. London School of Economics: Nanosatellite telecommunications: A market study for IoT/M2M applications, August 2017
12. Mazo, J.: Faster-than-Nyquist signaling. Bell Syst. Tech. J. 54, 1451–1462 (1975)
13. Mengali, A.: Optical feeder link satellite systems. In: Link Optimization in future generation satellite systems, chap. 4, pp. 61–86. Ph.D. thesis, University of Luxembourg, October 2018
14. Modenini, A.: Advanced transceivers for spectrally efficient communications. Ph.D. dissertation, January 2014
15. Northern Sky Research: M2M and IoT via satellite 10, December 2019
16. Rusek, F., Anderson, J.: Constrained capacities for Faster-than-Nyquist signaling. IEEE Trans. Inform. Theory $55(2)$, 764–775 (2009)
17. Ungerboeck, G.: Adaptive maximum-likelihood receiver for carrier-modulated data-transmission systems. IEEE Trans. Commun. $22(5)$, 624–636 (1974)
18. Viterbi, A.: Error bounds for convolutional codes and an asymptotically optimum decoding algorithm. IEEE Trans. Inform. Theory $13(2)$, 260–269 (1967)

Decentralized Brains: A Reference Implementation with Performance Evaluation

Aswin Karthik Ramachandran Venkatapathy[1,2]([envelope]) [iD], Anas Gouda[1] [iD],
Michael ten Hompel[1,2] [iD], and Joseph Paradiso[3] [iD]

[1] TU Dortmund University, 44227 Dortmund, Germany
{aswinkarthik.ramachandran,anas.gouda}@tu-dortmund.de
[2] Fraunhofer Institute for Material-Handling and Logistics,
44227 Dortmund, Germany
michael.ten.hompel@iml.fraunhofer.de
[3] Medialab, Massachusetts Institute of Technology, Cambridge 02139, USA
joep@media.mit.edu
https://flw.mb.tu-dortmund.de

Abstract. *Decentralized Brains* is a concept developed for multiple parallel control of decentralized collaborative swarms and systems. This systems communication paradigm comprises of local peer-to-peer control as well as the global state management which is required for large-scale collaborative systems. The scenarios vary from self-assembly protocols for aerospace structures to organizing a warehouse in a material-handling context where heterogeneous systems collaboratively accomplish a task. A reference implementation of the conceptualized protocol is developed and deployed in a 345 node test bed. A reliable broadcast communication primitive using synchronous broadcast is deployed in a dual-band System on Chip (SoC) micro-controller. The performance of the adopted synchronous broadcast for network-wide flooding and consensus is presented in this article. The firmware is based on the latest branch of Contiki-Open Source Operating System - Next Generation (Contiki-NG) to keep further open source implementations easier and modularized as per the ISO OSI networking model. Using the concepts of multi-hop mesh networking, network flooding using synchronous broadcasts from wireless sensor networks and multi-band radio controllers for cognitive radios, a hardware-software architecture is developed, deployed and evaluated. The synchronous broadcast has a success rate of more than 95% in network wide floods and the implicit network wide time synchronisation of less than 1 µs which is evaluated using experiments using a 345 node test bed is presented in this paper. The developed communication primitives for the target hardware CC1350 STK and the developed experiments are available at https://github.com/akrv/deBr.

Keywords: Wireless sensor networks · Decentralized communication · Network flooding · Constructive interference · Synchronous broadcast · Concurrent transmissions · Distributed consensus · Time synchronization

L. Peñalver and L. Parra (Eds.): Industrial IoT 2020, LNICST 365, pp. 80–99, 2021.
https://doi.org/10.1007/978-3-030-71061-3_6

1 Introduction

The terminology of *Decentralized Brains* is inspired by evolutionary biology. Cephalopods are a family of species from the molluscan class Cephalopoda such as a squid, octopus, or nautilus. From the perspective of evolution, the class of Cephalopoda has multiple brains and they work towards a common goal in a decentralized manner. The reason for such organisms to have separate brains or a *decentralized brains* is to delegate motor processes without detracting from other important functions. Neurons in an octopus are found in the arms, which can independently taste and touch and also control basic motions without the supervision of a central brain [1,2]. In other words, the decentralized brains of an octopus would order to grapple its prey after sensing it and the nerve cells in its tentacles would make the individually detailed control decisions regarding that action. This decentralized intelligence allows for autonomous task completion— an intent is broadcasted across the *brains* and respective nervous systems take action locally. Socially networked industry was a terminology coined to explicitly refer to the collaborative nature of industrial entities. Here a social network between the sensors, robots, drones and various workstations is established to exchange, negotiate and act on the information that is available in the network. Various scenarios of socially networked industries are explored in previous literature [3–6]. Collective behavior from a biological perspective often involves large numbers of autonomous organs or organisms interacting to produce complex assemblies [3]. *Kilobots*, an effort to mimic biology inspired self-assembly demonstrated the ability of self-assembly in a large-scale autonomous miniaturized robotic system [3]. It was achieved by creating and programming swarm behaviour to achieve a global behavior with the nodes i.e., the robots interacting between each other [3]. *Decentralized Brains* focuses on the communication

Fig. 1. Sensor floor 3d render showing the topology of the nodes.

between the nodes in scenarios of self-assembly and heterogeneous collaboration of nodes taking care of the communication payload dissemination. This allows the implementation of hardware-based extensions to existing centralized industrial scenarios to retrofit decentralized collaboration on a network level [2]. Using such a communication paradigm it becomes easier to implement and deploy multiple parallel control of decentralized systems. An abstract example from the perspective of networking and communication is when a node wants to discover and join a network and wants to start operating within the network to perform collaborative tasks. The collaborative task can be for self-assembly where the control systems have to exchange precise information between interacting nodes and disseminate the change in global states across all nodes in the network. We present this paper as a follow up to the *Decentralized Brains* concept [2], in advance of future large-scale integration of the communications architecture in diverse production systems. **Contributions** to this paper are (*i*) development of a networking architecture using well-proven, low-power, low data-rate industrial Cyber Physical Systems (CPS) and wireless communication standards applicable for self-assembly protocols, (*ii*) evaluation of a novel method for broadcasting and network flooding in a dual-band SoC and (*iii*) an implementation and performance evaluation on a 345 node test bed called the sensor floor deployed using commercially available off-the-shelf hardware (Fig. 1).

The background section gives insights on the concept of *Decentralized Brains* and low data-rate standards with some details on the software stacks used. Section 3 discusses the concept of synchronous broadcast which is the main concept *Decentralized Brains* is based on, followed by the hardware and software implementation where the core contribution of this paper exists. Section 4 presents our experimental test-bed and two experiments, first one shows that synchronous broadcast is possible for Sub-1-GHz band the second presents running our protocol for 50000 packets.

2 Background

In this section the elements that are required to form a low data-rate *Decentralized Brains* network are described with their respective architectures. The underlying architectures are well-known in the field of Wireless Sensor Networkss (WSNs). These architectures are implemented in a special dual SoC hardware to demonstrate the effects of *Decentralized Brains*. Leveraging the concept of time synchronization, a reliable synchronous broadcast approach is implemented by creating constructive interference that becomes the fundamental element for *Decentralized Brains*.

Few worth notable related-works that used the phenomenon of synchronous transmissions are Glossy [7], Low-power Wireless Bus (LWB) [8], Chaos [9], and Baloo [10]. The basic synchronous broadcast primitive was developed by Glossy [7] which is used in many other communication protocols such as LWB and Chaos. *Decentralized Brains* also proposes to use an adaptation of Glossy to the target hardware with dual-band SoC from Texas Instruments CC1350.

The method used for developing a reliable broadcast using synchronous transmissions is called the capture effect. Capture effect happens due to the intrinsic redundancy available in digital modulation schemes. Glossy [7] explores the nature of synchronous transmissions using constructive interference in low-power WSNs. The phenomenon of constructive interference based synchronous broadcast has been exploited in other works to develop routing-less networking for low-power WSNs. LWB turns a multi-hop low-power wireless network into an infrastructure similar to a shared bus, where all nodes are potential receivers of all data [8]. It achieves this by mapping all traffic demands on fast network floods, and by globally scheduling every flood using Glossy [7,8]. As a result, LWB inherently supports one-to-many, many-to-one, and many-to-many traffic [8]. Baloo is a flexible network stack design framework to facilitate the development of protocols based on Synchronous Transmissions to implement a wide variety of network layer protocols, while introducing only limited memory and energy overhead [10].

2.1 Decentralized Brains

The distributed cognition framework in [11], for collaborative efforts between humans, defines distributed cognition as cognitive activities viewed as computations which take place via the propagation of various information and knowledge transformation through media. The media here refers to both internal (e.g. individual memories) and external representations (wireless communication and other sensing capabilities). The states of the representations refer to various information and knowledge resources transformation during collaborative manoeuvres. According to the study [11], the way knowledge is propagated across different representational states is characterized by communicative pathways that are continuously interrupted and coordinated sequences of action by the demands of an ever-changing environment. Here, the evolution of the nervous system in an octopus is used as an inspiration and the notion of distributed cognition is used to conceptualize the idea of *Decentralized Brains*. The representational states are reliably replicated between the collaborating systems in a distributed wireless communication architecture [2]. This allows for local actuation without global coordination and facilitates multiple parallel control for collaborative maneuvers [2].

In distributed systems, the most common replication topology is to have a single leader that then replicates the changes to all the other nodes in the network with the benefit of avoiding conflicts caused by concurrent writes [2]. All the clients are writing to the same server, so the coherence in the data is maintained by the leader [2]. As shown in Fig. 2, our data replication spans two radio physical layers with multiple state transitions starting from network discovery. This helps in reducing channel contention while keeping lower bounds in latency [2].

The consensus protocol is inherently developed as a centralized protocol with network discovery and leader election methods. The main motivation of this architecture is to understand and identify the workhorse of a consensus protocol and to reliably develop those networking primitives in a modular manner.

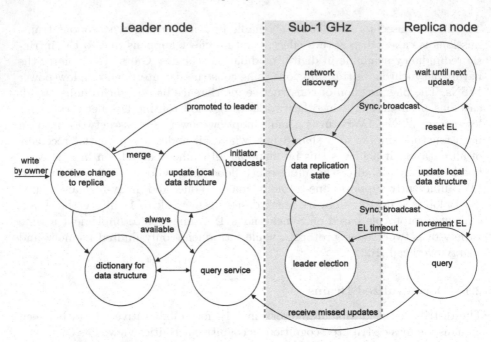

Fig. 2. *Decentralized Brains* networking architecture [2]

Modularity and reproducibility of the results in wireless sensor networks will facilitate further complex consensus algorithms to be implemented. From understanding and implementing a decentralized context broker [12], it can be drawn out that the fundamental requirement for a consensus protocol to reliably function is to have a robust atomic broadcast communication primitive within the network. Therefore, a method of reliable network flooding is identified in [2] and it is implemented taking into consideration the target hardware. An experiment is setup to prove that the broadcast communication primitive can be reliably deployed in Sect. 3.

The communication flow of the *Decentralized Brains* is illustrated in Fig. 2. There are two types of nodes in the network, the leader node and the replica node. Leveraging the fact that each node is equipped with a dual band networking, it is possible to operate two networking paradigms in parallel. One of the networks is deployed in 2.4 GHz networking which is a IPv6 over Low-Power Wireless Personal Area Networks (6LoWPAN) network and the other network is deployed in the Sub-1-GHz network which performs the data replication operation among the nodes [2]. A cohesive network spanning over two radio networks is developed in *Decentralized Brains* to increase the communication throughput and decrease the latency for replication [2]. The data replication state is met when networking flooding is performed using the synchronous broadcasts to propagate the same message across a large number of nodes that are sparsely deployed in a large spatial area or in a dense environment [2].

In this article we take into consideration the dense environment as usually seen in industry 4.0 scenarios [2]. The data that needs to be replicated is sent from the originator of the data to the leader node [2]. The leader node initiates the synchronous broadcast which results in a network flooding in the sub-1-GHz band [2]. The leader node also receives the changes to replica and it manages the most recent replica of the data structure which will be propagated throughout the network using the synchronous broadcasts [2]. For synchronous broadcasts, a strict clock synchronisation is required between the nodes which is implemented and tested in Sect. 4. 6LoWPAN is the networking layer provided by Contiki-NG which is used to create the 2.4 GHz network for one-to-one communication between the originator data and the leader node [13]. This networking layer provides a multi-hop mesh network, therefore the originator and leader nodes can reliably communicate in harsh environments [13]. Since there are extensive amount of literature available discussing the reliability and the performance of a large-scale 6LoWPAN based networking, the focus of this work is to present the performance evaluation of the synchronous broadcasts which is a newly developed networking primitive for this hardware. In the following Sect. 2.2, the idea for using Contiki-NG as the background for the networking layer of *Decentralized Brains*.

2.2   Why Use Contiki-NG?

The Contiki-NG official documentation states the following and also delivers on those points which is the main motivation for using Contiki-NG.

> Contiki-NG is an open-source, cross-platform operating system for Next-Generation IoT devices. It focuses on dependable (secure and reliable) low-power communication and standard protocols, such as IPv6/6LoWPAN, 6TiSCH, RPL, and CoAP. Contiki-NG comes with extensive documentation, tutorials, a road-map, release cycle, and well-defined development flow for smooth integration of community contributions.

Above all of this, it also liberates the developer and provides an operating system that is hardware agnostic. We strive to develop the *Decentralized Brains* also with the same philosophy as Contiki-NG to provide with the developers to apply synchronous broadcast communication primitive however possible in applications and not only for a distributed consensus in low-power WSNs. Moreover, the software support with well mature features that are required for developing the *Decentralized Brains* networking layer is provided by Contiki-NG. This allows for the extending the *Decentralized Brains* networking paradigm further into other hardware systems and applications. The network stack of Contiki-NG is shown in Table 1 which shows the necessary components that are developed for the IEEE 802.15.4 standard. It provides the Medium Access Control (MAC) layer for the 6LoWPAN networking using Carrier Sense Multiple Access (CSMA)/CA. The operating system also provides the flexibility to turn-off and on the features during run-time which is a requirement for developing the synchronous broadcasts communication primitive. Here the MAC layer is extended to provide the

Table 1. Contiki netstack along with *Decentralized Brains* netstack

OSI layers	Contiki-NG	Decentralized Brain implementation
Application	Web-socket, http-socket, coap.c	DeBr
Transport	udp-socket, tcp-socket	
Network, routing	uip6, rpl	Not required
Adaption	sicslowpan.c	
MAC	csma.c	Time synchronised scheduling
Duty cycling	nullrdc, contikimac	Synchronous broadcast
Radio	MSP430, CC1350, ...	CC1350 (Sub-1-Ghz)

functionality for synchronous broadcasts as the opposite of listen-before talk is required during this type of network flooding. In this network flooding, all nodes that are going to participate in the synchronous broadcast round will not listen to the channel rather transmit the payload as soon as the time constraints are met.

With a strict time synchronisation protocol, an effect called constructive interference is achieved between the nodes that are simultaneously transmitting in the medium [2,7]. The Radio Duty Cycling (RDC) layer and the MAC layer are the two layers that require flexible and scheduled operation using the synchronised time and the modularity provided by Contiki-NG in such granularity makes it easier to implement features that are necessary for *Decentralized Brains* communication layer. A reproducible, modular code base that can be used to develop applications is the goal of *Decentralized Brains* and Contiki-NG accelerates this process.

3 Communication Overview

In this section, the workhorse of the *Decentralized Brains* is presented. For any consensus algorithm to function reliably, a robust broadcast mechanism is required. Such a broadcast mechanism is identified and developed for the large-scale low power consensus [2]. In WSNs, network flooding a concept to distribute information updates quickly to every node in a large network. In the case of *Decentralized Brains*, we developed a method that was presented in [7] called Glossy, where the effect of constructive interference is achieved to reduce the time and reliably flood the network with the data that needs to be distributed across the network. The concept of synchronous broadcast is presented in the following Sect. 3.1. There are certain requirements for the design of the presented concepts which arise due to the choice of hardware. The features for low power operation which are considered as design choices for implementing the necessary components of *Decentralized Brains* are discussed in Sect. 3.2 followed by the implementation details in the target hardware which is discussed in the same Sect. 3.2.

3.1   Synchronous Broadcast

When a node is transmitting in a wireless medium, the node is broadcasting the packet information in the channel for all the nodes in the network. Due to this broadcast nature of wireless communications, interference occurs whenever stations are close enough to listen to each other and whenever they are transmitting concurrently [7]. Collision or interference is an effect due to the overlap of signals in both the time and space when the transmitting nodes share the same physical layer characteristics [7]. Digital wireless communication implements multiple factors for redundancy in radio communication to mitigate for interference. Therefore, the communication link reliability becomes a probability in success of transmission from a Boolean if the communication will be successful or not for a given scenario. Interference is one such factor that reduces the probability that a receiver will correctly detect the information embedded in the wireless signals [7]. Interference has been always considered as destructive in nature owing it to the fact that the communication reliability reduces due to interference. There are two types of effects due to interference which can be called *Constructive* and *destructive* interference [7].

We explore the nature of constructive interference in this case to develop the most important communication primitive of *Decentralized Brains*. If the overlap of the transmitted signals does not superpose with each other, then the interference is destructive and the probability of the transmitted data reaching the destination reduces. Whereas, when the base band signals from multiple transmitters superpose, the receiver detects the superposition of the transmitted signals that are generated by multiple transmitters [7]. For achieving the effect of the constructive interference it is necessary for the transmitted base band signals to be within a time window with respect to the carrier frequency used for communication to allow for the detection of superposition. The time window is strict as the mismatch in the temporal synchronisation will effect the transmission reliability due to destructive interference. To achieve the constructive effect, it is necessary for the transmitting stations to be time synchronised. Due to the complexity, cost for energy, and the hardware support for reliable software execution required for time synchronisation, the effect of constructive interference has not been extensively exploited in WSNs [7,14]. In [7], a low power time synchronisation algorithm is implemented to achieve the effect of constructive interference whereas in *Decentralized Brains* a different approach is used which is discussed in Sect. 3.2. Using the time synchronization, we enable nodes to synchronize their clocks which is required for waking up and listening to a broadcast, calculate any skew, correct the clock and wait for the predetermined delay to retransmit. By synchronizing to another transmitters clock, we exploit the nature of constructive interference which allows for concurrent multiple transmissions to take place in the same channel. Using CSMA/CA MAC strategy, the broadcast medium is used efficiently for contention based wireless transmission by avoiding any collisions of two transmitting stations in the medium. But to allow for concurrent multiple transmissions using constructive interference, we enable the devices to transmit into the wireless channel all at the same time. Even though

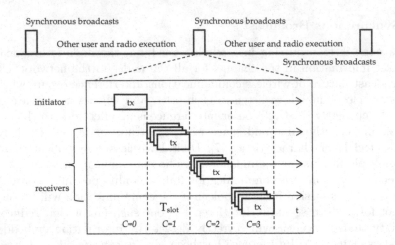

Fig. 3. Synchronous broadcast rounds with T_{slot} and counter C for number keeping track of number of transmissions [2, 7]

it is contrary to the operation of the well proven CSMA/CA MAC strategy, with the help of strict time synchronisation we make it possible for the devices to transmit simultaneously. By creating the opportunity for nodes to overhear packets from neighboring nodes using [7], nodes turn on their radios, listen for the transmitted packets over the wireless medium, and relay overheard packets immediately after receiving them with an allowed software delay where time synchronisation is performed amongst the nodes. Since the neighbors of a sender receive a packet at the same time, they also start to relay the packet at the same time. Here the time at which each node transmits after reception is governed by the time synchronisation and which nodes are allowed to transmit from the set of received messages are defined in the communication protocol. This again triggers other nodes to receive and relay the packet. In this way, glossy benefits from concurrent transmissions by quickly propagating a packet from a source node (initiator) to all other nodes (receivers) in the network [7]. Based on [7], the temporal offset among concurrent IEEE 802.15.4 transmitters must not exceed 0.5 μs to generate constructive interference with high probability.

As shown in Fig. 3, the radio transitions between three states looping between two states until the counter is exhausted. When a new node joins the network without using the network discovery, the node synchronizes its clock with the root node by listening to the broadcast. The broadcast frame carries a counter which is used for determining the number of transmissions the node has to make with the same packet. Once the counter is 0, the node goes to sleep until the next broadcast round.

3.2   Design and Implementation

There are two main differences between the implementation of Glossy [7] and synchronous broadcast in *Decentralized Brains* [2]. The target hardware where synchronous broadcast is developed is a dual-band SoC (2.4 GHz & Sub-1-GHz) which can run two radio networks in two different physical layers. We choose the 2.4 GHz for data communication in a multi-hop mesh network topology where the nodes communicate with addresses in a 6LoWPAN IPv6 networking paradigm. The synchronous broadcast is developed in the Sub-1-GHz physical layer. Two main reasons for such a choice in developing the synchronous broadcasts is to increase the range of each of the nodes and to reduce the strict temporal distance window to improve the reliability of synchronous broadcasts. Moreover, it leverages the flexible, hardware specific simplelink SDK for deploying a low power multi-radio network. We precisely developed the synchronous broadcast in the 868 MHz band because the temporal distance is higher to achieve the effect of constructive interference and it allows the nodes to be synchronized less frequently. Therefore, the precision of synchronisation required can be less compared to glossy [7].

Why CC1350? is because of the ability to run two different radio networks in two different physical layers and also that the simplelink SDK allows it to be ported to other micro-controllers from TI to allow developers to freely choose hardware depending on the application scenario.

Due to the choice of the hardware and the development of synchronous broadcast in 868 MHz, it is not necessary to implement the time synchronisation explicitly as required in Glossy [7] as the temporal distance required for performing reliable constructive interference increases. Here we choose to implement the time synchronisation using the two hardware clock sources and not using an extra hardware capability to track the clock changes using capture units as the requirements are performed inherently by the hardware.

Implementation: Time synchronisation is required for synchronous broadcasts to achieve constructive interference. It is implemented in [7] where time synchronisation depends on 2 clock sources which are the Real-Time clock (RTC) and another higher frequency clock. The high frequency clock is sourced from the micro-controller's internal clock. It is widely known that this clock is unreliable due to skew and micro-controller operations. RTC provides better accuracy against clock drifts on the long term and the higher frequency clock provides better time resolution to achieve accurate synchronous broadcasts. For the implementation in [7] the Virtual High-resolution Time (VHT) approach [15] was used, which uses both the RTC and an internal high-frequency Digital Controlled Oscillator (DCO) from MSP430 MCU. VHT ensures high precision in time synchronisation and low power consumption which has been thought to be an oxymoron in designing distributed low power electronics [15].

For our implementation Dual-band CC1350 MCU is used with TI Simplelink SDK. CC1350 is a dual band SoC that contains 2 ARM Cortex cores, one is the main MCU core that runs the user logic and the operating system and the second core is dedicated for the radio functions and dual operation. The dedicated radio core is implemented to power up and down depending on the radio usage for power conservation purposes.

CC1350 radio operations are scheduled and time stamped with a separate 4 MHz timer, called RAT timer. Therefore, radio operations scheduling resolution is limited to that frequency. This dedicated core/timer of CC1350 gives it an advantage of running flooding protocols as it guarantees exact timing of the execution of radio commands, hence it gives more deterministic control over temporal distance and required delays between Glossy floods.

VHT is used in Glossy but in the *Decentralized Brains* we use the hardware supported implicit clock synchronisation. This synchronization happens between the 4 MHz RAT timer and the 32 KHz RTC clock. As the RAT-RTC synchronization command is issued for the first time, the radio core waits for the next RTC tick to start the RAT timer. To handle the power downs of the radio core, every time before issuing the power down command a RAT stop command is issued. This command returns a synchronization parameter that is passed to the RAT start command at the next radio core power up. This method keeps consistency between RTC and RAT and preserves the required clock resolution and power limits.

Also another feature of CC1350 is that time stamping of received packets is done automatically by the RF core using RAT time. These two features simplify the calculations of time for the next flood and provide a deterministic behaviour of the temporal distance between the nodes. Instead of a software time stamping, calculating and waiting for a software-delayed time as in [7], *Decentralized Brains* implements a full hardware based approach on CC1350. To adhere to the requirements for low-power operational constraints, the *Decentralized Brains* software uses only event-based callbacks for scheduling of floods as well as other auxiliary run-time software components.

As soon as a non-initiator node receives its first flood packet, it stores its base time with the received packet time stamp, increments the packet relay counter and then transfers to transmission mode. The time between packets within a flood is fixed, so the node immediately issues a transmission command to the RF core to send after this fixed time. The RF core handles the power up and down and automatically wakes up before the transmission time. Depending on the specified number of transmissions, the node may switch to the receiving mode until the number of re-transmissions is done. Also as the time between floods is fixed, the node schedules the beginning time of the next flood with the last callback of each flood.

4   Experimental Setup and Results

This section presents the following three parts: *(i)* developing and performing experiments to prove the effect of concurrent transmissions, *(ii)* a large-scale experiment developed to analyse the performance of synchronous broadcasts and finally *(iii)* the performance analysis to understand the reliability of synchronous

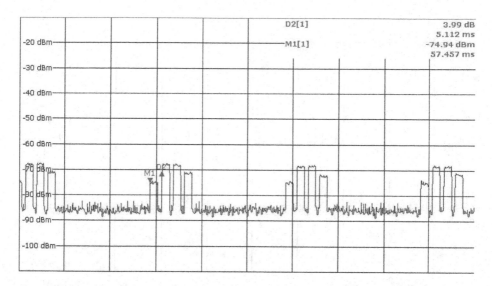

Fig. 4. Received signal power measured by spectrum analyzer. The X-axis is a time sweep of 2 s with distance between two vertical lines measuring 20 ms. The experiment is done using one initiator node and 3 non-initiator node.

broadcasts used in *Decentralized Brains* for developing decentralized consensus algorithms. Each experiment is performed with a different setup, hence the setup for each experiment will be explained individually. Initially the effect of concurrent transmission on received signal power and distortion are presented with the help of measurements using a spectrum analyzer. As discussed in Sect. 3.1, multiple nodes are transmitting simultaneously within an allowed window of time. This experiment visualizes the received signal power measured with the help of a spectrum analyzer listening at 868 MHz where nodes are placed away from the measuring antenna equidistantly.

4.1   Observing Effect of Concurrent Transmissions

Figure 4 shows the effect of concurrent transmission when there are two nodes which are the initiator node and only one non-initiator node. In Fig. 5, the same experiment is done with one initiator and 3 non-initiator nodes transmitting simultaneously with the allowed window of temporal displacement is shown. In both of the experiments including two nodes and four nodes, the nodes receiving the packets from the designated imitator node re-transmit the packet three times as soon as they receive it. The number of re-transmission is arbitrarily chosen as three to demonstrate the effect of constructive interference during synchronous broadcasts.

It can be observed from Figs. 4 and 5 that every time a transmission occurs, there are peaks in the signal acquisition which are marked by the markers *M1* and *D2*. During these transmissions, since there is more than one transmitting node, the received power of the signal and distortion increases with the number

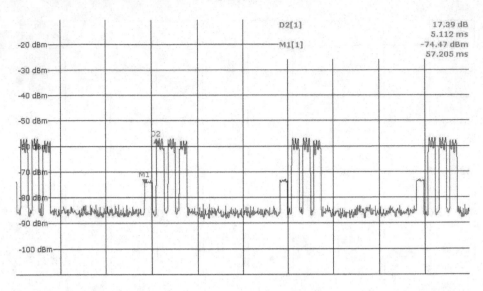

Fig. 5. Two nodes transmitting with different delays starting at 0 where absolute concurrent transmission occurs. The x-axis is the delay with a resolution of 0.25 μs. The experiment is performed for 20 times starting from 0.25 μs delay to 5 μs delay.

of concurrent transmissions. The first peak with the marker M1 is a packet transmitted by the initiator node hence, the measurement is not distorted and the received power is lower compared to the following peaks. The second and third peaks in the figures come from all of the nodes, hence they have the highest power and highest distortion. The last packet in each flood comes from non-initiator nodes, hence they have received a measured power slightly smaller than the previously received packets' measured power. This experiment is repeated for multiple rounds to ensure the effect of constructive interference.

In the *Experimental setup*, we present two experiments where both of the experiments were performed with a physical layer radio configuration of 50 Kpbs in a 2-GFSK modulation. The first experiment empirically quantifies the allowed temporal distance. This effect was already demonstrated for 2.4 GHz using the QPSK modulation in Glossy [7] but we perform the experiment in Sub-1-GHz band to prove the feasibility of constructive interference in this frequency band. Temporal distance is the allowed time window within which the effect of interference is constructive. The second experiment provides an insight into the effect of constructive interference due to the number of concurrent transmissions. It also helps in studying the effect of constructive interference in relation to the number of neighbors transmitting simultaneously.

The first experiment is performed in order to prove that constructive interference works for Sub 1-GHz and also calculates the minimum temporal distance. The experiment is performed by sending a signal from two nodes, one is delayed and the other one is non-delayed. To prove constructive interference and prevent the capture effect from making the receiving (RX) nodes capturing the

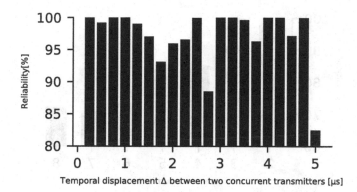

Fig. 6. The experiment studies the effect of temporal distance in case of two concurrent transmissions. The first transmitter sends the packet on the expected time and the other is delayed, The x-axis represents the amount of delay for each experiment with a resolution of $0.25\,\mu s$. The experiment is done for 20 times starting from $0.25\,\mu s$ delay to $5\,\mu s$ delay.

first signal, the non-delayed node sends at a power of $-10\,dBm$ and the delayed signal sends at a power of $0\,dBm$. The experiment is repeated multiple times increasing the delay by a step of $0.25\,\mu s$ each time. As observed in Fig. 6, the Sub-1-GHz behaves in a similar way to 2.4 GHz [7] where the shift in temporal distance results in several valleys and peaks. The signals get constructively and destructively interfered, but Sub-1-GHz (2-GFSK) seems to be prone to bigger temporal distances than 2.4 MHz as demonstrated in Glossy [7]. Figure 6 shows that the allowed temporal distance for Sub 1-GHz to reliably perform synchronous broadcasts due to constructive interference can be $1.25\,\mu s$. The signals can constructively interfere with a reliability of 97.06%.

The second experiment studies the effect of a number of neighboring nodes during synchronous broadcast rounds. The experiment starts with two nodes transmitting simultaneously. With each round of synchronous broadcast, the number of participating nodes is increased with an extra node. As observed in Fig. 7 flooding works at a 99.99% when there are 2 to 3 neighboring nodes. The behaviour starts to deteriorate in the experiment as more nodes join the synchronous broadcast round. After three nodes with a high reliability the nature of interference slowly shifts reaching a reliability of 72% when there are 8 neighboring nodes. Even though the reliability is above 70% for 8 nodes, this means that for every 10 packets sent, the constructive interference effect cannot be seen and three packets are lost. With a spatial long stretching, densely populated network for distributed sensing or collaborating control systems, this reliability can still offer certain capabilities that were not possible previously.

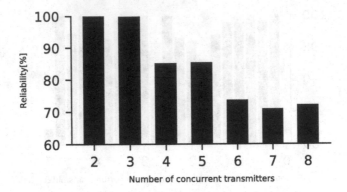

Fig. 7. This experiment studies the effect of the number of neighbours on the reliability of the packet received. The number of concurrent transmitters starts at 2 and increased by 1 for each next experiment.

4.2 Performance Evaluation

In this section we test our implementation on a local test bed (sensor-floor). We use a 345 node deployment to test the implementation. The 345 node deployment is called the sensor-floor which is a sensor network array embedded under the floor with CC1350 sensor tags. The floor contains 345 nodes, out of which, we choose a subset of 101 nodes randomly for every experiment run to count for the effect of spatial orientation and environment of the nodes for multi-path and scattering effects. 1 Initiator and 10 nodes for 10 concurrent transmissions are chosen randomly from the network of 345 nodes. Additionally these random patterns will allow for testing against different pattern arrangements of nodes along with the distance between nodes in the range of 1 to 30 m. The pattern choice and the sequence of transmissions performed for analysing the characteristics of constructive interference is listed in the Table 2.

As the Sub-1-GHz band can operate over greater distances which is greater than our test bed area. Therefore, we simulate the effect of hops as in the case of spatially distributed nodes in our experiments. Flood packets have their first byte used as a counter, this counter is set to zero by the initiator and incremented by 1 by all nodes with each re-transmission within a flood. Nodes are split into sequence groups, each group discards packets with a counter number less than a specific programmed number. As shown in Table 2 where the tests are presented, when the nodes are programmed to do 2 re-transmission ($N = 2$), with discarded packets marked as (x). Each sequence group keeps discarding flood packets until their programmed sequence number. When the sequence group identifier matches the counter byte then the sequence group joins the flood. In this manner a multi-hop test of 10 hops is simulated in our test bed for evaluating performance of spatially distributed nodes.

A flood is considered successful when a node receives the flood packet with the correct CRC (cyclic redundancy check) at least once, but we do not count floods in case no packets are received. The success rate is the rate of successful

Table 2. Testing on the sensor floor for re-transmissions (N = 2). For each of the 10 sequences, 10 nodes transmit concurrently. Each sequence is programmed to discard packets less than their sequence number based on the counter byte in the packet (First byte)

Node/re-transmission	0	1	2	3	4	5	6	7	8	9	10	11	12
Initiator	TX	RX	TX										
Sequence 0	RX	TX	RX	TX									
Sequence 1	x	RX	TX	RX	TX								
Sequence 2	x	x	RX	TX	RX	TX							
Sequence 3	x	x	x	RX	TX	RX	TX						
Sequence 4	x	x	x	x	RX	TX	RX	TX					
Sequence 5	x	x	x	x	x	RX	TX	RX	TX				
Sequence 6	x	x	x	x	x	x	RX	TX	RX	TX			
Sequence 7	x	x	x	x	x	x	x	RX	TX	RX	TX		
Sequence 8	x	x	x	x	x	x	x	x	RX	TX	RX	TX	
Sequence 9	x	x	x	x	x	x	x	x	x	RX	TX	RX	TX

Table 3. Overall success rate of testing on sensor floor

Concurrent transmissions (N)	Average success rate	Max no. of concurrent transmissions
N = 1	98.72%	10
N = 2	97.51%	20
N = 3	97.94%	30
N = 6	99.50%	50

floods over the overall number of floods averaged among all nodes on the floor. Each of the tests runs for 50000 packets.

Table 3 shows the result for the different number of re-transmissions. As it can be observed the increasing of re-transmissions helps in increasing the success rate. The success rate can reach 99.50% when there are 6 re-transmissions per synchronous broadcast flood round.

4.3   Energy Profile of *Decentralized Brains* Broadcast

In this section, the energy profile of the synchronous broadcast experiment is presented with the help of energy measurements using a oscilloscope. 1. as labelled in Fig. 8, startup phase or boot phase from the low energy mode to receive mode. Here initialization of all timers, clock synchronization, and the timers to extrapolate the high-speed clock from the slow clock are performed.

The second peak i.e., 2. as labelled in Fig. 8, is the reception of the first message from the initiator during the synchronous broadcast round.

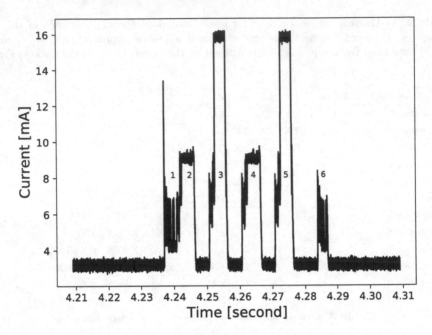

Fig. 8. Energy profile of synchronous broadcast

Until the third transient, label 3. in Fig. 8, the observed current draw, is the pre-defined software delay to synchronize all transmitters after message timestamping. The third peak is a decentralized synchronous transmission, where all other nodes are expected to be within the guaranteed temporal distance for effective constructive interference during transmission. The third peak observed in the figure is higher than the previous peak as transmission requires more energy than reception.

After taking part in the first transmission round, the node stays awake, listening to the next message to be transmitted again. There are four synchronous transmissions. The device under investigation will send only half the time as the alternating times; the node will listen for the same payload and clock synchronization.

The fifth peak (label 5 in Fig. 8) is the alternating second synchronous transmission attempt by this node. It is crucial to create an optimization plan across all nodes on the number of times a node can participate in synchronous broadcast transmission. In this scenario, a round is with four attempts, and every node can only participate two times. The larger and denser the network, the number of transmissions within a flood round should be increased. Reducing the participating nodes per round will optimize the network's overall energy cost.

The sixth peak (label 6 in Fig. 8) is the final round, where the node schedules its next network flood round to wake up if the application wants to conserve energy or allows other application-based processing and communication. The energy required is relatively lower than the reception and transmission since the

CPU schedules a timer enabling all the interrupts and returns to idle in this experiment scenario.

Cumulatively calculating the energy requirements from the measured energy profile, there are four synchronous broadcast rounds. We can calculate the overhead for decentralized synchronization as two transmissions and two receptions, each of which requires 13.4 mA at 10 dBm and 5.4 mA, respectively, as per the data sheet [16]. Use case dictates the frequency of decentralized synchronization that limits the recurrence of the synchronous broadcast. We can plan broadcast rounds with up to ten minutes of time delay between each round. This is the allowable limitation for time synchronization using message time stamping, after which the nodes cannot guarantee the temporal distance for synchronous broadcasts. Therefore, we can achieve decentralized synchronization at its highest level in the low-power wireless sensor networks with its calculated energy overhead required to perform the necessary communication primitives.

5   Conclusion

Decentralized Brains is a framework for developing distributed sensing and collaborative control systems in low-power, low data-rate WSNs networks [2]. In this article, the most important feature of *Decentralized Brains* called the synchronous broadcasts using constructive interference is developed, deployed in 345 low-power nodes and tested for performance. Various design choices and differences to existing implementations of constructive interference are discussed. The synchronous broadcasts module for *Decentralized Brains* is developed as part of the Contiki-NG to improve the transferable nature of the concepts and to make the features accessible for other industrial application developers. Leader election and network discovery are two further modules that leverage the synchronous broadcasts to create a decentralized network. When the network loses the initiator node which acts as the leader node due to energy constraints or because the network is highly mobile as discussed for self-assembly of space architectures [17], the network enters into a leader election phase where all nodes decide on another leader node using the same synchronous broadcast communication primitive [2].

5.1   Future Work

Porting Implementation to 2.4 MHz. As Simplelink SDK provides a unified API across several TI MCU, our implementation has the possibility to also be ported to 2.4 MHz devices that use the same SDK, for example TI CC2650. As per [7], the temporal distance for 2.4 MHz is 0.5 μs which is possible to be achieved with CC2650. As the radio clock of CC2650 is also 4 MHz the minimum allowed temporal distance is 0.25 μs. The SDK API for both CC1350 and CC2650 is identical, therefore the effort to port the code would only involve changes to the RF settings and time between the synchronous broadcast network floods.

This will allow for running the currently developed *Decentralized Brains* synchronous broadcast mechanism in CC2560.

Development of a Full Stack. As TI simplelink SDK has the option to run multiple radio instances as part of a single micro-controller core, we leverage it to implement the synchronous broadcasts. It also allows us to develop a network abstraction to run multiple radio protocols for communication. *Decentralized Brains* is communication protocol which leverages Glossy for synchronous broadcast, but the whole communication paradigm spans over two physical layers using the dual-band SoC for IPv6 based addressable communication within the network and a routing-less data replication scheme. The reliable synchronous broadcast is a crucial feature for the data replication scheme which was developed, implemented, and evaluated in this paper. To make this possible, to improve reproducibility of the results and to increase the use of constructive interference for network flooding in industrial applications it is proposed to write a dedicated MAC and NET layers in Contiki-NG for the target hardware. Since the target hardware SDK already supports multiple low-power micro-controllers the same code base can be compiled and reused out-of-the-box. This would allow to make the communication stack more code friendly and application realistic.

Acknowledgment. Part of the work on this paper has been supported by Deutsche Forschungsgemeinschaft (DFG) within the Collaborative Research Center SFB 876 "Providing Information by Resource-Constrained Analysis", project A4.

References

1. Godfrey-Smith, P.: Other Minds: The Octopus, the Sea, and the Deep Origins of Consciousness. Farrar, Straus and Giroux, New York (2016)
2. Ramachandran Venkatapathy, A.K., Ekblaw, A., ten Hompel, M., Paradiso, J.: Decentralized brain in low data-rate, low power networks for collaborative manoeuvres in space. In: Proceedings of the 6th IEEE International Conference on Wireless for Space and Extreme Environments (WiSEE 2018), pp. 83–88. IEEE (2018)
3. Rubenstein, M., Cornejo, A., Nagpal, R.: Programmable self-assembly in a thousand-robot swarm. Science **345**(6198), 795–799 (2014)
4. Ramachandran Venkatapathy, A.K., Bayhan, H., Zeidler, F., ten Hompel, M.: Human machine synergies in intra-logistics: creating a hybrid network for research and technologies. In: Federated Conference on Computer Science and Information Systems (FedCSIS 2017), pp. 1065–1068. IEEE (2017)
5. Ramachandran Venkatapathy, A.K., Riesner, A., Roidl, M., Emmerich, J., ten Hompel, M.: Phynode: an intelligent, cyber-physical system with energy neutral operation for phynetlab. In: Smart SysTech 2015; European Conference on Smart Objects, Systems and Technologies, pp. 1–8 (2015)
6. Ramachandran Venkatapathy, A.K., Riesner, A., Roidl, M., Emmerich, J., ten Hompel, M.: Phynetlab: architecture design of ultra-low power wireless sensor network testbed. In: Proceedings of the IEEE 16th International Symposium on A World of Wireless, Mobile and Multimedia Networks (WoWMoM 2015), pp. 1–6 (2015)

7. Ferrari, F., Zimmerling, M., Thiele, L., Saukh, O.: Efficient network flooding and time synchronization with glossy. In: Proceedings of the 10th ACM/IEEE International Conference on Information Processing in Sensor Networks, pp. 73–84 (2011)
8. Ferrari, F., Zimmerling, M., Mottola, L., Thiele, L.: Low-power wireless bus. In: Proceedings of the 10th ACM Conference on Embedded Network Sensor Systems, pp. 1–14 (2012)
9. Al Nahas, B., Duquennoy, S., Landsiedel, O.: Network-wide consensus in low-power wireless networks. In: SenSys: Proceedings of the 15th ACM Conference on Embedded Networked Sensor Systems (2017)
10. Jacob, R., Bächli, J., Da Forno, R., Thiele, L.: Synchronous transmissions made easy: design your network stack with baloo. In: Proceedings of the 2019 International Conference on Embedded Wireless Systems and Networks (EWSN 2019), pp. 106–117. Junction Publishing (2019)
11. Rogers, Y., Ellis, J.: Distributed cognition: an alternative framework for analysing and explaining collaborative working. J. Inf. Technol. 9(2), 119–128 (1994)
12. Ramachandran Venkatapathy, A.K., ten Hompel, M.: A decentralized context broker using byzantine fault tolerant consensus. Ledger, vol. 4 (2019)
13. Dunkels, A., Gronvall, B., Voigt, T.: Contiki - a lightweight and flexible operating system for tiny networked sensors. In: Proceedings of the 29th Annual IEEE International Conference on Local Computer Networks, pp. 455–462 (2004)
14. Swami, A., Zhao, Q., Hong, Y.-W., Tong, L.: Wireless Sensor Networks: Signal Processing and Communications Perspectives. John Wiley & Sons, Chichester (2007)
15. Schmid, T., Dutta, P., Srivastava, M.B.: High-resolution, low-power time synchronization an oxymoron no more. In: Proceedings of the 9th ACM/IEEE International Conference on Information Processing in Sensor Networks, IPSN 2010, pp. 151–161. ACM, New York (2010)
16. Texas Instruments: CC1350 datasheet: CC1350 SoC with RF Core (2016). http://www.ti.com/lit/ds/symlink/cc1350.pdf
17. Ekblaw, A., Paradiso, J.: Self-assembling space structures: buckminsterfullerene sensor nodes. In: AIAA/AHS Adaptive Structures Conference, p. 0565 (2018)

Wireless Sensor Network to Create a Water Quality Observatory in Coastal Areas

Sandra Sendra[1,2]([envelope]) [iD], Marta Botella-Campos[2] [iD], Jaime Lloret[2] [iD], and Jose Miguel Jimenez[2,3] [iD]

[1] Departamento de Teoría de la Señal, Telemática y Comunicaciones (TSTC), Universidad de Granada, C/ Periodista Daniel Saucedo Aranda, s/n, 18014 Granada, Spain
ssendra@ugr.es

[2] Instituto de Investigación para la Gestión Integrada de zonas Costeras (IGIC), Universita Politècnica de València, Camino de Vera, s/n, 46022 València, Spain
marbocam@etsid.upv.es, {jlloret,jojiher}@dcom.upv.es

[3] University of Haute Alsace, 2 rue des Frères Lumière, 68 093 Mulhouse Cedex, France

Abstract. Water is a natural resource necessary for life that must be taken care of. In coastal areas with near agricultural activity, it is very common to detect spills of chemical products that affect water quality of rivers and beaches. This water usually reaches the sea with bad consequences for nature and, therefore, it is important to detect where possible spills are taking place and water does not have enough quality to be used. This paper presents the development of a LoRa (Long Range) based wireless sensor network to create an observatory of water quality in coastal areas. This network consists of wireless nodes endowed with several sensors that allow measuring physical parameters of water quality, such as turbidity, temperature, etc. The data collected by the sensors will be sent to a gateway that will redirect them to a database. The database creates an observatory that will allow monitoring the environment where the network is deployed in real time. Finally, the developed system will be tested in a real environment for its correct start-up. Two different tests will be performed. The first one will check the correct operation of sensors and network architecture; the second test will check the network coverage of the commercial devices.

Keywords: Wireless sensor network · The Things Network (TTN) · Long Range (LoRa) · LoRaWAN · Water quality · Monitoring · Observatory

1 Introduction

Spain has approximately 8,000 kms of coastline. Along its entire coast, multiple areas classified as protected natural spaces can be found, as well as other areas which, despite not being classified as such, have a high ecological value due to their biodiversity; giving rise to one of the greater riches in landscape and coastal features of Europe. A large part of the Spanish population depends economically on coastal areas due to the presence of tourism and the productive activities carried out there, with more than 600 facilities,

© ICST Institute for Computer Sciences, Social Informatics and Telecommunications Engineering 2021
Published by Springer Nature Switzerland AG 2021. All Rights Reserved
L. Peñalver and L. Parra (Eds.): Industrial IoT 2020, LNICST 365, pp. 100–118, 2021.
https://doi.org/10.1007/978-3-030-71061-3_7

which include marinas, yacht clubs, and nautical and sport stations. Moreover, activities such as aquaculture and fishing, have also been an important source of income for the Spanish population [1].

Recently, different press publications highlighted problems in the quality of bathing water in coastal areas. In Oliva (Valencia-Spain) [2], for example, some bathing areas had to close because the water did not reach the required quality levels. Likewise, in Murcia (Spain) [3], the critical state of the Mar Menor where, in addition to chemical products such as zinc, a cloudy and greenish appearance of the waters can be found, as well as the increase in temperature of its waters. Another worrying case worth mentioning is the port activity, which can generate both atmospheric pollution (due to gas and CO_2 emissions, etc.) and water pollution (presence of hydrocarbons, suspended elements, etc.) [4]. Given the current situation and the constant publications of news regarding the poor quality of certain waters, we can deduce that it is necessary to apply corrective measures to try to solve and minimize the environmental impact that we are observing.

In order to apply corrective measures, the first essential point is to be able to detect, quantify and qualify any type of anomalies in our waters and environments that worsen their quality. This can be solved by using strategically located wireless sensor networks (WSNs) that continuously monitor water and atmospheric quality [5, 6]. WSNs are composed by a group of electronic devices with sensors and wireless communication capabilities that collaborate in a common task to detect a series of events or situations [7]. Their field of application is extremely wide, and it can be used in industrial environments, home automation, military environments, environmental detection, etc.

Nowadays, WSNs for marine monitoring systems [8] that store the collected information in a database and generate alarms are easily found. In this paper, we aim to go a step further from the simple generation of alarms. As summarized by G. Xu et al. in their review on the use of the Internet of Things (IoT) for environmental monitoring [9], the evolution of these networks must necessarily go through the application of novel data processing techniques and decision-making algorithms that allow the generation of intelligent actions to not only detect, but also solve unwanted situations.

For this reason, this paper presents the design, development, and start-up of a WSN based on LoRa (Long Range) technology for the creation of a water quality observatory in coastal areas. LoRa/LoRaWAN is a relatively new wireless technology that offers several important improvements over classic WiFi-based networks. LoRa/LoRaWAN is an LPWAN (Low Power Wide Area Network) technology that meets all the requirements of any IoT project. On the one hand, it offers us long-distance connectivity that ensures connections through triple encryption. It also allows the bidirectional sending of small data packets, which is more than enough for the purpose of this project. In addition, it has very low energy consumption, making it very suitable for the deployment of monitoring networks. Finally, it should be noted that LoRa is currently the only low-power technology capable of accurately geolocating outdoor and indoor locations and works on a free frequency band (making connectivity costs considerably lower than with any other methods). Our LoRa network will consist of a set of wireless nodes that will incorporate low-cost sensors to measure environmental parameters. The nodes will be in charge of monitoring water quality levels in terms of turbidity, temperature, salinity levels [10], and the presence of fuels and oils on the water [6]. The nodes will also be in charge of measuring meteorological parameters such as temperature, humidity, etc. [5]. These nodes will be located in the final sections of ditches/streams that flow into our beaches, ports and bathing areas, to collect environmental information. The collected data will be sent through a gateway to a database from which an Observatory will be created to enable real-time monitoring of data and allow the analysis of the evolution of the environment over time.

The creation of these observatories is extremely useful for the application of Big Data techniques and artificial intelligence algorithms to improve the sustainability of a productive area or sector. These decisions will be directly related to the adequacy of the recommendations for the quality of coastal waters in port areas [11]. The developed system will be deployed in a controlled environment for its testing and proper commissioning. The infrastructure proposed in this paper has many extensions and applications such as aquaculture [12], agriculture, and port activities management, among others. In addition, it can help promote the tourist activity in an area, bringing what is known as "blue tourism" and ensuring that aquatic activities are carried out in excellent quality waters. Finally, it should be noted that all the collected data can be displayed through a web portal, so that citizens have real-time access to the state of the waters and feel part of this project, to help preventing the pollution of our natural spaces.

The rest of the paper is organized as follows. Section 2 presents the related work on other existing water quality monitoring systems. Section 3 describes the developed system as well as the hardware and software resources used to implement the nodes. Tests and results are explained in Sect. 4. Finally, the conclusion and future work are presented in Sect. 5.

2 Related Work

In this section, some related works associated to our proposal are presented and analysed.

In 2017, Pule et al. performed a survey on the application of WSN to monitor water quality comparing and evaluating sensor node architectures in terms of monitored parameters, wireless communication standards, power supply architectures, and autonomy, among others [13]. Given the high rate of worldwide deaths caused by water borne diseases, ensuring water quality has become a major challenge. Depending on its application, the suitability of water relies upon its physical, chemical, and biological characteristics. Therefore, the acceptability of water requires collecting a large number of samples to compare its characteristic parameters with standards and guidelines and ensure a correct analysis. The use of WSNs allows real-time monitoring with relatively low maintenance costs, though this type of networks often lack processing power, energy, memory, and communication bandwidth if not addressed properly. Moreover, the use of repeaters might be necessary in order to improve their range capabilities.

Geetha et al. designed a power-efficient solution for in-pipe water quality monitoring based on IoT that analyses water samples and alerts remote users if water quality parameters suffer any deviations from standard values [14]. The proposed system monitors parameters such as turbidity, conductivity, pH, and water levels at a domestic level with sensors being directly interfaced to the controller unit. In this case, the collected data is displayed on an LCD screen and sent to the cloud through the controller. Moreover, a mobile application was implemented so that users can visualize real-time data and receive messages from the sensing device. Though an extensive research on techniques and tools used on pre-existing systems was performed, the lack of algorithms to detect anomalies in water quality parameters might prevent this approach from being applied on field environments.

In [15], Chen et al. presented a multi-parameter water quality monitoring system to collect real-time high-frequency data of Bristol Floating Harbour and display it online. In this case, researchers used the smart city infrastructure as a plug & play platform for wireless communication, data processing, storage, and redistribution. The designed system comprises several modules for data acquisition, data transmission, data storage and redistribution, as well as a power supply. This water quality monitoring probe is connected to a subnetwork using a serial to Wi-Fi server solution, and a software defined network and cloud computing for a fast and cost-effective deployment of the system. This project demonstrated how IoT can be used in environmental monitoring systems to provide details of water quality variations that can be useful for further evaluating water quality parameters.

Ngom et al. depicted a LoRa-based measurement station to monitor water quality parameters at the Botanical Garden pool of UCAD's Faculty of Science in Canada [16]. This low-cost system is composed of a remote station that uses a LoRa module, powered by a solar power source, and a web-platform for data visualization. The remote measurement station involves an acquisition node with a micro-controller and four sensors to monitor pH, conductivity, water temperature, and oxidation/reduction potential, and transmit the data to a gateway. In this case, it was decided to send structured frames to the gateway through a LoRa network and store them in a database of the local server using the Ethernet interface of the gateway. If the internet connection is available, the collected data will also be stored in a cloud database to enable direct access to the data and have a backup system. Although the designed system allows to effectively monitor some water quality parameters, the lack of physicochemical and bacteriological parameters prevents this system from surveying possible water borne diseases.

In [17], Simitha et al. developed a monitoring system based on IoT and WSN to collect real-time water quality data to better preserve and manage water resources. The proposed approach aims to achieve a low cost and low power consumption system using LoRa modules and LoRaWAN communication protocol to transmit sensor values to the ThinkSpeak platform and perform further analysis. However, this system is divided into two phases: water quality monitoring, and air quality monitoring together with streetlight energy saving. Among the water quality parameters monitored in the first phase of this project, we encountered that only temperature, pH and turbidity are being monitored whereas the dissolved oxygen (DO) is calculated using the temperature-DO dependency equation. As a result, researchers designed a long-range communication system capable of successfully monitor the established water quality parameters.

In 2019, Wu et al. proposed a mobile water quality monitoring system based on LoRa and IoT that uses unmanned surface vehicles (USVs) to monitor several water parameters in Lake Dardanelle, Arkansas [18]. Although this lake is a major destination for tourist activities and game fishing, it also includes areas with intensive crop agriculture, timberlands, and industrial units. However, it lacks monitoring systems to ensure that water quality parameters obey the necessary health standards. By integrating a set of sensors on a mobile platform that will pass the collected data to a LoRa transceiver module, researchers designed a low-cost long-range system that communicates with the LoRa gateway to send data to The Things Network (TTN) cloud.

In [19], Jia introduced a real-time monitoring system based on a multi-sensor combination to monitor water and air quality in wetlands. The water sensor combination uses six types of sensors to monitor temperature, pH, conductivity, turbidity, water levels, and DO. The collected data is sent to the base station using a LoRa module; thus, allowing a high speed and wide coverage system. Although LoRaWAN protocol is used to communicate acquisition nodes and sink, a data fusion algorithm was implemented on the acquisition nodes to reduce the amount of data being sent, improving the network throughput, and reducing power consumption. However, since this system was not tested in site-specific environments, its robustness needs to be verified. Moreover, no solution was provided for data management and analysis.

Unlike existing works, this paper shows the design, development, and implementation of a wireless sensor network in a real environment for water quality monitoring. In addition, a web-based user interface has been developed. This user interface made citizens part of this project to see and know the quality of water in rivers and, thus, make them aware of the importance of keeping rivers clean and avoiding uncontrolled discharges.

3   System Description

This section describes the developed system as well as the hardware and software resources used to implement it.

3.1   System Overview

The developed network is based on LoRa technology, which is a widely used wireless technology for monitoring tasks, and it is included into the category of a low-power wide-area networks (LPWAN) [20]. It is characterized to be a low power technology able to transmit up to hundreds of kilometres with adequate and unobstructed direct vision in the Fresnel area between the devices [21, 22]. The range for rural surroundings is around 20 km. However, in urban surroundings, it is reduced to 5 km due to the high dependence on the environment and the building materials. Additionally, it is possible to send small packets of data between 0.3 kbps and 5.5 kbps.

The network topology used is an infrastructure architecture where a LoRa Gateway will be in charge of collecting data from LoRa nodes and forward it to a server to store and/or process the data from the sensors. The collected data will be stored in a network storage server. In this case, the Data Storage integration service provided by The Things Network (TTN) [23] was used. It offers the necessary tools to collect and store the data in a database (DB) at a minimum cost for a period of 7 days. On the other hand, we can easily visualize the data in real time using Ubidots Platform.

Finally, a dashboard through a web application has been developed to allow users to see the monitored parameters. Figure 1 shows the network architecture of our system.

The dashboard takes the data from the different nodes and sensors and presents it as a graph. Furthermore, the position of nodes is displayed in a map.

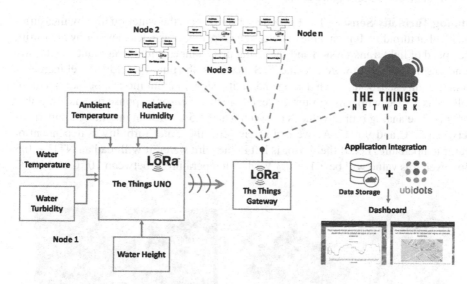

Fig. 1. Proposed system

3.2 Hardware

This subsection exposes the main features of the different devices and elements used to deploy our nodes.

Network Devices. The Things Gateway [24] is a LoRaWAN base station that permits connecting LoRa devices, such as sensors and embedded computers, to them access to the internet. It is based on open source hardware and software standards and operates at 868 MHz for use in the EU and 915 MHz for use in US. This model uses an antenna of 14 dB gain. The Things Gateway implements its own security systems through https connections and embedded mechanisms in the LoRaWAN protocol. According to the manufacturer indications, a single device can serve thousands of nodes inside a coverage wireless range of up to 10 km (6 miles).

The Things Uno module [25] is based on the Arduino Leonardo board with a Microchip LoRaWAN RN2483 module and on-board antenna. It is fully compatible with the Arduino IDE and existing shields. The Arduino Leonardo is a board with an ATmega32U4 microcontroller that allows IoT designs. It has native USB by hardware and therefore does not need any serial-USB conversion. It has 20 digital input/output pins (with a maximum current of 40 mA per pin) of which 7 of them can be used as PWM outputs and 12 as analog inputs. The clock speed is 16 MHz. It contains 32 KB Flash Memory (4 KB used for the bootloader), 2.5 KB SRAM and 1 KB internal EEPROM. A supply voltage between 7–12 V is recommended.

Combining The Things Gateways and The Things UNO nodes, it is possible to deploy IoT networks for embedded, sensing and connected city applications, with up to 10 km range coverage. Figure 2 shows the network devices used in this system.

Analog Turbidity Sensor. The turbidity sensor detects the water quality by measuring the level of turbidity. It is capable of detecting suspended particles in water by measuring the speed of light transmission and scattering that changes with the amount of total suspended solids (TSS) in water. As the TTS increases, the liquid turbidity level increases. This turbidity sensor has both analog and digital signal output modes. Sensor operating voltage is 5 VDC with a maximum current of 40 mA. Sensor response time is lower than 500 ms. The analog output value is between 0 and 4.5 V with an operating temperature between 5 °C and 90 °C. As we can see in [26], the water turbidity is dependent on water temperature, i.e., if the sensor is left in the pure water, it will read an NTU < 0.5. However, this value will be 4.1 ± 0.3 V when temperature is between 10 °C and 50 °C.

Fig. 2. LoRa Gateway and Nodes used to deploy our network

DHT11 Temperature and Humidity Sensor. In order to measure the environmental temperature and relative humidity, the system includes a DHT11 sensor [27]. This sensor offers a digital output due to a small 8-bit microcontroller that is already calibrated by the factory. The DHT11 sensor is able to measure temperature in the range of 0 °C to 50 °C with an error of ± 2 °C and relative humidity in the range of 20% to 90% with an error of $\pm 5\%$.

3 Wire PT100 Temperature Sensor. This sensor is a 3-wire RTD resistance thermometer. The sensor is made up of a stainless-steel housing that provides great robustness to the sensor. Its size is 50 mm long and has a diameter of 6 mm with a cable length of 2 m. The working range of this sensor is from $-50\,°C$ to $+300\,°C$. The temperature measurement is based on the common characteristic of all conductors and semiconductors, i.e., the electrical resistance is modified itself when temperature varies. The PT100 sensor has an ohmic value of 100 Ω at a temperature of 0 $°C$ and its coefficient of variation is 0.00385 $\Omega/°C$.

Infrared Distance SHARP GP2Y0A21 Sensor. The Sharp GP2Y0A41SK0F [28] distance sensor allows obtaining the distance between the sensor and some object within the range of 4 to 30 cm. It integrates three devices: An infrared emitting diode (IRED), a sensitive position detector (PSD) and a signal processor circuit. The device delivers a voltage output proportional to the sensed distance. The difference in the reflectivity of the materials, as well as the operating temperature, does not greatly affect the operation of this sensor due to the detection method used based on triangulation.

After analysing the features and working ranges of each sensor, they were combined and mounted to perform the tests. Figure 3 shows a diagram of the deployed node while Fig. 4 shows a picture of the sensor node in a plastic drum with real river water sample.

3.3 The Things Network Platform

The Things Network (TTN) [23] is an organization/community that has created a distributed and decentralized network of LoRa Gateways for the Internet of Things with open source hardware and software philosophy. The particularity of this scenario is that the network is created from the collaboration of citizens who install gateways that provide coverage and allow communications between the nodes and the Internet. Currently the TTN community is made up of more than 12,800 gateways and more than 117,000 across 150 countries.

The LoRaWAN [29] network architecture is based on a star topology. The main component of this topology is a gateway that forwards messages between an end device and the network server. The network server forwards the packets of each device in the network to an application server. The security of the network is provided by a symmetric model of session keys derived from keys associated with each device. The gateways are connected to the Internet through the conventional TCP/IP network protocol, while the end devices are connected to the Internet using LoRaWAN and communicate with one or more gateways. The Gateway's function is collecting data from the different nodes included in the network and connecting them to the rest of the network. Finally, the users can access the data by using the TTN supported protocols such as HTTP or MQTT (Message Queuing Telemetry Transport).

3.4 Web-Based User Interface

Web-based user interfaces allow users to interact with the content stored on remote or cloud servers through web browsers. In this acquisition method, the web browser acts as a client and, therefore, it is in charge of downloading the stored data to present it to the user. As it is said before, in this case, Ubidots platform was used as it allows

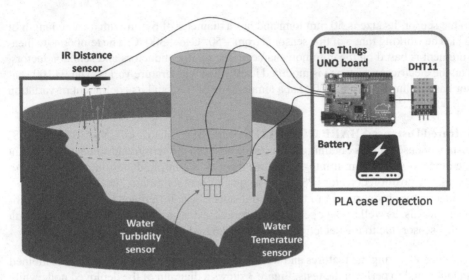

Fig. 3. Diagram of the designed LoRa node

Fig. 4. Sensor node in a plastic drum with real river water sample.

affordable and reliable end-to-end IoT solutions through HTTP, MQTT, TCP and UDP protocols [30]. Figure 5 presents the developed website. As the figure shows, the main page displays the position of the nodes in a map. These nodes are clickable and they allow the user to have an overview of the sensed data in the form of a small pop-up window that exhibits real time data of the sensors connected to that node.

In this project, the collected data is retrieved from the server using HTTP protocol and Node.js JSON parser to execute request methods for real time asynchronous events. Figure 6 displays the flow diagram of the web application. Although the web browser executes HTTP methods to retrieve information from the server, the solicited data is sent to the TTN storage site in the form of a JavaScript Object Notation (JSON) file, which is the format type that Ubidots platform manages. To effectively connect TTN and Ubidots platforms, TTN payload formats need to be configured in our application console to decode this type of messages. After integrating Ubidots to TTN, we will be able to retrieve data from the database and display it in the dashboard. Furthermore, this setup allows the nodes to push information over the LoRa network up to the TTN server, and from the TTN server to Ubidots. Since the main page will display de position of the nodes, this data will be converted into a csv file that includes name, geolocation, id, and the token of each device. In order for the user to enter the dashboard and visualize real time data of each node, the selected node needs to be clicked. This action will open a pop-up window with real time values of the monitored parameters and a button to access the dashboard and observe the historical data of the sensors plotted in different graphs to see their evolution over time.

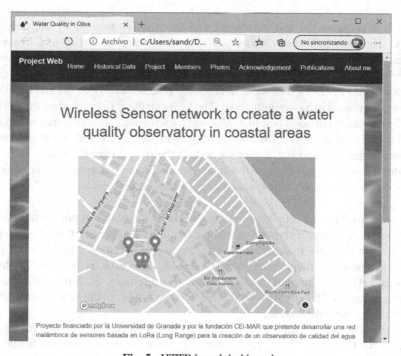

Fig. 5. HTTP-based dashboard.

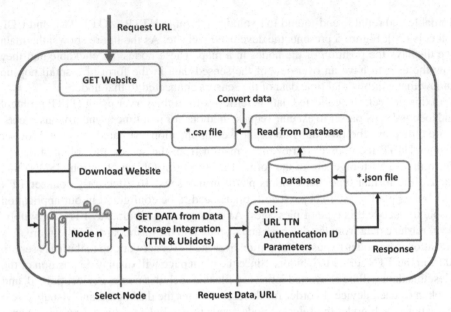

Fig. 6. Scheme of the developed website.

4 Results

This section presents the test performed and the results obtained by the developed network. The tests have been performed in a semi-urban scenario, in Oliva Beach (Valencia-Spain). In this scenario, single-family semi-detached houses are predominant.

In order to carry out the measurements, we used three different nodes placed on the green points of Fig. 7. Two of these nodes were placed directly in the river while the other one was placed in a swimming pool. The LoRa gateway (identified by the red point in Fig. 7) was placed inside a building. Moreover, each node was configured to send data every 5 min. The rest of time, the node is in sleep mode. Figure 7 shows the placement of nodes and gateway and Fig. 8 shows a node in the river during the tests.

In the following figures, we will display the monitored parameters to compare the results of two scenarios: cloudy pool water (Node 1), and ditch water (Node 2 and Node 3).

Figure 9 displays the relative humidity sensed by the nodes in pool water and real river water. As this graph shows, the relative humidity levels sensed by Node 1 (pool water) are considerably lower than the ones measured by Node 2 and Node 3 (ditch water). The reason for these differences is the location of each node during the testing process as well as the amount of sun exposure. Furthermore, the humidity sensor has a working range of 20% to 90% with a ±5% error, which is the reason why relative humidity levels saturate at 95%.

Additionally, DHT11 sensor also measures environmental temperature in the range of 0 °C to 50 °C with a ±2 °C error. Figure 10 shows the sensed ambient temperature in pool water (Node 1) and real river water (Node 2 and Node 3). As the figure shows,

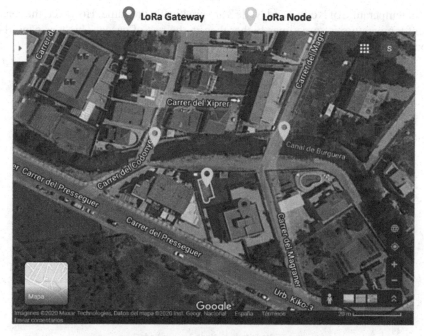

Fig. 7. Position of nodes and gateway.

Fig. 8. Sensor node in the river to perform the tests.

ambient temperature of Node 2 and Node 3 are practically the same. However, the sensed ambient temperature is sometimes higher than in the rest of cases. This was caused by the location of the water samples during the tests.

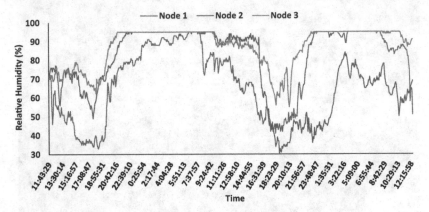

Fig. 9. Relative humidity in %.

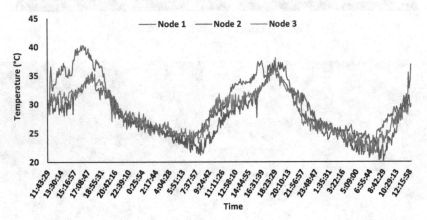

Fig. 10. Ambient temperature in °C.

Water levels were measured using Sharp GP2Y0A41SK0F analog distance sensor that features a detection range of 4 cm to 30 cm, indicated by the output voltage. Though in this case water levels in pool water and ditch water are not significant for the sake of this study, Fig. 11 helps demonstrate the functioning of this sensor. As it can be seen, water levels measured by Node 1 (pool water) are much lower than the ones measured by Node 2 and Node 3 (real river water). The reason for this is that the buckets used in each test were different. However, this graph shows some fluctuations of water levels that can be explained by the sensor's sampling rate.

Water temperature was measured using PT100 3-wire sensor that allows a reading range from −25 °C to +250 °C. Figure 12 displays water temperature of pool water (Node

1) and real river water (Node 2 and Node 3). As the figure shows, water temperature in ditch water is generally higher than in pool water. The reason for this is that real river water contains a full biodiversity of aquatic invertebrates and particles that contribute to the increase of temperature, while pool water is often cleaner.

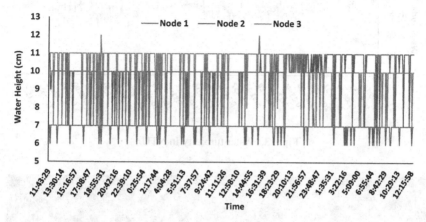

Fig. 11. Water height in cm.

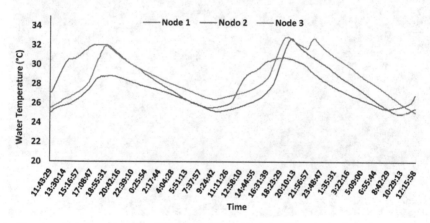

Fig. 12. Water temperature in °C.

Finally, water turbidity is displayed in Fig. 13. Gravity turbidity sensor SEN0189 allows measuring turbidity thanks to its relationship with output voltage [28]. When comparing this graph with temperature, one can easily observe that turbidity levels rise with the increase of temperature. This may be due to the increase of activity of the aforementioned invertebrates and suspended particles.

Finally, the coverage of LoRa nodes was tested. In order to carry out these measurements, TTN Mapper mobile application [31] was used. Figure 14 shows the surface covered to check the signal levels detected by our node, and the Received Signal Strength Indicator (RSSI) measured. The maximum distance at which the node managed to send data was 910 m.

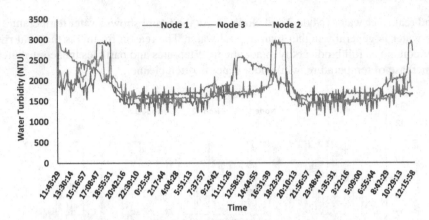

Fig. 13. Water turbidity in NTU.

Fig. 14. Values of RSSI measured during the test.

Figure 15 shows the results of RSSI obtained as a function of the distance, while Fig. 16 shows the results of SNR obtained as a function of the distance.

The distance was measured from the gateway (which is our reference point), to the node that collects the data. It should be taken into account that the selected area to perform this test has several buildings with a height lower than 10 m. In spite of this, the height of the buildings obstruct the signal propagation, significantly reducing the SNR and RSSI levels. As we can see, it was possible to collect data at 910 m from the gateway. Moreover, the average value of SNR was around 0 dB, which indicates that the signal levels are balanced with the received noise levels. Therefore, we can conclude that these devices can correctly deploy a network area of 900 m of diameter.

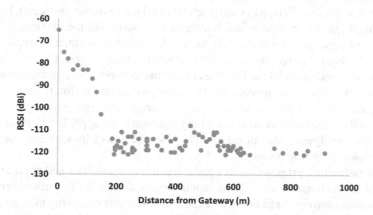

Fig. 15. Values of RSSI as a function of the distance to the gateway.

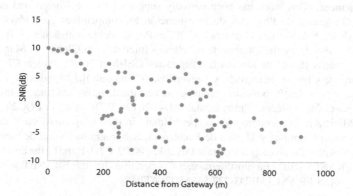

Fig. 16. Values of SNR as a function of the distance to the gateway.

5 Conclusion and Future Work

The conservation of natural resources, such as water, is currently a hot topic. However, this task must be carried out not only by researchers but also by citizens. Therefore, it is interesting to apply current technology to monitor the state of these resources and bring this type of project closer to the population. This way, we would be able to make the population aware of the importance of conserving our natural areas. To this end, this paper presented the design and development of a hardware and software platform that allows real-time monitoring of different water parameters, at different points of a river network. The system is made up of a LoRa-based network with different wireless nodes that send data to a central database that allows its visualization through a website. The entire network has been tested in a real environment with three nodes and results have shown interesting results. On the one hand, we have noticed that water turbidity is closely related to water temperature. On the other hand, LoRa coverage tests have demonstrated that it is very difficult to reach the coverage distances indicated by manufacturers. According to the device's specifications, we could reach up to 10 km (without obstacles). However, we performed the coverage tests in a semi-urban scenario and the maximum distance reached in our experiments was only 910 m, which is much lower than the expected one.

Currently, there is a growing trend in the creation of these observatories to apply Big Data techniques and artificial intelligence algorithms to improve the sustainability of an area or productive sector using real data. Therefore, an interesting future work would be improving the network performance in terms of coverage, integrating more gateways and nodes, as well as other sensors, to create a bigger network and apply Big Data techniques and artificial intelligence algorithms to make intelligent decisions, create alarms, and correct possible pollution problems.

The infrastructure proposed in this paper has many extensions and applications. A network of these characteristics allows monitoring water quality in harbours and areas with aquaculture activity. In addition, it can help promote tourist activity in an area ("blue tourism") and ensure that water activities are carried out in waters of excellent quality.

Acknowledgement. This work has been partially supported by the Universidad de Granada through the "Programa de Proyectos de Investigación Precompetitivos para Jóvenes Investigadores. Modalidad A jóvenes Doctores" of "Plan Propio de Investigación y Transferencia 2019" (PPJIA2019.10), by the Campus de Excelencia Internacional Global del Mar (CEI•Mar) through the "Ayudas Proyectos Jóvenes Investigadores CEI•Mar 2019" (Project CEIJ-020), by the "Ministerio de Ciencia, Innovación y Universidades" through the "Ayudas para la adquisición de equipamiento científico-técnico, Subprograma estatal de infraestructuras de investigación y equipamiento científico-técnico (plan Estatal I+D+i 2017–2020)" (project EQC2018-004988-P), by the "Ministerio de Economía y Competitividad" in the "Programa Estatal de Fomento de la Investigación Científica y Técnica de Excelencia, Subprograma Estatal de Generación de Conocimiento" within the project under Grant TIN2017-84802-C2-1-P and by the European Union through the ERANETMED (Euromediterranean Cooperation through ERANET joint activities and beyond) project ERANETMED3-227 SMARTWATIR.

References

1. Instituto Nacional de Estadística (INE): España en cifras 2018. https://www.ine.es/prodyser/espa_cifras/2018/files/assets/common/downloads/publication.pdf?uni=4f7e7b429c56ccb c4bf56b3e93ebc47b. Accessed 29 Aug 2020
2. Vera Oliva, M.C.: Oliva prohibirá el baño en tres ríos al hallar restos fecales procedentes de acequias, 2 August 2018. https://www.lasprovincias.es/safor/oliva-prohibira-bano-201808 02002812-ntvo.html. Accessed 29 Aug 2020
3. Belmonte Espejo, P.: El Mar Menor, en la encrucijada, 4 June 2018. https://www.eldiario.es/murcia/murcia_y_aparte/Mar-Menor-encrucijada_6_778732142.html. Accessed 29 Aug 2020
4. Autoridad Portuaria de Melilla – Puerto de Melilla: Estudio Medioambiental. https://www.puertodemelilla.es/images/documentos/ampliacion_puerto/estudio_impacto_ambiental.pdf. Accessed 29 Aug 2020

5. Sendra, S., Parra, L., Lloret, J., Jiménez, J.M.: Oceanographic multisensor buoy based on low cost sensors for Posidonia meadows monitoring in Mediterranean Sea. J Sens. **2015**, 23 (2015). Article ID 920168
6. Parra, L., Sendra, S., Jimenez, J.M., Lloret, J.: Smart system to detect and track pollution in marine environments. In: Proceedings of the 2015 IEEE International Conference on Communication Workshop (ICCW), London, UK, 8–12 June 2015, pp. 1503–1508 (2015)
7. Lloret, J., Garcia, M., Bri, D., Sendra, S.: A wireless sensor network deployment for rural and forest fire detection and verification. Sensors **9**(11), 8722–8747 (2009)
8. Gupta, P., Batra, J., Sangwan, J., Khatri, A.: Marine monitoring based on WSN: application and challenges. Int. J. Adv. Stud. Sci. Res. **3**(12), 322–324 (2018)
9. Xu, G., Shi, Y., Sun, X., Shen, W.: Internet of Things in marine environment monitoring: a review. Sensors **19**(7), 1711 (2019)
10. Parra Boronat, L., Sendra, S., Lloret, J., Bosch Roig, I.: Development and test of conductivity sensor for monitoring groundwater resources to optimize the water management in Smart City environments. Sensors **15**(9), 20990–21015 (2015)
11. Ministerio de Fomento: Recomendaciones para obras marítumas ROM 5.1-13 - Calidad de las aguas litorales en áreas portuarias. https://www.puertos.es/gl-es/BibliotecaV2/ROM%205.1-13.pdf. Accessed 29 Aug 2020
12. Parra, L., Sendra, S., Lloret, J., Rodrigues, J.J.: Design and deployment of a smart system for data gathering in aquaculture tanks using wireless sensor networks. Int. J. Commun. Syst. **30**(16), e3335 (2017)
13. Pule, M., Yahya, A., Chuma, J.: Wireless sensor networks: a survey on monitoring water quality. J. Appl. Res. Technol. **15**, 562–570 (2017)
14. Geetha, S., Gouthami, S.: Internet of Things enabled real time water quality monitoring system. Smart Water **2**, 1–19 (2017)
15. Chen, Y., Han, D.: Water quality monitoring in smart city: a pilot project. Autom. Constr. **89**, 307–316 (2018)
16. Ngom, B., Diallo, M., Gueye, B., Marilleau, N.: LoRa-based measurement station for water quality monitoring: case of botanical garden pool. In: Proceedings of the 2019 IEEE Sensors Applications Symposium (SAS), Sophia Antipolis, France, 11–13 March 2019, pp. 1–4 (2019)
17. Simitha, K.M., Subodh Raj, M.S.: IoT and WSN based water quality monitoring system. In: Proceedings of the 2019 3rd International Conference on Electronics, Communication and Aerospace Technology (ICECA), Coimbatore, India, 2–14 June 2019, pp. 205–210 (2019)
18. Wu, N., Khan, M.: LoRa-based Internet-of-Things: a water quality monitoring system. In: 2019 SoutheastCon, Huntsville, Alabama, USA, 11–14 April 2019, pp. 1–4 (2019)
19. Jia, Y.: LoRa-based WSNs construction and low-power data collection strategy for wetland environmental monitoring. Wirel. Pers. Commun. **114**(2), 1533–1555 (2020). https://doi.org/10.1007/s11277-020-07437-5
20. LoRa Documentation. https://lora.readthedocs.io/en/latest/. Accessed 29 Aug 2020
21. Benites, B., Chávez, E., Medina, J., Vidal, R., Chauca, M.: LoRaWAN applied in Swarm Drones: a focus on the use of fog for the management of water resources in Lima-Peru. In: Proceedings of the 5th International Conference on Mechatronics and Robotics Engineering, Rome, Italy, 16–19 February 2019, pp. 171–176 (2019)
22. Sanchez-Iborra, R., Sanchez-Gomez, J., Ballesta-Viñas, J., Cano, M.D., Skarmeta, A.F.: Performance evaluation of LoRa considering scenario conditions. Sensors **18**, 772 (2018)
23. The Things Network website. https://www.thethingsnetwork.org/. Accessed 29 Aug 2020
24. The Things Gateway features. In The Things Network website. https://www.thethingsnetwork.org/docs/gateways/gateway/. Accessed 29 Aug 2020
25. The Things UNO features. In The Things Network website. https://www.thethingsnetwork.org/docs/devices/uno/. Accessed 29 Aug 2020

26. Analog Turbidity Sensor features. https://wiki.dfrobot.com/Turbidity_sensor_SKU__SEN 0189. Accessed 29 Aug 2020
27. Datasheet of DTH11 Sensor. https://components101.com/dht11-temperature-sensor. Accessed 29 Aug 2020
28. Sharp GP2Y0A41SK0F sensor features. https://www.farnell.com/datasheets/2364614.pdf?_ga=2.92005150.540766343.1598431848-1376214988.1597914665. Accessed 29 Aug 2020
29. LoRaWAN™ Architecture. In Microchip website. https://microchipdeveloper.com/lora:lorawan-architecture. Accessed 29 Aug 2020
30. UBIDOTS Platform. https://ubidots.com/platform/. Accessed 29 Aug 2020
31. TTN Mapper application. https://ttnmapper.org/. Accessed 29 Aug 2020

Session 3

An Intelligent Predictive Maintenance Approach Based on End-of-Line Test Logfiles in the Automotive Industry

David Vicêncio[1,2,3]($\boxtimes$) (iD), Hugo Silva[2] (iD), Salviano Soares[1,4] (iD), Vítor Filipe[1,3] (iD),
and António Valente[1,3] (iD)

[1] University of Trás-os-Montes and Alto Douro, Vila Real, Portugal
{salblues,vfilipe,avalente}@utad.pt
[2] Continental Advanced Antenna, Sociedade Unipessoal, Lda., Vila Real, Portugal
{david.2.vicencio,hugo.2.silva}@continental.com
[3] INESC TEC, Porto, Portugal
[4] IEETA, Aveiro, Portugal
https://www.inesctec.pt/
http://www.ieeta.pt/

Abstract. Through technological advents from Industry 4.0 and the Internet of Things, as well as new Big Data solutions, predictive maintenance begins to play a strategic role in the increasing operational performance of any industrial facility. Equipment failures can be very costly and have catastrophic consequences. In its basic concept, Predictive maintenance allows minimizing equipment faults or service disruptions, presenting promising cost savings. This paper presents a data-driven approach, based on multiple-instance learning, to predict malfunctions in End-of-Line Testing Systems through the extraction of operational logs, which, while not designed to predict failures, contains valid information regarding their operational mode over time. For the case study performed, a real-life dataset was used containing thousands of log messages, collected in a real automotive industry environment. The insights gained from mining this type of data will be shared in this paper, highlighting the main challenges and benefits, as well as good recommendations, and best practices for the appropriate usage of machine learning techniques and analytics tools that can be implemented in similar industrial environments.

Keywords: End-of-Line Testing Systems (EOL) · Service monitoring and log operation data · Industry 4.0 · Predictive Maintenance (PdM) · Machine learning (ML)

Supported by Continental Advanced Antenna (CAA), Portugal (a Continental AG Group Company).

L. Peñalver and L. Parra (Eds.): Industrial IoT 2020, LNICST 365, pp. 121–140, 2021.
https://doi.org/10.1007/978-3-030-71061-3_8

1   Introduction

Nowadays, facing through a so globalized and competitive environment, industries are constantly challenged to look for new ways to differentiate themselves and improve their effectiveness and efficiency, in order to remain competitive and sustainable. Maintenance management policies are a relevant aspect in the evaluation of the production processes of any industrial plant, and, therefore, it has become an interesting and relevant topic of scientific research. The effectiveness and internal efficiency of an industrial plant can be directly influenced by the role of maintenance and its impact in other areas, as *e.g.*, production and quality processes. According to [1], between 15% and 70% of the total production costs comes from maintenance activities. However, the vast majority of industries still opt for outdated and inefficient maintenance policies, which, consequently, leads to a loss in productive quality and efficiency [2]. Today, with the technological advances that have been made in areas such as Computer Science (CS) and Artificial Intelligence (AI), as well as the increased usage of sensors and monitoring systems, Predictive Maintenance (PdM) approaches can be made in any industrial equipment, allowing a forecast relatively reliable about its Remaining Useful Life (RUL). PdM is relatively of interest in the environment of Industry 4.0 and it can increase drastically the efficiency of modern production facilities. The usage of monitoring sensors provides us a set of historical data on the operational state of industrial equipment, as well as corrective actions that may have occurred. This information is extremely valuable for PdM actions or models, which use both historical and operational data to make diagnostics and predictions, as presented by [1–3].

The possibilities of PdM applications connected with other parts of the production process are increasing, now even more in the context of Industry 4.0 and the Internet of Things (IoT) [3–5]. Generally, PdM models run through prior knowledge about the equipment's normal operation. This knowledge can be acquired through the installation of monitoring sensors for recording relevant signals of degradation, as *e.g.*, vibration, temperature, or voltage. Sometimes, the inclusion of sensors or major hardware upgrades is impractical on industrial equipment, due to expensive implementation costs, effort, or regulatory hurdles. In alternative, we can obtain knowledge about the functioning regions of a device by studying its logs. For example, in the case of an End-of-Line (EOL) testing system, all device operations, from measurement, test environment, signal analysis or calibration, are controlled through different applications. These applications can produce tons of logs during their operation. Theoretically, it's possible to understand the normal operating regions of industrial equipment through the study of its logs. The extraction and analysis of such information through the usage of Analytical methods can help in the preventive detection of system disruptions. The usage of logfiles as a way to prevent equipment malfunctions has not yet been fully explored and is still posing computational challenges given its complex structure and its huge amount of data [5–7]. Later on, in the next sections, as our main contributions, we will focus on the way we formulate our problem, from data gathering to the algorithm selection and results, through a case study developed in a real automotive industry facility (CAA).

This paper is structured in seven sections, according to the following: Sect. 1 gives a brief introduction to the main topic, exploring the principal goals intended; By Sect. 2, we will address the topic with some recent publications, where other works, recently presented by other authors dealing with PdM will be presented and discussed; In Sect. 3, a review of the state of the art is made, trying to fit the topic with some European Norms (EN) and recent publications, that support this paper; The methodology applied in this study is described in Sect. 4; The case study experiments, through the usage of a real operational dataset, obtained from an EOL testing system, are described in Sect. 5; Principal conclusion are shared on Sect. 6, as well as the list of future work in this actuation area is explored.

2   Related Works

This section reviews the related work on data-driven approaches, based on multiple-instance learning to predict equipment or service disruptions. For the majority of the scientific papers published recently, the theme of PdM is approached as a way of assisting in the attentive detection of equipment failures, which are generally being monitored in critical systems. PdM uses a variety of approaches and ML techniques to study data in order to identify and interpret abnormal operating patterns. As *e.g.*, Z. Li *et al.* [8], attempt an approach to predict the RUL of an aircraft engine based on advanced ensemble algorithms, as *e.g.*, Random Forests (RF), Classification and Regression Tree (CART), Recurrent Neural Networks (RNN) and Relevance Vector Machine (RVM). In his study, a variable selection approach using RF was used to determine an optimal set of variables, whose approximation served as the basis for this paper. Also, Z. Weiting [4], conduct a comprehensive survey of PdM in industrial equipment. This publication, propose a PdM scheme for automatic washing equipment and compares different models and algorithms accuracy from the aspects of ML and Deep Learning (DL) techniques. The study was conducted collecting data from four type of sensors that should represent the equipment performance (*i.e.*, vibration, temperature, electrical signal and rotating speed). One of the main challenges of predictive models, used in maintenance purposes, is that they are based on the assumption that there are certain contexts in the equipment lifetime where the failure rate is increasing. The vast majority of PdM studies that have been made, focus on the application in mechanical components or induction motors, whose specificities are directly influenced by several known factors, as *e.g.*, increasing operating temperature or vibrations. Also, J. Yan et al. [1], tried to predict the RUL of key components of a CNC machining center, where the input variables collected were vibration, acoustical signals, and power data. With the increasing of IoT systems and the more frequently usage of sensors, it's becoming easy to collect pre-treated information about the status of any device over a certain time-frame. In industrial operational context, there are patterns in which the failure probability does not increase, but remains constant during the equipment lifetime, and therefore the equipment can fail at any time, as *e.g.*, electrical and electronic components. There is also the case where the direct factors or variables that may influence the operating regions of an equipment are unknown, or even the case where it's impractical to place sensors to collect information. One of the notable previous works dealing with industrial log analysis to predict anomalies is that of R. Sipos *et al.* [9], in which main contributions served us as a guide in the methodology chosen. However, in our case, the impossibility to calculate the RUL of EOL systems due to the insincerity of data coming from the in-service maintenance database (DB), lead us to do a different approach. Our approach can then be applied in industrial cases, where the collection of logging data is available and whose analysis of such information represents a viable low cost alternative compared to the installation of sensors, or even in the impracticality of installation. Log data can be used to understand operational regions of any equipment and understand common patterns. The conduct of our study was based on unsupervised clustering techniques to analyse operational logfiles and then use Principal Component Analysis (PCA) algorithms to identify the variables, that we assume, with the greatest impact on possible anomalies.

3   State of the Art Review

In this section, a review of the state of the art will be carried out, through the approximation to the main European Standards (Std.), serving as support for the framework and justification of the problem in the next sections.

3.1   Maintenance Approach Classification

Maintenance has suffered different evolutions from the first corrective approaches to nowadays more complex predictive applications. So, according to the principal European Norms (EN), the NP EN 13306:2007 Std. [10], the theoretical and principal foundations of maintenance approaches could be divided, essentially, according to three different categories, *i.e.*, corrective, preventive and predictive maintenance. As a summary, Fig. 1 shows a high-level maintenance approach classification.

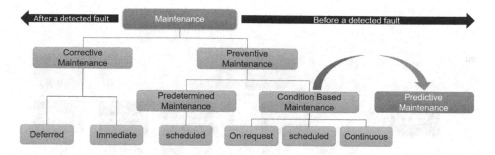

Fig. 1. Maintenance approach classification [2].

1. **Corrective Maintenance:** Taking as reference what is shown in Fig. 1, we can say that the corrective maintenance could be classified according two different categories, *i.e.*, immediate and differed. According to [10], and regarding the first category, it is said that this is an **"emergency maintenance that is made immediately** after a detection of a state of fail, to avoid unacceptable consequences". It is also intended as reactive maintenance. Regarding the second category, the **differed maintenance** is the maintenance that is not immediately made after the detection of a state of fail, but is retarded according to the policies of maintenance established.

2. **Preventive Maintenance:** This type of maintenance could be classified in two main categories, *i.e.*, predetermined maintenance and condition based-based maintenance (see Fig. 1). Regarding the **predetermined maintenance**, it's defined by [10] as a "preventive maintenance carried out at pre-established time intervals or according to a maximum number of uses allowed, but without prior control of the condition". Regarding the **condition-based maintenance**, it's defined by [10] as a "preventive maintenance which includes a combination of condition monitoring and/or inspection and/or testing, analysis, and the ensuing maintenance actions". This technique is fundamentally used to collect data from equipment in order to execute a better repair approach. Some techniques used in this type of maintenance are, as *e.g.*, the monitoring of vibrations, performance, temperature, humidity, tribology, or even visual inspections and tracking of Key Process Indicators (KPI) for health management to discover trends that lead to abnormal operating conditions.

3. **Predictive Maintenance:** As represented schematically in the maintenance approach classification diagram (see Fig. 1), and according to [10], PdM it's defined as a "condition-based maintenance carried out following a forecast derived from repeated analysis or known characteristics and evaluation of the significant parameters of the degradation of the item". This type of maintenance is a sub-classification of the condition-based maintenance. PdM uses a

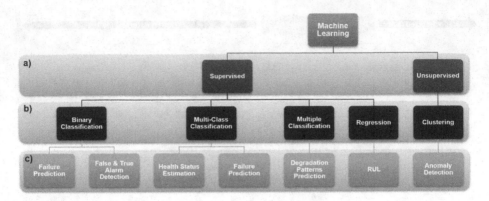

Fig. 2. ML techniques for PdM approaches: (a) ML approaches, (b) ML Techniques and (c) PdM information [2].

set of different ML techniques to learn with historical and recent operational data and make accurate prediction failures in specific equipment. The application of PdM is possible when any equipment has a "symptom" that can characterize the system failure.

3.2 Development Techniques of Data-Driven Models for Maintenance Purposes

The first step of the development phase of a learning model is to understand the business requirements or the specific application context in a more comprehensive way. According to [9,11,12], we can classify different ML approaches in order to obtain a specific PdM result. This information is shown in Fig. 2. The basic steps of a data-driven approach for PdM applications are discussed in this section.

1. **Data Collection and Transformation:** The collection of data is the process of gathering data from relevant sources regarding the analytical problem, as *e.g.*, raw data from monitoring sensors or even operational logfiles. The principal of predictive modelling is to learn patterns from historical data, based on statistical trends, and try to predict future outcomes based on these observations. Collected data can be very complex and the efficiency of a predictive model is directly influenced by the quality of the input data. So, before applying any learning model, it's important to explore it first. The exploration of data can lead us to understand some hidden trends in the data. According to [9,11,12], we can divide data transformation methods in two main tasks, *i.e.*, **processing** and **data analysis**.

2. **Algorithm Selection:** In its concept, according to [9,11,12], "predictive modelling is a mathematical approach to create a statistical model to forecast future behaviour based on input test data". Predictive Modelling can be classified in three main phases, *i.e.*, algorithm selection, training model and evaluation. As shown in Fig. 2, ML techniques are essentially classified in two main approaches: (a) **supervised learning**, where the information about the occurrence of failures is present in the modelling dataset; and (b) **unsupervised learning**, where there is no historical data of maintenance operations. Supervised learning techniques can be grouped in two main areas: (i) **classification methods**, which are generally used in PdM to classify groups of normal and abnormal operation, *i.e.*, Decision Trees, RF, Nearest Neighbors (NN) or Support Vector Machine (SVM); and (ii) **regression methods**, as *e.g.*, LASSO Regression, are usually employed to predict the RUL of equipment. On the other hand, unsupervised learning models, combining **clustering techniques** are valid arguments to detect patterns, behaviours or deviations in what are considered the regions of normal operation. Some unsupervised learning techniques are, as *e.g.*, K-means and PCA.

3. **Model Training and Evaluation:** In order to test the performance of a built model, according to [2,3], there are two types of evaluation metrics capable of quantify its applicability: (a) **offline**, that is generally employed on training datasets, using historical data to obtain performance metrics like F1-score, precision and recall; and (b) **online**, that is used to estimate business metrics through real-time data in deployed models. According to [2,3], a good practice should be to split data sampling into training and cross-validation datasets. In the case of models that learn from very unbalanced datasets, the confusion matrix is also applied as a way to understand, with more detail, the percentage of correct and incorrect classifications. Some confusion matrix insights are, as *e.g.*, the AUC-ROC Curve, F1-score, precision, recall and accuracy.

3.3 Ensemble Learning-Based Predictive Modelling

According to [8,13–15], ensemble learning methods could be defined as "meta-algorithms that combine multiple base learners into a single predictive model in order to improve prediction performance". Ensemble learning methods can be classified into two main categories, *i.e.*, parallel and sequential ensemble methods. The parallel ensemble techniques, as *e.g.*, PCA or RF, generates parallel base learners independently and then average their predictions or take a weighted sum of their predictions. **Parallel ensemble methods** can be implemented, for *e.g.*, using a Dempster–Shafer framework [16] or a Bayesian [17] where the weights are interpreted as probabilities. In the other hand, **sequential ensemble methods** such as AdaBoost construct base learners sequentially and then reduce the bias of the combined base learners. In our case study, the development of the ensemble learning algorithm was based in PCA. This framework is sequenced in four phases: (a) variable selection; (b) model training; (c) model validation; and (d) test. A greater weight will be assigned to the base learner with better performance.

3.4   End-of-Line (EOL) Testing Systems

The development of this paper was made in CAA, an industrial automotive facility, dedicated and specialized in the development of automotive intelligent antennas. Therefore, considering the example of the automotive industry where this case study was developed, in all the Final Assembly (FA) area, there are test equipments, or machines, that measures all the functionalities of each antenna produced at the plant. These equipments, End-of-Line (EOL) Testing Systems (see Fig. 3), are responsible for one of the most crucial parts of the production process, once they perform the screening of defective parts, or, whose measurements do not fall within the limits considered as accepted for the final customer. In this way, the least number of EOL faults, interventions or unavailability, is crucial for the manufacturing process.

Fig. 3. Example of a real EOL test system station. EOL MT460 Motortester [18].

Essentially, we can say that EOL maintenance is accomplished considering: (a) the maximum number of cycle operations recommended by the manufacturer - preventive maintenance; or (b), when physical anomalies are detected in the test equipment - corrective maintenance. In the second case, this could lead to a considerable increase in the number of parts evaluated incorrectly, increasing the First Time Quality (FTQ), as well as an increase in the number of secondary evaluations, and, in the last case, the possibility of shipping defective parts to the customer.

There are some factors that can lead to the predictive detection of EOL anomalies: (a) temperature increase; (b) number of EOL cycle operations;

(c) impurity detection on the test needles; (d) detection of patterns or deviations in the curves from the electrical test signals originated by the antennas; (e) Angle of contact with the test needles.

However, as most of these equipments are working 24×7, it's impractical to place physical sensors, capable of collecting information that can be considered useful for the preventive detection of malfunctions. Thus, the analysis structure of this paper will be based on the collection of information present in the logfiles, produced during their operation.

4 Problem Description

In this section we will describe, in detail, the methodology applied, the logging structure, the PdM approach and the requirements take in consideration on this paper.

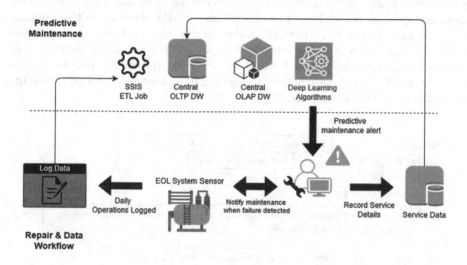

Fig. 4. EOL operation life cycle and PdM workflow interactions.

4.1 Log Data Description

During the normal life cycle service, the EOL operates normally until a detection of a state of fail. When the problem is identified in the FA area by the operator, the maintenance service team is notified and then a repair service is created/scheduled in the maintenance service DB. After the intervention, the maintenance technician updates the scheduled service details, such as component consumption, time spent, repair description, and then closes the service intervention. During the whole process, the EOL still records all component testing information into logfiles. This life cycle (bottom part of Fig. 4) gets repeated over and over for all the FA area in more than fifty equipment units. The dataset used in this study contains all the information present in the logfiles, collected in the past recent years[1]. Logfiles recorded during the EOL's operation (see Fig. 5), are, essentially, a collection of measure points, recorded during the test of each antenna produced. So, essentially, for each antenna produced on the plant, there's a logfile with its measurement results. In detail, EOL's logfile are constituted by: (a) a timestamp (indicating when an antenna was tested); (b) the partnumber and serial number of the antenna tested; (c) the EOL number; (d) test specification, name and results; and (e) the antenna final electrical result (indicating if the antenna is according to the std., and then, can be shipped to the client). In the EOL's normal operation, for each different antenna model (partnumber), there's different test specifications, and each EOL can test more than one antenna partnumber.

Logfiles are differential in some aspects, they are temporal, and can be seen both as symbolic sequences and as numeric time series, with some specific deviations from test signals over some window, e.g. time or days. EOL logfiles can give us important feedback, when for a specific measurement there's deviation considering the all population. The old-fashioned PdM approach in this domain, is to manually create PdM patterns for a specific electrical test, based on the boolean combination of a few relevant samples. This approach is heavily time consuming and experience-based, but it's representative that component failures (e.g. test needles) can be predicted by checking daily logs for patterns, consisting in the EOL's electrical curve results.

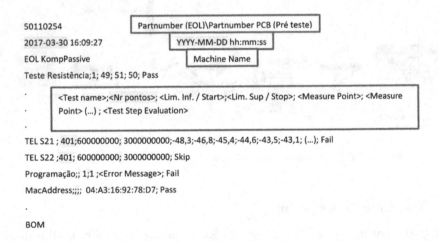

Fig. 5. Example of a real std. logfile from an EOL testing operation.

---

[1] To demonstrate this approach, the authors used datasets from in-service EOL devices, nevertheless, this methodology can also be applied to other research fields, as e.g., IT infrastructures or any industrial equipment, in which such sort of logs could be collected.

4.2   PdM Approach

The PdM approach adopted in this study can be seen in the top part of Fig. 4. A central DB is at the core of the PdM workflow. This central DB combines the information that was originated from the EOL's operation, as well as the information recorded about the history of disruptions and maintenance support from the in-service DB. The ML module processes data from the central DB. The analytics methodology used in this paper was based on the approach made by [9], and it can be classified into four different stages: (a) data acquisition and transformation; (b) model building; (c) model evaluation; and (d) monitoring. In order to build a model, the analytics module first loads the relevant data from the central DB, extracts predictive features (see Sect. 5), forms and represents the data in a matrix format for learning algorithms. Learning algorithms can then build the model and pass it for evaluation. To do this evaluation, the model needs to be compared against historical known data and scored against Key Performance Indicators (KPI). After evaluation, the model needs to be revised or trained until its acceptable performance is considered to be placed in production environment. In the monitoring stage, the system pulls the new daily logfiles from the EOL system and predict a component failure using a model. If, the predicted score exceeds a predefined threshold, an alert will be sent to the maintenance support in order to make some visual inspections locally in the equipment suspected of malfunction.

5   Case Study

This work was conducted in a complex intelligent manufacturing system, CAA, in order to detect patterns in test measurements coming from EOL systems, in an attempt to predict eventual failures. More information about EOL systems can be found in Sect. 3. The proposed case study can be divided essentially in two different parts, but are complementary to each other. The first part of the project consists in the data acquisition and archive solution of the logfiles, produced during the EOL's operation. This solution aims to fill one of the existing fails in maintaining the history of the test curves, necessary for the analysis and development of new products, as well as in the case of complaints from customers for specific antennas. This part is essential for the next step, once that the archive DB was used in order to develop ML techniques for the EOL PdM.

5.1   Methodology and Materials

The range of Software (Sw) used in this work were chosen taking into account the Sw licensing available, and in compliance, according to the Std. defined by the company. In this sense, regarding the data acquisition, the Sw used for the Extractions, Transformations and data Loads (ETL), was the Microsoft SQL Server Integration Services (SSIS) with SQL Server Data Tools (SSDT) 2015, integrated with data storage, performed in a SQL Server 2016 (RTM-GDR) DB.

Regarding the reporting development, the v13 of QlikSense was the Sw chosen. Lastly, for data analytics and machine learning algorithms, the Sw used was MATLAB R2019b. Both solutions are running in different servers, with the same characteristics, this is, Windows Server 2016 with 64 GB of Ram and Intel(R) Xeon(R) CPU ES-2667 v4. The methodology approach and problem description where already addressed on this paper, and can be found in Sect. 4 and Fig. 4.

5.2   Data Acquisition and Preparation

The data acquisition methodology implemented in this case study, can be found in Fig. 6. Logfiles are collected from two different workflows. According to Fig. 6, in (1), the EOL testing system directly stores the antenna test results (raw data) on a primary Staging Area (SA) DB, avoiding the usage of text (.txt) files. This data acquisition is fully integrated with the traceability system, the Manufacturing Execution System (MES). For this purpose, specific .dll methods were developed, in order to get data automatically from the EOL's operation. On the other hand, for the FA workcenters with no MES traceability system, the .txt logfiles are imported by SSIS into the primary SA DB (2). In (3,4), a Daily Job is collecting the last 24h of information (stored on different SQL Server instances) into the Archive DB, and cleaning redundant info from the SA DB. Data should be cleaned, transformed and stored into a Data Warehouse (DW) containing the last 3 week's info. In (5), the treated info is imported from the DW DB into .Qvd files, for in-memory reports; (6) Qlik Report available for usage; (7) Web App for Archive Solution. Search for period or antenna should be available. User Alert (via e-mail) after solution reloaded. (8) MES DataSErver does all the validations on production environment and inserts the results at PMSE DB.

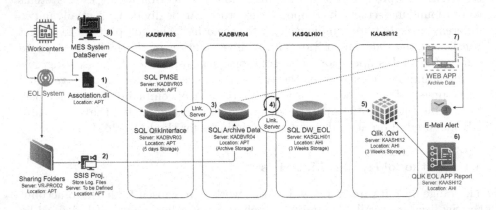

Fig. 6. EOL logfile data acquisition, data storage and archive solution diagram.

5.3 Dataset Overview and Principal Component Analysis

After the first phase of the project complete, it was intended to find a dataset that could fit the overall behaviour of the EOL on the plant. The dataset overview that was chosen for this use case, can be consulted on Table 1. For this analysis, the EOL18 was the chosen one, and the dataset overall includes the collection of information regarding the operation of this equipment, from October 2019 to April 2020. During this period, this equipment performed the validation test for 12 different antenna partnumbers, covering a total of 162.744 produced antennas (see Table 1). It should also be noticed that the overall value for the First Time Quality (FTQ) indicator, for this equipment, reached values above 95%. Achieving, by that, a good ratio between the number of parts rejected during the manufacturing process, versus the total number of pieces attempts.

Table 1. Dataset overview for EOL18, total tested parts by partnumber and FTQ.

Station	Partnumber	Total tested parts $[inUn.]$	FTQ $[in\%]$
EOL18	011031	23.838	99.0
EOL18	011032	22.902	97.9
EOL18	011038	5.624	94.9
EOL18	011039	14.287	98.0
EOL18	011065	11	81.8
EOL18	011066	10	80.0
EOL18	020013	112	95.5
EOL18	020014	2	50.0
EOL18	226944014	110	99.1
EOL18	50010990	1.417	95.4
EOL18	50010991	94.151	93.7
EOL18	52512577	281	94.3
Total		**162.744**	**95.5**

In the model training stage, not all the variables are useful. On the contrary, some variables may even reduce prediction accuracy, because these variables may not be correlated to the degradation behaviour of EOL test systems. To select the most effective variables, PCA mathematical procedures were used to measure the importance of measurement variables with respect to their performance on prediction accuracy. More information about PCA and RF can be consulted on Sect. 3. The list of variables considered in the dataset used in this case study are presented on Table 2.

Table 2. List of variables considered in the case study dataset.

Var. ID	Symbol	Description	Unit
1	RTR	Resistance Test Results	(Ω)
2	TTR	Test Time Results	(s)
3	RKECR	RKE Curr. Results	(A)
4	RKETXFR	RKE TX Freq ECE Results	(Hz)
5	RKETXPR	RKE TX Power Results	(db)

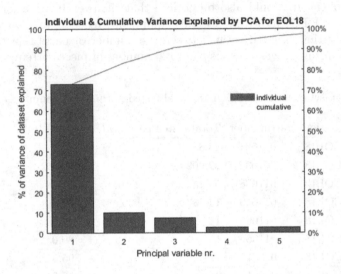

Fig. 7. Individual and cumulative variance on principal variables explained by PCA for EOL18.

Figure 7 illustrates the variable importance. Based on this criterion, the most important variable is the RTR (the variable importance is above 70%). The least important variable is RKETXPR (the variable importance is lower than 5%). In this study, only the three variables with the highest percentage of importance were considered on the analysis, covering a percentage, representative of the all dataset, above 90%.

As shown in Fig. 7, the measurement variables, including RTR, TTR and RKECR, were selected for the predictive models. This result is partially consistent to the methods applied on [1,6], where three measurement variables were selected according to the lognormal distributions of the measurement data.

Figure 8 shows the correlation between the three principal variables, resulted from PCA methods. Notice that only five groups of different partnumber where considered on the analysis, covering the majority of the test measurements performed by the EOL18. So, according to Table 1, only the partnumber: 01103; 011032; 011038; 011039 and 50010991 where chosen, corresponding to data1 until data5, respectively, on Fig. 8. Analysing the Fig. 8, it can be seen that the

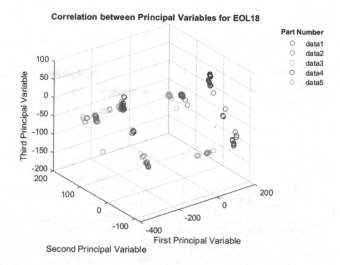

Fig. 8. Correlation between three principal variables for EOL18, considering five different datasets, representing five different antenna partnumber.

behaviour is quite similar for each of the dataset samples. The normal functioning region is in a cluster with a larger number of samples, with some clusters forming around it, with a less concentrated population, moving from the normal operating region. This type of behaviour could be better understood through a two-dimensional analysis, considering only the first two principal variables from the dataset (RTR and TTR).

Figure 9 and Fig. 10 shows how the collection data evolved over time, regarding the principal variables, RTR and TTR, respectively. Notice that, analysing Fig. 9, it's possible to verify, in spite of the noise that is noticed, a pattern in all the analysed partnumber (*i.e.* 011031, 011032, 011038 and 011039). Analysing the RTR variable, its possible to see a peak and a constant increase in the monitored values. This constant increasing in the monitored values may be representative of a malfunction, as well as wear of parts, or damage, caused by improper operation or maintenance.

5.4   EOL Operation Regions Classification and RUL

As planned in Sect. 4 and described in Fig. 4, it was intended on this scope, to collect data of in-service DB, with precious information about the history of faults and maintenance schedules. However, this analysis has become unsuccessful, due to the uncertainty of the records collected and the inaccuracy of the historical data, since they are manual input data. In this sense, without the inclusion of this data in the ML algorithm, it became impossible to implement and detect the RUL of the equipments under analysis. Thus, according to Fig. 2, a different approach was taken into account, as it is not possible to calculate the

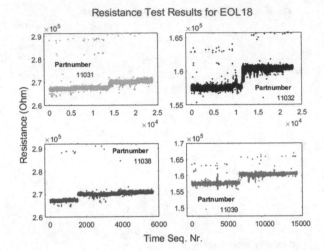

Fig. 9. Resistance test results discretization for EOL18, considering four different samples.

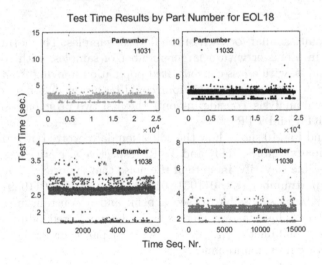

Fig. 10. Operation test time results discretization for EOL18, considering four different samples.

RUL, but the detection of anomalies through the usage of Unsupervised Learning algorithms. Through the analysis of the correlation between the first two principal variables resulted from PCA, it was possible to trace the normal and degradation regions of operation on EOL18. Notice that for the construction of Fig. 11, only the analysis of the results obtained for a partnumber (data1) were taken into account, in which it's possible to see the formation of different clusters moving away from the normal region of operation.

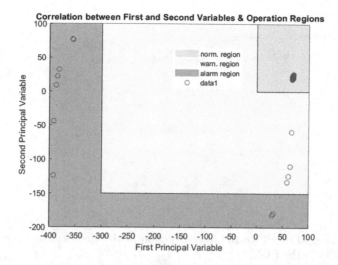

Fig. 11. Correlation between the first two principal variables for dataset1, on EOL18, and different operation regions (*i.e.*: normal, warning and alarm regions).

5.5 EOL Testing Curves Dashboard and Statistical Measurements Information

With the automation made with the data acquisition, it was possible to reconstruct the test signal curves, resultant for each antenna. Despite not being the main part of the project, this phase made it possible to fill one of the main flaws in the storage of information of this type, necessary not only for the development and continuous improvement of products, but also in the archive of information, and made consultation available always when needed (in the case of customer complaints about a particular product). Considering specific regions of the electrical test curve results for each antenna, proved to be a relevant aspect for the PdM analysis. Despite the test measurements, shown in Fig. 12(b), be within the stipulated limits, the analysis of specific points of the curves may indicate that after some time, there may have been some deterioration in the test needles. The analysis of patterns at specific points or regions on the measurement curves, can then be applied as a way to teach the PdM algorithm. Figure 12 shows the final result of the dashboard implemented in QlikView. It was possible to consult the test curves for a specific antenna serial number, Fig. 12(a), as well as check some trends in measurements during the operation time, Fig. 12(b).

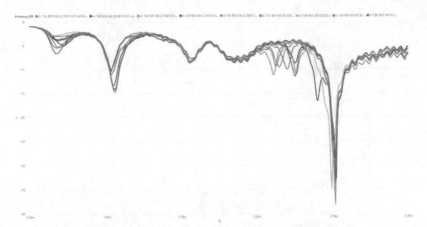

(a) *E.g.* of the final result for the reconstruction of the electrical test curves for the antennas tested in the EOL28.

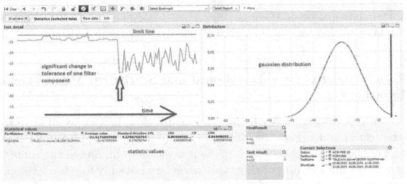

(b) Significant change in tolerance of one filter component during time operation.

Fig. 12. Final *e.g.* of the dashboard developed for the EOL electrical test result consultation. Notice that it's possible to filter data by partnumber, EOL, test name or date.

6   Conclusion and Future Work

This paper presents a data-driven approach, based on multiple instance learning, for predicting EOL disruptions, through the analysis of equipment operational logfiles, which was applied, and validated, through a use case in a world leader automotive industry for intelligent antenna systems (CAA). This study was conducted with some state-of-the-art ML techniques to build PdM models from an EOL testing operation log dataset. The presented application on EOL testing machines shows that, major breakdowns can be predicted or anticipated, by the identification of different operation regions of these equipments. Thus, many corrective and preventive maintenance operations can be precisely scheduled and resources, for example, "spare parts", can be managed in a better way to be provided according to the needs. It was also clear from this study that maintenance costs can be optimized and, depending on the applicability, costs for installing sensors and creating physical models can be avoided. On the other hand, as well as other studies carried out in the field of PdM based on log analysis, as *e.g.*, C. Gutschi *et al.* [11], this study showed that creating stable data-driven log-based models is very time-consuming and its profitability has to be proven.

The comparison of feature selection techniques showed a significant impact on the results regardless of the applied prediction methods. Although feature selection was not in the major scope of this paper, log-based PdM is highly influenced by the applied feature selection algorithm. Thus, further investigations should also consider features combined with other prediction methods into account. It's also intended, as future work, with the inclusion of data from the equipments' in-service maintenance records, to be able to do another type of approaches, such as supervised learning models, in order to obtain a more approximate method regarding the RUL of the equipments, as described in Sect. 3.

Acknowledgements. This work is financed by National Funds through the Portuguese funding agency, FCT - Fundação para a Ciência e a Tecnologia within project UIDB/50014/2020. Special thanks to all the personnel involved, that gave the support necessary to make the publishing of this work possible, in particular to the Continental Advanced Antenna and the University of Trás-os-Montes and Alto Douro.

References

1. Yan, J., Meng, Y., Lu, L., Li, L.: Industrial big data in an Industry 4.0 environment: challenges, schemes, and applications for predictive maintenance. IEEE Access **5**, 23484–23491 (2017). IEEE Special Section on Complex System Health Management Based on Condition Monitoring and Test Data, USA
2. Merkt, O.: On the use of predictive models for improving the quality of Industrial maintenance: an analytical literature review of maintenance strategies. In: 2019 Federated Conference on Computer Science and Information Systems (FedCSIS), Germany, vol. 18, pp. 693–704. ACSIS (2019)
3. Krupitzer, C., et al.: A survey on predictive maintenance for Industry 4.0. Cornell University Computer Science Article, Germany (2020). https://arxiv.org/abs/2002.08224
4. Weiting, Z., Dong, Y., Hongchao, W.: Data-driven methods for predictive maintenance of industrial equipment: a survey. IEEE Syst. J. **13**, 2213–2227 (2019)
5. Cachada, A.: Intelligent and predictive maintenance in manufacturing systems. IPB MSc dissertation, Portugal (2018). http://hdl.handle.net/10198/18301
6. Markiewicz, M., Wielgosz, M., Tabaczynski, W., Konieczny, T., Kowalczyk, L.: Predictive maintenance of induction motors using ultra-low power wireless sensors and compressed recurrent neural networks. IEEE Access **7**, 178891–178902 (2019). IEEE Special Section on Intelligent and Cognitive Techniques for Internet of Things, Poland

7. Ding, H., Yang , L., Yang, Z.: A predictive maintenance method for shearer key parts based on qualitative and quantitative analysis of monitoring data. IEEE Access **7**, 108684–108702 (2019). IEEE Special Section on Advances in Prognostics and System Health Management, USA

8. Li, Z., Goebel, K., Wu, D.: Degradation modeling and remaining useful life prediction of aircraft engines using ensemble learning. J. Eng. Gas Turbines Power Trans. ASME **141**, 041008 (2019)

9. Sipos, R., Fradkin, D., Moerchen, F., Wang, Z.: Log-based predictive maintenance. In: KDD 2014: Proceedings of the 20th ACM SIGKDD International Conference on Knowledge Discovery and Data Mining, USA, pp. 1867–1876. ACM (2014)

10. European/Portuguese Standard. Norma Portuguesa NP EN 13306:2007 (Registo no. 20294). (Portugal) IPQ, Terminologia da Manutençã (2007). https://biblioteca.isel.pt/cgi-bin/koha/opac-ISBDdetail.pl?biblionumber=20294

11. Gutschi, C., Furian, N., Suschnigg, J., Neubacher, D., Voessner, S.: Log-based predictive maintenance in discrete parts manufacturing. Procedia CIRP **79**, 528–533 (2019). 12th CIRP Conference on Intelligent Computation in Manufacturing Engineering, Italy

12. Kadechkar, A., Moreno-Eguilaz, M., Riba, J.-R., Capelli, F.: Low-cost online contact resistance measurement of power connectors to ease predictive maintenance. IEEE Trans. Instrum. Meas. **5**(12), 4825–4833 (2019)

13. Proto, S., et al.: REDTag: a predictive maintenance framework for parcel delivery services. IEEE Access **8**, 14953–14964 (2020). IEEE Special Section on Intelligent and Cognitive Techniques for Internet of Things, Italy

14. Kennedy, J., Eberhart, R.: Particle swarm optimization. IEEE Access **4**, 1942–1948 (1995). Proceedings of ICNN'95 - International Conference on Neural Networks, Australia

15. Li, Z., Wu, D., Hu, C., Terpenny, J.: An ensemble learning-based prognostic approach with degradation-dependent weights for remaining useful life prediction. Reliab. Eng. Syst. Saf. **184**, 110–122 (2019)

16. Goebel, K., Eklund, N., Bonanni, P.: Fusing competing prediction algorithms for prognostics. In: Accepted for Presentation and Publication in Proceedings of 2005 IEEE Aerospace Conference, USA. AERO, Big Sky, MT, p. 10 (2006). https://doi.org/10.1109/AERO

17. Chen, H.: A multiple model prediction algorithm for CNC machine wear PHM. Int. J. Prognostics Health Manage (2011). http://works.bepress.com/huimin_chen/5/

18. DEUTRONIC. End of Line (EOL) e-motor test system. DEUTRONIC, Modern test concepts for various electro mobility components, Germany (2020). https://www.deutronic.com/testsystem/end-of-line-eol-motor-test-system/

Towards Construction Progress Estimation Based on Images Captured on Site

Peter Hevesi[1]($\boxtimes$), Ramprasad Chinnaswamy Devaraj[2], Matthias Tschöpe[1], Oliver Petter[1], Janis Nikolaus Elfert[1], Vitor Fortes Rey[1], Marco Hirsch[1], and Paul Lukowicz[1,2]

[1] German Research Center for Artificial Intelligence (DFKI), Kaiserslautern, Germany
{peter.hevesi,matthias.tschoepe,oliver.petter,janis_nikolaus.elfert, vitor.fortes_rey,marco.hirsch,paul.lukowicz}@dfki.de
[2] University of Kaiserslautern, Kaiserslautern, Germany
ramprasad.devaraj@gmx.de, lukowicz@cs.uni-kl.de

Abstract. State of the art internet of things (IoT) and mobile monitoring systems promise to help gathering real time progress information from construction sites. However, on remote sites the adaptation of those technologies is frequently difficult due to a lack of infrastructure and often harsh and dynamic environments. On the other hand, visual inspection by experts usually allows a quick assessment of a project's state. In some fields, drones are already commonly used to capture aerial footage for the purpose of state estimation by domain experts.

We propose a two-stage model for progress estimation leveraging images taken at the site. Stage 1 is dedicated to extract possible visual cues, like vehicles and resources. Stage 2 is trained to map the visual cues to specific project states. Compared to an end-to-end learning task, we intend to have an interpretable representation after the first stage (e.g. what objects are present, or later what are their relationships (spatial/semantic)). We evaluated possible methods for the pipeline in two use-case scenarios - (1) road and (2) wind turbine construction.

We evaluated methods like YOLOv3-SPP for object detection, and compared various methods for image segmentation, like Encoder-Decoder, DeepLab V3, etc. For the progress state estimation a simple decision tree classifier was used in both scenarios. Finally, we tested progress estimation by a sentence classification network based on provided free-text image descriptions.

Keywords: Construction progress estimation · Neural networks · Computer vision

This work has been partly funded by the Federal Ministry of Education and Research of Germany (BMBF) within the framework of the project ConWearDi (project number 02K16C034).

L. Peñalver and L. Parra (Eds.): Industrial IoT 2020, LNICST 365, pp. 141–161, 2021.
https://doi.org/10.1007/978-3-030-71061-3_9

1   Introduction

Connecting digital models and plans with physical reality has been a key application of Internet of Things. In the industrial domain it is at the core of the Industry 4.0 concept that is currently driving a wave of transformation that is often compared to the original industrial revolution [6]. Concrete applications range from monitoring progress of specific tasks to optimally support the worker and prevent errors, through process optimization to predictive maintenance.

While IoT has been very successful in the industrial domain, it has so far had much less impact on the construction sector. This is certainly not due to the lack of potential applications. Construction planning and reporting is increasingly digital. Connecting such digital plans and reports to the physical reality on the construction site is today done mostly manually which is not only time consuming but also error prone. Process monitoring is another important and necessary step for management of large construction projects and their resource optimization. Again, classical analogue "pen and paper" approaches are time consuming and error prone.

The problem with using IoT to connect construction sites to the digital domain is a combination of high instrumentation effort with only limited structure and high degree of dynamism. Thus a factory floor is in most cases a very well defined, highly structured environment with complex technical infrastructure into which sensors can be easily integrated. The infrastructure and structure tends to remain unchanged for long periods of time. As a consequence many processes taking place on the factory floor are highly structured. A construction site on the other hand is set up temporally with limited infrastructure. Sites tend to significantly differ from each other and evolve. As a consequence work processes tend to be much more adaptive.

As a consequence of the instrumentation difficulties the use of image processing techniques, in particular in conjunction with aerial, drone-based surveillance of construction sites is a growing field. The potential market value of business services that may benefit from drones has been predicted to reach several billion dollars [14]. Drones have been used in physical infrastructure (energy, roads, railways, oil and gas, construction) to examine terrain, record progress, inventory assets, inspect facilities for maintenance [14]. Drone surveillance can be eventually automatized (in some countries, there are legal restrictions), allowing a cost effective way to capture the project state frequently.

In previous work, we explored site monitoring for the earth-movement phase of projects using various sensors in the participating vehicles [3]. Building on the experience from that previous work in this paper we investigate how the increased accuracy of image based object detection techniques can be leveraged to facilitate processes tracking much like embedded sensors allow process tracking on factory floors. Specifically we aim to infer the state of a building process as defined by a human expert from images of the construction site.

The idea is based on the observation that domain experts are often able to quickly assess the current state of the site by visual inspection. This implies the existence of visual cues correlating strongly with specific steps in the process [10].

We propose a two-stage model leveraging state-of-the-art components representing human experts knowledge about project states in different types of construction processes. The first stage involves image processing to extract information about the visual cues related to the targeted process. As we present, this step can be implemented by different types of methods, e.g., semantic segmentation or object detection models. The second stage focuses on predicting the current project state based on the detected object and resources on the images. For this work, we selected two scenarios to evaluate and present the approach:

1. Road Construction
2. Wind Turbine Construction

While this model alone is insufficient to replace complex monitoring systems involving real time sensor data collection, 3D scanning and comparison with Building Information Models (BIM), it is a lightweight approach that aims to map an experts' capability to judge project states based on a single 2D image taken from the right perspective.

2 Related Work

2.1 Use Case

Sensor-based monitoring of road constructions has been proposed in the literature [12,13], where the authors use RFID and GPS information to estimate the progress. In other approaches, activity recognition on movement and location data of vehicles was used to detect progress in the earth movement operations [3].

The authors of [1] propose an advanced recording setup using autonomous drones to collect real time 3D information and compare these with the available building information model. In contrast to our approach, this requires the collection of very accurate data points across the construction site and assumes the availability of accurate planing models.

Unmanned Aerial Vehicles (UAV) have been used by [5] for calculating stockpile volume and pavement characteristics. In another paper, the authors use convolutional neural networks (CNNs) to detect existing roads from UAV images [8]. Similar techniques are proposed by [24] to use UAVs to automatically detect and assess the health condition of civil infrastructure such as bridges and pavements. The authors of [22], used data from UAVs to progress estimation based on height profile in road construction scenarios.

2.2 Methods

In our approach, we build upon state-of-the-art models for image segmentation, object detection and sentence classification. For the image segmentation task, we included networks like AdapNet [21], PSPNet [27], GCN [16], SegNet [2] and DeepLabV3 [4] in our work. We used the YOLOv3-SPP implementation by Jocher et al. [7], which is an improvement of the original YOLO, which was invited by Redmon and Farhadi [17–19]. For these networks, there are various pre-trained model weights available, that can be leveraged when training on a data set with low amount of examples and were therefore well suited for our concept.

A combination of a deep vision CNN with a language generating RNN was proposed by Vinyals et al. In their "Show and Tell" paper [23], the authors demonstrated that their NIC (Natural Image Caption) approach significantly outperformed previous state-of-the-art solutions in automatic image captioning. Consecutive research in this field has led to steady improvements in captioning quality [25,26]. Hence, we explored an initial approach towards using natural language descriptions as input for the progress estimation. It should be noted that the majority of the methods described in literature aim at captioning a wide variety of images from different contexts as opposed to the use cases in this work with a low diversity of meaningful scenarios.

3 Scenarios

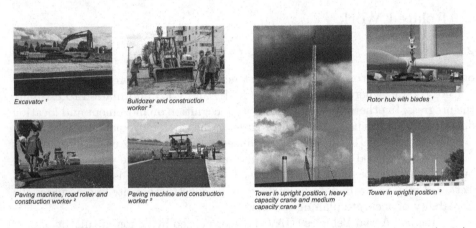

Fig. 1. Example scenarios: road construction (left) and wind turbine assembly (right). Most process steps involve a different set of vehicles, machines, materials or parts that can be observed on the image. A person familiar with the process often can identify the currently performed process step by observing only a single image. [1]sample images from unsplash.com, [2]sample images from pixabay.com

The approach could be applied to every real world scenario to estimate progress where there are existing visual cues that are specific to a given progress step. Many construction processes meet that criterion and are therefore ideal candidates for an initial evaluation. Most of them are of a linear nature, as previous steps must be completed before the next ones start. Furthermore, the progress of construction as well as material, vehicles, tools and workers, that are involved in the construction process, can be visually observed in every state. This is especially true, because just in time delivery and deployment is highly relevant in construction projects, due to the costs and expenditure that are associated with storing materials at the construction site and renting vehicles.

In this work, we considered two different construction processes to prove the feasibility of our approach; the construction process of roads and the installation process of wind turbines. Some example images found on the internet including different states in these two scenarios are depicted on Fig. 1.

3.1   Road Construction

The first scenario is the process of road constructions, more specifically the construction of roads with flexible pavement asphalt. The construction process of roads differs, based on the pavement type that is used. The focus on asphalt pavement roads was selected because of the sufficient complexity and visual variations during the process steps. A typical process for a road construction is comprised of five sequential stages, the first five in the list provided below. In order to cover the scenario of road reconstruction and maintenance, we have included milling process as part of the construction stages. Milling is used to remove the damaged layers of the road and enables thorough repair by removing surface irregularities. Depending on the depth of surface removed during reconstruction, the other stages are carried out sequentially to complete the road construction.

1. Preparation - Excavation
2. Subgrade layer construction
3. Subbase layer construction
4. Base layer construction
5. Pavement layer construction
6. Milling

The assumption here is, that each of these steps can be usually identified by the occurrence of specific objects found on the construction site during its execution. We divided these objects into three main categories. These categories are 1) construction workers 2) vehicles or machines used during the process and 3) construction resources and materials. The category *construction worker* (or person) does not include any further sub-classes for now.

The following construction vehicles were identified to be involved in the process during individual steps of applying asphalt pavements: *Excavator, Dump truck, Bulldozer, Motor-grader, Paving machine, Distributor, Milling machine, Road roller.*

The construction materials relevant in the use-case are *Sand, Asphalt, Aggregate, Natural soil or clay and Gravel.*

The exact mapping of resources to progress states are not presented in this paper, since in the idea this representation is learnt automatically during the training step.

3.2 Wind Turbine Installation

As a second application scenario, the installation process of wind turbines was selected. Similar to the road construction, this involves a number of steps performed in sequence. The typical construction process for this scenario consists of the following stages:

1. Site preparation - Excavation
2. Foundation stage: (a) Inserting steel reinforcement, (b) Pouring concrete, (c) Curing and compacting the foundation with soil
3. Installation of Tower sections
4. Rotor Blades and Generator Installation (top): (a) installation of Nacelle section, (b) Installation of Blades to Rotor hub, (c) Installation of Rotor

During these steps, various transportation vehicles and heavy machinery are utilized. For the progress estimation, following construction and transport vehicles were identified to be relevant:

- For construction site preparation and to lay foundation: Excavator, Dump truck, Bulldozer, Road roller, Concrete mixer truck, Concrete pump truck
- For transportation: flatbed or dropdeck truck
- For installation: Heavy capacity crane (>150 ton), Medium capacity crane (≥20 ton and ≤150 ton), Low capacity crane (<20 ton)

In addition to the vehicles, the presence of different parts and materials is assumed to be also relevant to the progress estimation. For the wind turbine assembly these parts are the following: *Reinforcing steel, Concrete basement, Embedded ring, Tower parts (e.g. in horizontal, tilted or upright positions), Nacelle, Rotor hub, Blade - can also subdivided into two sub-classes based on horizontal or tilted/vertical positions.*

Similar to the road construction use case, a direct mapping of these categories to the process step is not provided, but learnt during the training phase.

4 Progress Estimation

4.1 Concept

The core idea for the progress estimation is to use a single image that contains a representative view of the site. Images, such as those on Fig. 1, provide enough information for understanding the current state in the progress towards completion.

We propose a model divided into two main stages. The first stage is responsible of extracting the available visual information from the image. In an intermediate step, the image processing results are filtered (e.g. removing false positives based on low confidence or size filters) and mapped to the format expected by the second stage. The second stage receives the previously extracted information from the image processing (e.g., what machines and resources can be seen),

Fig. 2. Overview of the estimation pipeline. The two major parts of the system are an image processing network (e.g., for semantic segmentation) and a stage classification to predict the project's state.

and maps these to the project's state. An overview of the proposed pipeline is presented on Fig. 2.

The main reason for the division into two separate stages is to have a modular, extendable system, where the parts can be trained on different data sets. By doing so, the image processing part can be independently optimized to recognize construction resources and machines in general, and the second stage can be just trained scenario specific to evaluate presence, co-location and other spatial relations of those. Ideally, this would lead to an easier knowledge transfer to new scenarios.

4.2   Stage 1: Image Processing

Goal of the first stage is to extract relevant visual information from the provided image by detecting machines, materials and other for the scenario relevant resources. For this step to provide meaningful output, the image should fulfill minimum requirements like:

- Image quality (e.g., brightness, contrast, sharpness) should be good enough to be able to recognize relevant objects on it.
- The image should be taken from an appropriate angle and distance that captures all relevant parts of the scene.
- Vehicles and objects should not be occluded by each other in a way that prevents useful detection of other items.

For this processing step, there are different alternative approaches to extract data from images:

- Object detection: detecting specific object's bounding boxes (and with it presence) on the image.
- Semantic segmentation: assigning a class to each pixel of an image, ideally segmenting it into meaningful regions.
- Image captioning: generating a human readable textual description of the scene.

Depending on the complexity of the scenario, the appropriate method can be different. Simple object detection models are well suited to predict the presence of objects on the image. For detecting surfaces (e.g. asphalted road segment), or estimating more detailed object information (like orientation, size, relation to other objects), image segmentation models are eventually a better choice. In this paper, we focused on evaluating methods for semantic segmentation and object detection in the scenarios. Image captioning models were not included in this initial work.

Object Detection. For object detection, we used the YOLOv3-SPP implementation by Jocher et al. [7] and modified the code for our purposes. We computed new anchors, added random crop, motion blur and random noise as new augmentation methods, and reduced the input images to a size of 864×486. We also used the pretrained weights from Jocher et al. [7], which were trained on the MS COCO data set [11].

An advantage for this method is the simple and fast annotation process, compared to semantic segmentation. A disadvantage can be the limited information about the objects. Sometimes the bounding box is very large, even if the object is rather small, e.g. if a blade occurs diagonally in the image.

Image Segmentation. In this task, the goal is to identify regions of the image belonging to different entities. Typically the output is a class label for each image pixel. Neighbouring pixels with the same class can be merged into a bigger region. For image segmentation, we compared network architectures like *PSP-NeT, DeepLabV3, AdapNet, Global Convolutional Network (GCN)* and *Encoder-Decoder* network. The models were pretrained using ILSVRC2012 data set [20].

When working well, the output of the model is able to provide accurate object boundaries, and thus for example could be used for estimating the object's pose. On the other hand, image segmentation methods are typically more resource intensive in training and inference phase as well. Annotation task is typically a highly time consuming task, since requires accurate ground truth information for the whole image.

Some expected output examples for the semantic segmentation are shown on Fig. 3.

Filtering. In this intermediate step, the outputs of the first stage are filtered and prepared as an appropriate input for the second stage. In particular, one step here is an attempt to remove some of the false positives. In case of object detection network, candidates can be filtered by confidence of the network for the outputted label. Removing the objects with low predicted confidence, typically reduces the amount of wrong detections. For image segmentation, we applied simple size filters, where certain objects are known to have at least a specific size, e.g., an excavator need to contain more than just a couple of pixels to be accepted as an excavator instance.

To input the intermediate results into a simple classification model, we generated feature vectors for each image in a format such as $x = [0, 1, ...0, 1]$, where each position in the array represents a specific entity that could be relevant for the scenario (e.g. *crane*, etc.). At the given index of the feature vector, we use

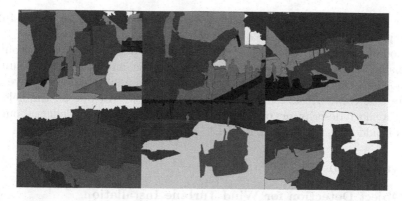

Fig. 3. Examples for semantically segmented images in the road construction scenario. Different colors represent parts of individual classes (e.g. excavator, worker, asphalt etc.).

the value 1 if the object is present on the image and 0 if not. For both results of the segmentation, and object detection, we used this simple "presence" representation in this work.

4.3 Stage 2: Progress Estimation

In the second stage, the progress of the construction process is determined using the information from images in the previous stage. An additional label is introduced in addition to the project's progress classes called "Need Additional Information" (NAI). The label is used in case the provided input for stage 2 is insufficient to assign one of the project's states to it, for example when the image was taken from an unfavorable perspective where the image detection fails to predict one of the key items.

Progress Estimation Using a Decision Tree. To predict the class label of the project stage, we trained a model using the binary feature vector provided by the filter step of stage 1 as an input. In preliminary experiments, we tried various different common classification algorithms and could not observe any significant difference in performance. The results shown in this paper are from a simple decision tree classifier we chose for its intuitive representation of different object presence to project stage label.

Progress Estimation with a Sentence Classification Network. While stage 1 presented in this paper solely provides a binary feature vector, we tested an initial approach using natural language descriptions as an intermediate representation. Descriptions of the images created by humans are used as an input for an alternative stage 2 model consisting of a sentiment analysis for sentences utilising convolutional neural networks, which have shown to be successful for these type of tasks in the past [9].

Encoding the image information into a free text adds information about the relationship of objects to each other which can be interpreted by a suitable model. Additionally, the form of natural language enables an alternative approach in case camera usage is not possible or feasible. Anyone on the field can provide a short description of the scene and the expert knowledge about the process is added by the stage 2 model.

5 Evaluation

5.1 Object Detection for Wind Turbine Installation

Performance of a custom trained YOLOv3-SPP network was evaluated on detecting relevant entities on images taken on wind turbine constructions.

Data Set. For this evaluation, we created a custom data set, acquired from videos available on the internet. To capture the most important categories, as described in Sect. 3, we annotated the following seven classes with bounding boxes on the image:

crane := {Low capacity crane, Medium capacity crane, Heavy capacity crane }

tower := {Tower-horizontal, Tower-tilted, Tower-vertical, Embedded ring }
blade := {Blade-horizontal, Blade-tilted }
motor := {Nacelle, Rotor hub }
fbm := {Excavator, Dump truck, Bulldozer, Road roller, Concrete mixer truck, Concrete pump truck }
trans := {Flatbed truck, Dropdeck truck }
found := {Concrete Foundation, Reinforcing steel, Concrete }

where fbm is our abbreviation for *foundation building machine*, trans stands for *transport truck* and found for *foundation*.

In total, we labeled 911 images, containing 2285 objects from 31 videos. These objects are allocated to the above classes as follows: crane 577, tower 567, blade 337, motor 315, fbm 242, trans 114 and found 133. We used a random train-val-split with 90% training and 10% validation images. Our test set consists of frames of four independent videos, i.e. there is not a single frame in the test set that is also in the training set or validation set. Under those preconditions, we picked the test-videos in such a way, that the class-ratio distribution of the test-set is similar to the class-ratio distribution of the whole data set. This leads to a test-set with 101 images containing 72 crane, 68 tower, 38 blade, 28 motor, 23 fbm, 17 trans and 17 found objects. Notice, the column *support*, used in Table 1 is described in [15] and denotes the number of positive ground truth labels, which is equivalent to TP+FN. However, since we prefiltered some predictions by setting the Class-Specific Confidence Score to 0.1, not all of these numbers match to the numbers mentioned above.

Fig. 4. Examples of detected objects by YOLOv3-SPP after re-training with our annotated images from wind turbine construction videos. Instances of the class "foundation
building machines" (e.g. excavator) are as well detected on road construction images.

Results. In the current phase of evaluation, we reduced the object detection
output to the presence of an object on the image. This leads to a multi-label
classification problem where we can use Precision, Recall and F_1 score for each
class. The results for this are shown in Table 1. Best results were achieved for
the *crane* class with a Precision, Recall and F_1 score of over 90%. Since *cranes*
were the most commonly represented and visually distinct class in the data set,
this result was expected.

The second last row (weighted mean) in Table 1 indicates the weighted metrics,
i.e. taking the respective sums of TP, FP, FN and TN values from the seven classes
and compute the metrics with those totals. Thus, the metrics of smaller classes
(like transport truck) have smaller TP, FP, FN and TN values and therefore less
impact of the metrics. The last row (mean) averages the metrics over all seven
classes, and therefore weights each class equally. In addition to Table 1 Fig. 4 shows
some object detection results applied on each single image from Fig. 1. Since we
trained YOLOv3-SPP on a 16:9 ratio, we embedded each image from Fig. 1 to a
16:9 background. This was especially important for the upright image.

Considering that our data set is rather unbalanced and relatively small, the
results indicate that with proper training set sizes, we can achieve good results
detecting construction process related objects.

5.2   Semantic Segmentation for Road Construction

Semantic segmentation methods for detecting construction vehicles and materials were evaluated on a custom image data set for road constructions.

Data Set. To evaluate the performance of the networks as given in Sect. 4.2,
a custom data set on road construction resources is created by acquiring image
frames from videos available on the internet. The construction vehicles and
materials as described in Sect. 3.1 are of unique nature and are important in

Table 1. Step1: evaluation results, object detection

	Precision	Recall	F_1 score	Support
Crane	0.98	0.93	0.95	70
Tower	0.78	0.77	0.77	66
Blade	0.70	0.70	0.70	37
Motor	0.46	0.59	0.52	27
Fbm	0.75	0.82	0.78	22
Trans	0.29	0.24	0.26	17
Found	0.92	0.65	0.76	17
Weighted mean	0.75	0.75	0.75	256
Mean	0.70	0.68	0.69	256

determining the current ongoing process at construction site. Therefore are annotated as separate class labels. Further, the background information observed during road construction is categorized into one of the following class labels: 1) Sky, 2) Vegetation, 3) Signboard, 4) Car, 5) Barricade 6) Building. The parts of the image that does not belong to the above classes are annotated as Unlabeled.

A total of 330 images of size 800×576 covering all processes involved in road construction are pixel-wise annotated. Data augmentation methods are followed to improve the data set size. Augmentation techniques such as varying brightness intensity, flipping images horizontally and introducing blur and noise in the images are used. With this, the size of the data set is increased to a total of 1650 images. Out of which 1200 images are used for training and 300 images for validating. The test set consists of 150 images with an even distribution of 25 images per road construction stage as described in Sect. 3.1. The image frames in test set are not used for training or validation.

Results. Performance of a semantic segmentation model is normally evaluated using metrics such as Intersection of Union(IoU), Precision, Recall and F_1 score. Due to class imbalance issue in the data set, pixel accuracy is not used to evaluate the model. As the road construction scenario involves determining several classes as described in Sects. 3.1 and 5.2, it is a multi-class segmentation problem. Therefore, Mean Intersection of Union (mIOU) of the image is calculated by taking the IoU of each class and averaging them.

The performance of the networks on the road construction data set are provided in Table 2. The mIoU values provided in the second column from the left suggests that Encoder-Decoder network performs better than the other networks on the custom road construction data set. Since the Stage2: Progress estimation relies on the accuracy of predicted construction resources from this stage. It is important to obtain good predictions. Considering the size of the data set, the results are significant and can be further improved by increasing the training set size and covering more possibilities of real world scenarios.

Table 2. Image segmentation results using different network types on the road construction data set

	mIOU	Precision	Recall	F_1 score
AdapNet	0.65	0.88	0.87	0.87
PSPNet	0.64	0.84	0.85	0.84
Encod.-Decod	0.75	0.94	0.93	0.93
GCN	0.49	0.70	0.72	0.69
DeepLabV3	0.33	0.57	0.56	0.53

5.3   Progress Prediction - Road Construction

For evaluating the second stage in the road construction scenario, we defined two test cases, when generating the feature vectors:

1. using perfect image processing results (the ground truth labels for the images)
2. using predicted objects on the images by the best performing image segmentation network (Encoder-Decoder)

Data Set. For evaluating the second stage, we did not use any of the augmented images. In total we had 330 images with available progress labels. These labels correspond to the 6 possible progress states of road constructions as listed in Sect. 3.1. For every target class, we selected half of the available images randomly to be in the training set, and the rest was dedicated to be used for training. In total 165 images were used in training the classifier.

For testing the performance of the classification using the results of the image processing stage, we only had 30 images that were in the test set of the image processing and are original images without data augmentation. These 30 images include 5 examples for every project steps, which led to a rather small data set. Therefore, we let the training of the second stage run with the ground truth detections and used the 30 detections solely for testing.

Results. The trained progress classification decision tree model could provide a perfect classification when tested with feature vectors generated out of the ground truth objects (filtered and prepared image segments). These results are displayed in Table 3. This result for road construction was not unexpected, since we assumed an perfect mapping of resources and machines to the target classes beforehand.

The results for applying the progress estimation on realistic output of the image processing stage are listed in Table 4. Here, we used the results of the *encoder-decoder* network, since this seemed to be the most promising image segmentation method for the use case. The progress classification has only one mistake, a confusion between excavation and sub-base stages, which can be rooted

Table 3. Progress prediction results for road construction assuming perfect object detection results

	Precision	Recall	F_1 score	Support
Base	1.00	1.00	1.00	17
Excavation	1.00	1.00	1.00	30
Milling	1.00	1.00	1.00	29
Paving	1.00	1.00	1.00	31
Subbase	1.00	1.00	1.00	28
Subgrade	1.00	1.00	1.00	30

back to a partly wrong image segmentation result. Other mistakes from the segmentation did not influence the final performance. The small data set however only allows limited significance and will be subject of future work to further test with more diverse scenes.

Table 4. Progress prediction results for road construction using predictions from the Encoder-Decoder network's output as a feature vector

	Precision	Recall	F_1 score	Support
Base	1.00	1.00	1.00	5
Excavation	0.83	1.00	0.91	5
Milling	1.00	1.00	1.00	5
Paving	1.00	1.00	1.00	5
Subbase	1.00	0.80	0.89	5
Subgrade	1.00	1.00	1.00	5

5.4   Progress Prediction - Wind Turbine Construction

For evaluating the second stage in the wind turbine construction scenario, we defined two test cases, when generating the feature vectors:

1. Assuming perfect image processing results by using the ground truth labels
2. Using predicted objects by the fine-tuned YOLOv3-SPP network

Data Set. For each of the 911 images in the wind turbine data set, we assigned the process step label as one of the following classes:

- Excavation: earthwork phase of site preparation
- Foundation: building the foundation
- Tower Installation: building the tower parts

- Rotor Installation: assembly of the rotor blades, mounting of nacelle and rotor to the top of the tower
- NAI: the image does not contain enough information to be able to assign it to a single process step

For test case 1, we performed a split of the data set randomly selecting 319 instances for test to contain approximately 35% of each class and the remaining instances for training. The feature vector for each instance was created using the list of annotated objects on the image - to see how well the classifier performs with no errors coming from the first stage.

For test case 2, we wanted to evaluate the classifier under realistic conditions, where we do not have image annotations at all. For this test, we used object detection results of the YOLOv3-SPP on the test set for images (not included in the training of the network's weights). This was the basis for training and testing the second stage completely. Out of the 256 instances (feature vector representing the detected object on the image and corresponding progress class label), we selected randomly 104 for the test-set, and trained a new decision tree classifier on the remaining 152 examples.

Table 5. Progress prediction results for wind turbine construction assuming perfect object detection results used as an input

	Precision	Recall	F_1 score	Support
Excavation	0.71	0.97	0.82	30
Foundation	0.84	0.77	0.80	60
Tower installation	0.93	0.54	0.68	98
Rotor installation	0.57	0.92	0.70	88
NAI	0.67	0.37	0.48	43

Results. Results for test case 1 are shown in Table 5. Excavation and Foundation classes achieve an F_1 score of approximately 0.8, Tower and Rotor installation classes are around 0.7. A look at the confusion matrix on Fig. 5 reveals that these two pairs of sequential process step's classes are also responsible for most of the *confusions*. Probable reason for these inaccuracies, is that the simplified information about presence of objects is not enough anymore, to perfectly distinguish the classes and especially in the early project phases, similar vehicles (like excavator) are still in use or at site, when next steps are performed.

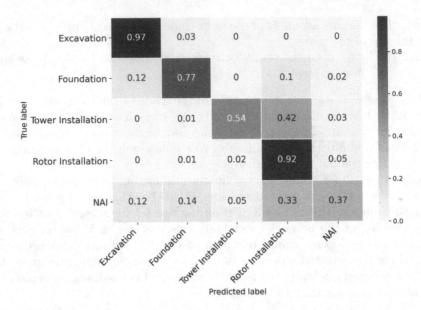

Fig. 5. Confusion matrix of the progress predictions for the wind turbine data set assuming perfect object detection results.

Table 6. Progress prediction results for wind turbine construction using detected objects by a custom trained YOLOv3-SPP network

	Precision	Recall	F_1 score	Support
Excavation	0.67	1.00	0.80	20
Foundation	0.92	0.67	0.77	18
Tower installation	0.65	0.76	0.70	29
Rotor installation	0.61	0.55	0.58	20
NAI	0.44	0.24	0.31	17

In test case 2, using only the predicted object detections for feature vector generation, we performed the same training workflow. Results are summarized in Table 6 and in the confusion matrix on Fig. 6. With exception of the class *Rotor Installation*, that has worse results, the scores are in a similar range as in test case 1.

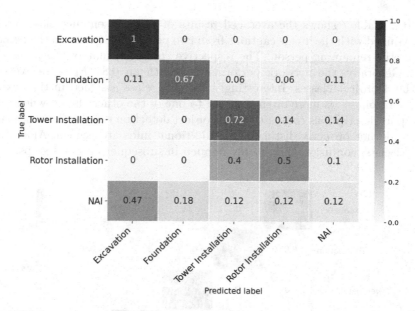

Fig. 6. Confusion matrix of the progress predictions for the wind turbine data set when using objects detected by YOLOv3 model.

5.5 Wind Turbine Construction - Using Image Captions

Data Set. We selected a subset of images throughout all the stages from 4 different construction sites and let 3 people describe the image content in text form leading to 633 annotations for 211 images, like the following examples.

- "An excavator digs a hole into a field."
- "A construction sign, with a tower section hanging on a heavy capacity crane next to the vertical tower parts in the background."
- "A road roller is behind an excavator, that is performing earth moving operations."
- "A blue heavy capacity crane is next to a half-built tower."

It should be noted that the annotators had no expert knowledge about the processes nor were they associated with the construction industry but they have been shortly briefed for the task. In addition to explaining the purpose of the labels, they were briefly explained what the construction scenario is about. The description should be focused on the visible objective representation of the image, with no interpretation or mentions regarding the process state. Additionally, they were asked to use predefined names for the key objects, like "heavy capacity crane" or "rotor blade" whenever possible. The total description text length was limited to a maximum of 200 characters per image, which seemed to be more than sufficient for most of the cases. Apart from that, the annotators could write freely without any restrictions regarding language complexity sentences or grammar.

Results. Table 7 shows the averaged results of using a sentence classification CNN, trained with the image captions from two people and tested on the descriptions of the remaining person. The respective confusion matrix can be seen in Fig. 7. Generally, the network performs well with an 0.84 F_1 score averaged over the 4 project classes. Interestingly, the NAI class assigned in the "expert assessment phase" is more often assigned to one of the other classes when using non-expert descriptions compared to the object detection results. Hence, the network could not properly distinguish if additional infos are needed. Apart from the NAI class, confusion almost only happen in subsequent process steps.

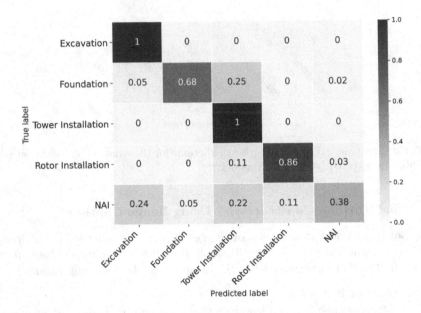

Fig. 7. Confusion matrix of the progress predictions with sentence classification CNN using image captions.

Table 7. Progress prediction results for wind turbine construction using a sentence classification CNN with image captions

	Precision	Recall	F_1 score	Support
Excavation	0.77	1.00	0.87	36
Foundation	0.93	0.68	0.78	40
Tower installation	0.74	1.00	0.85	62
Rotor installation	0.89	0.86	0.87	36
NAI	0.88	0.38	0.53	37

6   Conclusion

Construction projects present in most cases a changing and for IoT systems an often challenging environment. This makes remote, automatic monitoring difficult task. In this paper, we propose a lightweight, alternative path for automatically predicting the construction project's state based on images taken at the construction site. This initial work describes a modular, two stage model and evaluates some state-of-the-art techniques that could be used in the different stages of the pipeline.

The core idea is to apply a suitable image processing model in the first stage, that extracts a human readable representation of the relevant visual cues from the image. For simple use case scenarios, the *visual cue* can be just the presence of specific objects on the image. The second stage can be independently optimized to map the extracted cues to the project state.

For object detection tasks, we evaluated the usage of a YOLOv3-SPP network re-trained specifically to recognize key objects for a wind turbine construction use case. Even with a small amount of images in the data set (911 in total during different phases of the construction process), results look promising, with one of the classes (crane) even performing above 0.9 precision and recall values when focusing on presence of objects.

We also performed an initial evaluation of different image segmentation networks, by annotating images from the road construction scenario and comparing them to alternative models for the task. An Encoder-Decoder network could achieve precision and recall scores above 0.9 on average over all classes. The approach of image segmentation can be particularly interesting later in use cases where more information is necessary than just the presence of certain objects.

The progress detection step in the second stage utilized a simple *decision tree* classifier for both scenarios. In the road construction scenario, this approach seems to be able to provide perfect classification results assuming a perfect prediction from the image processing stage. The wind turbine scenario proved to be more challenging. However, the classifier performs reasonably well, the tower and rotor installation classes show a lot of confusion. The issue here seems to be in the nature of the underlying data, hinting that a simple presence of objects might be insufficient information to predict this project's states.

Motivated by this outcome and the idea to keep a human readable intermediate data representation, we explored if and how well manually generated free text image captions can be mapped to the project state. For this task, a sentence classification CNN was utilized, what could learn to map given input texts to the output class label. For 3 classes, this image caption interpreter achieved a F_1 score above 0.84. This shows that a free text written by a human observer can be mapped to a more abstract process state even if the observer does not have expert knowledge about the process itself.

Initial results, included in the paper, provided helpful insights for the way towards a practically useful system. The two stage model seems to be very helpful because its modular nature makes it possible to always select state-of-the-art specialized methods for the sub-tasks. Looking at the initial wind turbine results, we assume that many scenarios will require more detailed information like object relationships (spatial and semantic). Hence, besides training on larger image data sets with a higher variety of construction related entities (material, tools, vehicles) and exploring other use case scenarios, in future work, we want to evaluate the performance of automated image captioning models and their potential of mapping to process stages.

References

1. Anwar, N., Izhar, M.A., Najam, F.A.: Construction monitoring and reporting using drones and unmanned aerial vehicles (UAVs). In: The Tenth International Conference on Construction in the 21st Century (CITC-10) (2018)
2. Badrinarayanan, V., Kendall, A., Cipolla, R.: SegNet: a deep convolutional encoder-decoder architecture for image segmentation. IEEE Trans. Pattern Anal. Mach. Intell. **39**(12), 2481–2495 (2017)
3. Bucchiarone, A., et al.: Smart construction: remote and adaptable management of construction sites through IoT. IEEE Internet Things Mag. **2**(3), 38–45 (2019). https://doi.org/10.1109/IOTM.0001.1900044. https://ieeexplore.ieee.org/document/8950968, print ISSN: 2576-3180 Electronic ISSN: 2576-3199
4. Chen, L.C., Papandreou, G., Schroff, F., Adam, H.: Rethinking atrous convolution for semantic image segmentation (2017)
5. Congress, S.S.C., Puppala, A.J.: Novel methodology of using aerial close range photogrammetry technology for monitoring the pavement construction projects. In: International Airfield and Highway Pavements Conference 2019, pp. 121–130. American Society of Civil Engineers (2019). https://doi.org/10.1061/9780784482476.014
6. Drath, R., Horch, A.: Industrie 4.0: Hit or hype? [industry forum]. IEEE Ind. Electron. Mag. **8**(2), 56–58 (2014)
7. Jocher, G., et al.: ultralytics/yolov3: Rectangular Inference, Conv2d + Batchnorm2d Layer Fusion (2019). https://doi.org/10.5281/zenodo.2672652
8. Kestur, R., et al.: UFCN: a fully convolutional neural network for road extraction in RGB imagery acquired by remote sensing from an unmanned aerial vehicle. J. Appl. Remote Sens. **12**(1), 016020 (2018). https://doi.org/10.1117/1.JRS.12.016020
9. Kim, Y.: Convolutional neural networks for sentence classification. In: Proceedings of the 2014 Conference on Empirical Methods in Natural Language Processing (EMNLP), pp. 1746–1751. Association for Computational Linguistics, Doha, Qatar, October 2014. https://doi.org/10.3115/v1/D14-1181, https://www.aclweb.org/anthology/D14-1181
10. Kopsida, M., Brilakis, I., Vela, P.: A review of automated construction progress monitoring and inspection methods. In: Proceedings of the 32nd CIB W78 Conference on Construction IT (2015)
11. Lin, T.-Y., et al.: Microsoft COCO: common objects in context. In: Fleet, D., Pajdla, T., Schiele, B., Tuytelaars, T. (eds.) ECCV 2014. LNCS, vol. 8693, pp. 740–755. Springer, Cham (2014). https://doi.org/10.1007/978-3-319-10602-1_48
12. Navon, R., Shpatnitsky, Y.: Field experiments in automated monitoring of road construction. J. Constr. Eng. Manage. **131**(4), 487–493 (2005). https://doi.org/10.1061/(ASCE)0733-9364(2005)131:4(487)

13. Navon, R., Shpatnitsky, Y.: A model for automated monitoring of road construction. Constr. Manage. Econ. **23**(9), 941–951 (2005). https://doi.org/10.1080/01446190500183917
14. Otto, A., Agatz, N., Campbell, J., Golden, B., Pesch, E.: Optimization approaches for civil applications of unmanned aerial vehicles (UAVs) or aerial drones: a survey. Networks **72**(4), 411–458 (2018). https://doi.org/10.1002/net.21818
15. Pedregosa, F., et al.: Scikit-learn: machine learning in Python. J. Mach. Learn. Res. **12**, 2825–2830 (2011)
16. Peng, C., Zhang, X., Yu, G., Luo, G., Sun, J.: Large kernel matters-improve semantic segmentation by global convolutional network. In: Proceedings of the IEEE Conference on Computer Vision and Pattern Recognition, pp. 4353–4361 (2017)
17. Redmon, J., Divvala, S., Girshick, R., Farhadi, A.: You only look once: unified, real-time object detection. In: Proceedings of the IEEE Conference on Computer Vision and Pattern Recognition, pp. 779–788 (2016)
18. Redmon, J., Farhadi, A.: YOLO9000: better, faster, stronger. In: Proceedings of the IEEE Conference on Computer Vision and Pattern Recognition, pp. 7263–7271 (2017)
19. Redmon, J., Farhadi, A.: YOLOv3: an incremental improvement. arXiv preprint arXiv:1804.02767 (2018)
20. Russakovsky, O., et al.: ImageNet large scale visual recognition challenge. Int. J. Comput. Vis. **115**(3), 211–252 (2015). https://doi.org/10.1007/s11263-015-0816-y
21. Valada, A., Vertens, J., Dhall, A., Burgard, W.: Adapnet: adaptive semantic segmentation in adverse environmental conditions. In: 2017 IEEE International Conference on Robotics and Automation (ICRA), pp. 4644–4651. IEEE (2017)
22. Vick, S., Brilakis, I.: Road design layer detection in point cloud data for construction progress monitoring. J. Comput. Civ. Eng. **32**(5) (2018). https://doi.org/10.1061/(ASCE)CP.1943-5487.0000772
23. Vinyals, O., Toshev, A., Bengio, S., Erhan, D.: Show and tell: a neural image caption generator. In: Proceedings of the IEEE Conference on Computer Vision and Pattern Recognition, pp. 3156–3164 (2015)
24. Wu, W., et al.: Coupling deep learning and UAV for infrastructure condition assessment automation. In: 2018 IEEE International Smart Cities Conference (ISC2), pp. 1–7. IEEE, 16–19 September 2018. https://doi.org/10.1109/ISC2.2018.8656971
25. Xiao, X., Wang, L., Ding, K., Xiang, S., Pan, C.: Deep hierarchical encoder-decoder network for image captioning. IEEE Trans. Multimed. **21**(11), 2942–2956 (2019)
26. Yao, T., Pan, Y., Li, Y., Mei, T.: Exploring visual relationship for image captioning. In: Ferrari, V., Hebert, M., Sminchisescu, C., Weiss, Y. (eds.) Computer Vision – ECCV 2018. LNCS, vol. 11218, pp. 711–727. Springer, Cham (2018). https://doi.org/10.1007/978-3-030-01264-9_42
27. Zhao, H., Shi, J., Qi, X., Wang, X., Jia, J.: Pyramid scene parsing network. In: Proceedings of the IEEE Conference on Computer Vision and Pattern Recognition, pp. 2881–2890 (2017)

Integration of Wireless Communication Capabilities to Enable Context Aware Industrial Internet of Thing Environments

Imanol Picallo[1,2], Peio López Iturri[1,2], Mikel Celaya-Echarri[3], Leyre Azpilicueta[3], and Francisco Falcone[1,2(✉)]

[1] Electrical, Electronic and Communication Engineering Department, Public University of Navarre, Pamplona, Spain
francisco.falcone@unavarra.es
[2] Institute of Smart Cities, Public University of Navarre, 31006 Pamplona, Spain
[3] School of Engineering and Sciences, Tecnologico de Monterrey, 64849 Monterrey, Mexico

Abstract. In order to provide interactive capabilities within the context of Internet of Thing (IoT) applications, wireless communication systems play a key role, owing to inherent mobility, ubiquity and ease of deployment. However, in order to comply with Quality of Service (QoS) and Quality of Experience (QoE) metrics, coverage/capacity analysis must be performed, in order to account for the impact of signal blockage as well as multiple interference sources. This analysis is especially complex in the case of indoor scenarios, such as those derived from Industrial Internet of Things (IIoT). In this work, a fully volumetric approach is employed in order to provide precise wireless channel characterization and hence, system level analysis of indoor scenarios. The proposed methodology will be tested against a real measurement scenario, providing full flexibility and scalability for adoption in a wide range of IIoT capable environments.

Keywords: Industrial Internet of Things · Wireless channel characterization · Coverage/Capacity estimations

1 Introduction

The implementation of scenarios with context-awareness capabilities is being progressively adopted with the aid of elements such as Internet of Things and novel heterogeneous communication networks. Multiple applications are envisaged within these scenarios, such as Smart Grids, Intelligent Transportation Systems or Smart Health, to name a few. Out of these, one of the most promising applications is related with Cyber Physical systems and Industry 4.0, giving rise to the paradigm of Industrial Internet of Things. In this sense, communication play a key role in order to enable data processing, inference, prediction or real time interaction, among others. Wireless communication systems are being employed in order to provide data exchange capabilities, owing to their flexibility, mobility and ubiquity. Moreover, the adoption of different types of wireless

© ICST Institute for Computer Sciences, Social Informatics and Telecommunications Engineering 2021
Published by Springer Nature Switzerland AG 2021. All Rights Reserved
L. Peñalver and L. Parra (Eds.): Industrial IoT 2020, LNICST 365, pp. 162–170, 2021.
https://doi.org/10.1007/978-3-030-71061-3_10

communication systems with variable coverage/capacity ranges provide a set of multiple options in order to provide different types of connectivity, as a function of node config- uration, location and network topological requirements. In this way, different services such as logistic handling, maintenance, location, tracking or diagnostics can be provided by means of wireless personal area networks (e.g. Bluetooth, NFC, RFID, etc.), wireless sensor networks (ZigBee, Sigfox, LoRa-LoRaWAN), wireless local area networks or mobile networks (with emphasis on 4G and 5G systems, including specific networks for IoT based communications, such as NB-IoT or Cat M1-M2) [1–3].

Despite the advantages in the use of wireless communication systems in terms of rapid deployment, integration and high mobility, they also face multiple challenges, owing to highly vulnerable wireless channel characteristics. Wireless communication channels are subject to highly variable losses given by different mechanisms, such as fading due to blockage, absorption or multi-path propagation. Moreover, other effects are given by the existence of different types of interference sources, as well as by time related phenomena, such as Doppler shift or high levels of delay spread. In the case of indoor industrial environments, these effects are increased, mainly given by the predom- inance of non-line of sight links owing to high levels of clutter, as well as by strong multi-path components, owing to high density of metallic objects in the environment [4–9]. These phenomena lead eventually to degradation in terms of service level met- rics, in which coverage areas tend to decrease given by degradation in signal to noise ratio values detected at the receiver side. In order to adequately address the deploy- ment and design of wireless systems it´s therefore required to perform radio planning tasks in order to carefully assess transmitter signal levels, as well as distribution of non- desired interference sources. There are multiple methods in order to analyze wireless channel behavior, spanning from deterministic based techniques to empirical/statistical methods. The first ones solve Maxwell equations in a given simulation model of the Sce- nario Under Test (SUT), providing very accurate field estimation values. These methods, such as Full Wave electromagnetic simulation (e.g., FDTD, FITD, MoM, etc.) require precise scenario description as well as very large computational cost. The later meth- ods exhibit much lower computational cost but exhibit large errors, requiring intensive measurement-based calibration. As a mid-term solution between these two there are techniques based on the approximation of field propagation based on GO-UTD, such as ray tracing and ray launching methods. These methods balance computational cost with accuracy, enabling the analysis of relatively large scenarios with complex scatterer distributions with feasible computational cost.

In this work, wireless channel characterization within complex indoor scenarios with large scatterer levels is presented, with the aid of an in-house implemented 3D ray launch- ing code. The SUT is a large sized laboratory called Luis Mercader, at UPNA in Spain, which has been selected in order to emulate potential scatterer densities within indus- trial environments. The 3D RL simulation code has been extensively tested with multi- ple types of scenarios, in order to perform frequency/power calculations, time domain parameters extraction and with subsequent processing, quality of service (QoS)/quality of experience (QoE) metrics [10–12]. The code is implemented in Matlab and the SUT is recreated, considering the dimensions of all objects, as well as assignment of the frequency dispersive properties, in terms of dielectric constant as well as conductivity values, for each one of the elements within the scenario. In this work, the simulation scenario that has been implemented is shown in Fig. 1, where the detail of all the indoor elements within the scenario can be observed.

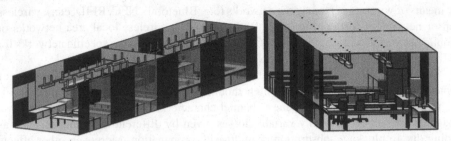

Fig. 1. Schematic representations of the Scenario Under Test for validation of volumetric wireless channel characterization.

2   Wireless Channel Simulation in the Scenario Under Test

Once the scenario has been defined, wireless channel estimation values corresponding to different network systems are obtained. Simulation parameters such as ray launching volumetric angular resolution ($\Delta\phi = \Delta\theta = 1°$), maximum number of reflected rays until extinction (N = 6) or cuboid size resolution ($\Delta l = 10$cm) are defined, following previous convergence analysis studies [12]. Potential transmitter/receiver sources have been located within the SUT, considering WBAN/WLAB/WSN/PLMN systems operating within the frequency bands of 433 MHz, 868 MHz, 2.4 GHz and 3.5 GHz (in order to include frequency range 1 5G network services). In this way, received power levels can be estimated within the total SUT volume. For the sake of clarity, specific cut-planes providing the bi-dimensional RX power level distributions have been depicted. The cut-plane height selected correspond to h = 0.6 m, h = 1.2 m, h = 1.8 m and h_2.4 m. The results obtained for each one of these cut-planes for all operational frequencies are depicted in Figs. 2, 3, 4 and 5. It can be observed, depending on the selected height and the operating frequency, received power level distributions vary, being strongly dependent on the specific location and material properties of the distribution of objects within the SUT. It's worth noting that the selected simulation sources can represent transmitters as well as any type of interfering source, including intra-system interference, inter-system interference or external interference sources, such as appliances, motors or other type of electro-mechanical devices. This is given by the fact the simulation code enables the use of hybrid simulation techniques as well as Huygens box emulation of equivalent radiating sources, in which full wave simulation techniques, like FDTD, can be employed to obtain the current sources of an equivalent array of transmitting sources, that can be embedded within the 3D RL code.

In order to validate the accuracy of the estimations obtained by means of 3D RL simulation, measurement results of receiver power level distributions have been obtained for the frequency bands under consideration. To this end, a wide band voltage controlled

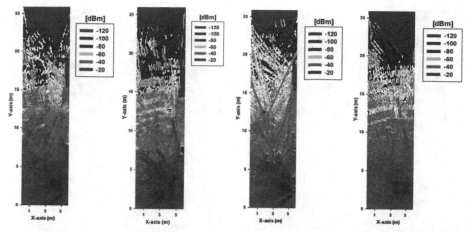

Fig. 2. Received power levels estimations for the SUT, corresponding to a frequency of operation of 433 MHz, and cut-plane heights of a) 0.6 m, b) 1.2 m, c) 1.8 m and d) 2.4 m respectively.

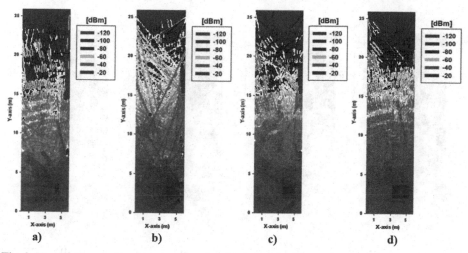

Fig. 3. Received power levels estimations for the SUT, corresponding to a frequency of operation of 868 MHz, and cut-plane heights of a) 0.6 m, b) 1.2 m, c) 1.8 m and d) 2.4 m respectively.

oscillator (Mini-Circuits ZX95 VCO) has been connected to a wide band transmitter antenna (Antenova Omni LOG up to 8 GHz) and measurement results have been obtained with the aid of a portable spectrum analyzer (Rohde Schwarz FSH20, up to 20 GHz). Images from the measurement setup employed are depicted in Fig. 6. The comparison between simulation and measurement results for linear TX/RX distributions are depicted in Figs. 7, 8, 9, 10 corresponding to the four frequency bands under consideration. It can be seen that in all cases, simulation and measurement results are in good agreement, with average errors in the order of 3–5 dB for all cases.

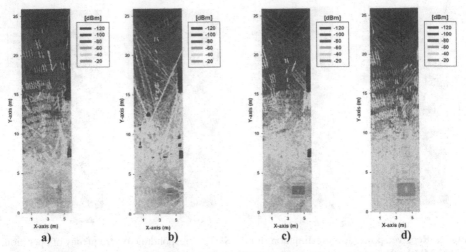

Fig. 4. Received power levels estimations for the SUT, corresponding to a frequency of operation of 2.4 GHz, and cut-plane heights of a) 0.6 m, b) 1.2 m, c) 1.8 m and d) 2.4 m respectively

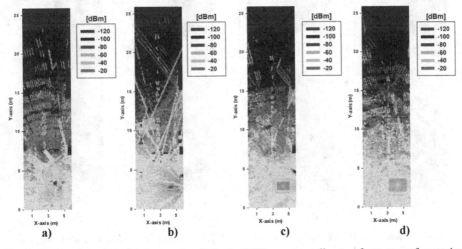

Fig. 5. Estimation of received power levels for the SUT, corresponding to a frequency of operation of 3.5 GHz, and cut-plane heights of a) 0.6 m, b) 1.2 m, c) 1.8 m and d) 2.4 m respectively

The results obtained show that received power levels are once again strongly dependent on the configuration of the scenario, as well as on the frequency of operation. As expected, path losses are higher as frequency increases. The proposed methodology can be readily extended to consider multiple aspects, such as transceiver design (in terms of antenna configuration, transmitter power range or receiver sensitivity thresholds), variations within the configuration of the scenario in terms of scatterer distribution, the configuration of the network topology as a function of node location or the existence and behavior of multiple interference sources, among others.

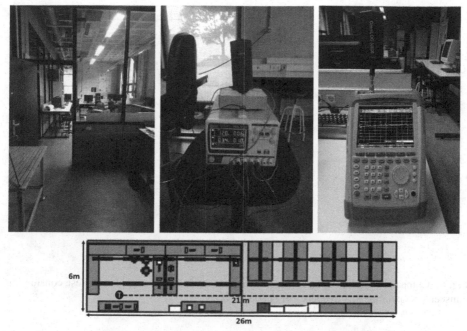

Fig. 6. Measurement scenario and schematic description of the measurement points within the Scenario Under Test, located at the Luis Mercader laboratory, at the Public University of Navarra.

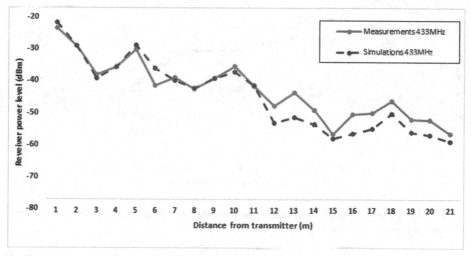

Fig. 7. Comparison of simulation vs measurement results for the Scenario Under Test, considering transceivers operating at a frequency of @433 MHz.

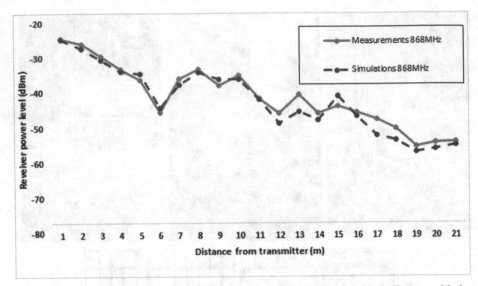

Fig. 8. Comparison of simulation vs measurement results for the Scenario Under Test, considering transceivers operating at a frequency of @868 MHz.

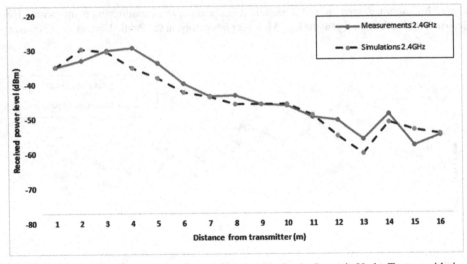

Fig. 9. Comparison of simulation vs measurement results for the Scenario Under Test, considering transceivers operating at a frequency of @2.4 GHz.

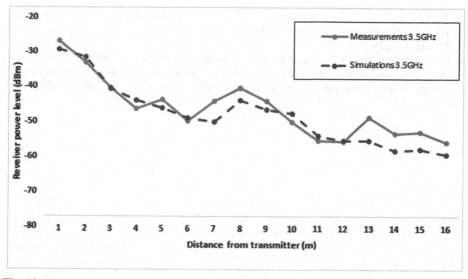

Fig. 10. Comparison of simulation vs measurement results for the Scenario Under Test, considering transceivers operating at a frequency of @3.5 GHz.

References

1. Colombo, W., Karnouskos, S., Kaynak, O., Shi, Y., Yin, S.: Industrial cyber physical systems: A backbone of the fourth industrial revolution. IEEE Ind. Electron. Mag. **11**(1), 6–16 (2017)
2. Lu, C., et al.: Real-time wireless sensor-actuator net-works for industrial cyber-physical systems. Proc. IEEE **104**(5), 1013–1024 (2016)
3. Stenumgaard, J., Chilo, J., Ferrer-Coll, J., Angskog, P.: Challenges and conditions for wireless machine-to-machine communications in industrial environments. IEEE Commun. Mag. **51**(6), 187–192 (2013)
4. Candell, R.: Industrial wire-less systems: radio propagation measurements. In: NIST Tech. note 1951, NIST, Gaithersburg, MA, USA, January 2017
5. Cheffena, M.: Industrial wireless sensor networks: channel modeling and performance evaluation. EURASIP J. Wirel. Commun. Netw. **2012**(1), September 2012 https://doi.org/10.1186/1687-1499-2012-297
6. Cardieri, P.: Modeling interference in wireless Ad Hoc networks. IEEE Commun. Surv. Tuts. **12**(4), 551–572 (2010)
7. Savazzi, S., Rampa, V., Spagnolini, U.: Wireless cloud networks for the factory of things: Connectivity modeling and layout design. IEEE Internet Things J. **1**(2), 180–195 (2014)
8. Garcia, M., Tomas, J., Boronat, F., Lloret, J.: The development of two systems for indoor wireless sensors self-location. Ad Hoc Sens. Wirel. Networks **8**(3–4), 235–258 (2009)
9. Garcia, M., Martinez, C., Tomas, J., Lloret, J.: Wireless sensors self-location in an indoor WLAN. In: International Conference on Sensor Technologies and Applications. SENSORCOMM, Valencia, Spain, 14–20 October 2007
10. Azpilicueta, L., Rawat, M., Rawat, K., Ghannouchi, F.M., Falcone, F.: A ray launching-neural network approach for radio wave propagation analysis in complex indoor environments. IEEE Trans. Antennas Propag. **62**(5), 2777–2786 (2014)

11. Azpilicueta, L., Falcone, F., Janaswamy, R.: A hybrid ray launching-diffusion equation approach for propagation prediction in complex indoor environments. IEEE Antennas Wirel. Propag. Lett. **16**, 214–217 (2017)
12. Casino, F., Azpilicueta, L., Lopez-Iturri, P., Aguirre, E., Falcone, F., Solanas, A.: Optimized wireless channel characterization in large complex environments by hybrid ray launching-collaborative filtering approach. IEEE Antennas Wirel. Propag. Lett. **16**, 780–783 (2017)

Power-Based Intrusion Detection for Additive Manufacturing: A Deep Learning Approach

Michael Rott and Sergio A. Salinas Monroy[✉]

Wichita State University, Wichita, KS 67260, USA
MJRott@shockers.wichita.edu, Sergio.SalinasMonroy@wichita.edu

Abstract. Due to the ability of 3D-printers to build a wide range of objects at low costs, many industries are rapidly adopting additive manufacturing. However due to their sensing and communications capabilities, 3D-printers are Internet of Things (IoT) devices that are vulnerable to sophisticated cyberattacks, such as defect injection attacks. By maliciously manipulating the behavior of a 3D-printer, an attacker can compromise the integrity of a manufactured objects. To avoid detection, the adversary also compromises the sensor data reported by the 3D-printer that the operator could use to detect the attack. In this paper, we design a deep neural network that can detect such attacks by predicting the power consumption of a 3D-printer based on the object design and previous power consumption observations. By analyzing the difference between the predicted power consumption and the observed one, we can determine if the 3D-printer is under attack. By measuring the power consumption of the 3D-printer at the power line with an independent sensor, we can determine the true behavior of the 3D-printer without relying on sensor data reported by the potentially compromised 3D-printer. Compared to previous works, our proposed detection technique only requires cheap power sensors that can be easily installed. We conduct extensive experiments on a real-world additive manufacturing testbed and observe that our proposed method can detect defect injection attacks with up to 96% accuracy.

Keywords: Security · Intrusion detection · Side-channel defense · 3D-printing · Additive manufacturing

1 Introduction

Additive manufacturing (AM) is rapidly being adopted by many industries including healthcare [1,2], aerospace [3], and automotive [4]. In AM, 3D-printers manufacture objects by depositing material in a layer-by-layer fashion, which allows them to build a wide range of objects with complex geometries, and various levels of tensile strength, heat transfer, etc. Compared to traditional manufacturing where machines need tool retrofitting each time they build a new object, AM can redirect 3D-printers to produce entirely different types of objects without changing any of their parts [5]. Moreover, 3D-printers are Internet of Things (IoT) devices

L. Peñalver and L. Parra (Eds.): Industrial IoT 2020, LNICST 365, pp. 171–189, 2021.
https://doi.org/10.1007/978-3-030-71061-3_11

equipped with sensing and communications capabilities that allow factory managers to monitor and control their AM operations in real-time [6,7].

However, the use of 3D-printers to build objects for safety-critical industries such as healthcare and transportation raises major cybersecurity concerns. Sophisticated cyber attackers regularly target industrial control systems aiming to steal intellectual property or sabotage their physical processes [8,9]. Standard security controls, e.g., firewalls, intrusion detection systems, encrypted communications, etc. [10], can protect against many non-sophisticated attacks, such as an adversary stealing object designs from an unencrypted source. Unfortunately, standard security controls are inadequate to address sophisticated attacks where the adversary has enough knowledge and resources to bypass these controls. Therefore, it is crucial to design IoT-enabled AM systems that not only allow operators to enhance their systems with improved monitoring and control but also prevent malicious adversaries from compromising their operations.

A particularly serious sophisticated cyberattack against 3D-printers is the defect injection attack [11,12]. In a defect injection attacks, the adversary introduces defects into the additively manufactured objects to affect their integrity, and ultimately lead to premature (and potentially life-threatening) failure. To inject the defects, the adversary maliciously modifies the machine instructions used to build the object in such a way that it changes the manufactured object's geometric or material properties. To avoid detection, the adversary replaces the original sensor data transmitted by the 3D-printer to the operator with sensor data that appears normal. For example, the adversary can collect sensor data reported during normal operation, and then replay it during the attack while deleting the true sensor data. Such attacks can be launched by compromising the 3D-printer firmware, launching a man-in-the-middle attack, or by compromising the PC that controls the 3D-printer. Similar attacks where the adversary compromises both the physical process and the sensor data have been observed in industrial control systems, e.g., [13]. Thus, to detect defect injection attacks, we need access to information about the 3D-printer's behavior that is independent from the potentially compromised 3D-printer.

To detect defect injection attacks, researchers have proposed to analyze sidechannel signals that carry information about the behavior of the 3D-printer. By measuring the side-channel with a device that is independent of the 3D-printer, it is possible to observe the behavior of the 3D-printer and detect when it is compromised. Some works measure the acoustic emissions with microphones [14–17] to measure the movements of the 3D-printer tools. However, they need sophisticated microphones placed near the 3D-printers and can be affected by interference from other nearby machines. Researchers have also proposed to measure the power consumption of the 3D-printers to detect defect injection attacks [12,18]. Unfortunately, these works either require a complicated retrofit of the 3D-printer to measure the consumption of individual components [7], or rely on an energy consumption model [18].

In this paper, we propose to use a deep neural network to analyze the electrical power consumption of a 3D-printer using a single off-machine sensor. Specifically, our proposed deep neural network takes as input the object design and the previously observed power consumption measurements to predict the power consumption measurement. By analyzing the difference between the predicted power consumption and the observed one, we can determine if the 3D-printer is deviating from the known object design, and thus injecting defects into the object. By measuring the power consumption of the 3D-printer at the power line with an independent device, we can determine the true behavior of the 3Dprinter without relying on sensor data reported by the potentially compromised 3D-printer. Compared to previous works that employ sophisticated hardware, our proposed detection technique only requires power sensors, which can be acquired at low cost and can be easily installed on the power lines without retrofitting the 3D-printer. We conduct extensive experiments on a real-world additive manufacturing testbed. We measure the performance of our proposed detection method under different types of defect injection attacks in terms of accuracy, precision, and recall. We observe that it can successfully detect defect injection attacks with up to 96% accuracy.

The rest of this paper is organized as follows. In Sect. 2, we present the system model. Section 3 describes our use of deep learning and detection methodology. Section 4 presents the implimentation and results of our model testing. Section 5 and 6 provide a conclusion and reference to future works to be done on this subject.

2   Related Works

In this section, we provide a brief overview of works relating to additive manufacturing security.

Cybersecurity issues in additive manufacturing have received increased attention from researchers in recent years. Specifically, Yampolskiy et al. [19] describe several attacks against 3D-printers, including defect injection attacks and how they can be used to compromise the additively manufactured object's shape and material properties. Sturm et al. [20] describe void injection attacks, where the adversary creates empty spaces within the objects. This type of attack is particularly challenging to detect since it requires complex imaging such as computerized tomography (CT) scans, to observe the voids. Graves et al. [21] discuss how defect injection attacks can be used to sabotage industrial control systems and the consequences of these attacks. Do et al. [22] demonstrate how an attacker can remotely manipulate the behavior of a 3D-printer. Belikovetsky et al. [11] implement a defect injection attack that introduces voids into a 3D-printed object.

Some researchers have designed methods to detect defect injection attacks. Sturm et al. [23] propose to detect defects in a metallic additively manufactured objects by comparing its impedance to that of a control defect-free object. Unfortunately, this verification method only works with metallic objects, and must be done after building the object, which can result in expensive material waste. Wu et al. [14] propose machine learning methods that analyze acoustic and visual data from the additively manufactured objects. In [16], Belikovetsky et al. propose to compare the acoustic emissions of a 3D-printer to a recording of the same 3D-printer when it built a defect-free object. Gao et al. [17] used acceleration, visual, audio, and magnetic field measurements to create an accurate estimate of the 3D-printer's movements. The observed movements were compared to the defect-free objects to detect the attack. In [12], Belikovetsky et al. propose to monitor the power consumption of individual stepper motors inside the 3D-printer. However, these defect injection methods require the installation of multiple sophisticated sensors near, or inside, the 3D-printer, and thus are expensive, difficult to implement, and subject to interference from nearby machines. In particular, the method proposed in [12] requires opening the 3D-printer and separating the wires that feed electrical power to each stepper motor inside the 3D-printer. This poses a significant challenge to system operators since they could have multiple machines, and disassembling them could be cumbersome, complicated, and costly.

Salinas et al. [18], propose to identify defect injection attacks in a system of multiple 3D-printers by observing their aggregate power consumption with a single power consumption sensor installed on the power lines that feed the machines. However, this approach only focuses on isolating the compromised machine and assumes that an energy consumption model already exists.

In this work, we design a deep neural network mechanism that can detect defect injection attacks and only requires a single power consumption sensor that is cheap and can be easily installed on the power lines feeding the 3D-printer. These power measurements are independent from the potentially compromised measurements reported by the 3D-printer.

3   System Model

In this section, we develop a model that describes the operation of a 3D-printer, and describe our considered threat model.

3.1   3D-printer Operation Model

We consider a 3D-printer that is controlled by a PC. The 3D-printer operates an extruder head mounted on a gantry with three degrees of freedom. The planes are denoted by x, y, and z, respectively, as shown in Fig. 1. To build the objects, the extruder head deposits material on the printing bed. The 3D-printer creates objects from the bottom up in a layer by layer fashion. A set of tool-path instructions transmitted from the controller PC to the 3D-printer determines the extruder head's speed and direction of movement. Besides the tool-path instructions, the controller PC sends several build parameters to the 3D-printer, such as the temperature of the printing bed, speed of material extrusion, cooling fan speed, etc. Figure 1 shows the planes of movement of the extruder head.

Fig. 1. 3D-printer axes.

The 3D-printer implements the tool-path instructions by actuating a set of stepper motors that, in turn control the position of the extruder head and the material deposition. Let $m_0^x, m_0^y, m_0^z, m_1^z, m_0^e$ denote the motors of the 3D-printer. Motor m_0^x and motor m_0^y move the extruder head along the x and y axes, respectively. Both motor m_0^z and m_1^z drive the motion of the extruder head along the z-axis. Motor m_0^e controls a gear that feeds material into the extruder head.

Besides the stepper motors, the 3D-printer also controls two heaters and two cooling fans. The first heater is used to maintain a constant temperature at the baseplate to help keep the print in place as well as to aid in the bonding of layers [24]. The second heater melts the material filament as it is fed through the extruder head. The cooling fans are placed near the extruder head to promote bonding between layers by reducing the temperature of the deposited material [17].

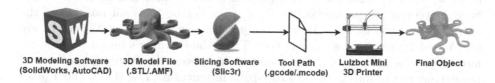

3D Modeling Software (SolidWorks, AutoCAD)   3D Model File (.STL/.AMF)   Slicing Software (Slic3r)   Tool Path (.gcode/.mcode)   Lulzbot Mini 3D Printer   Final Object

Fig. 2. 3D printing process chain.

3.2 Tool-Path Instruction Model

The 3D-printer builds objects by following tool-path instructions that specify the path its extruder head needs to follow and the amount of material it needs to deposit. To find the tool-path instructions, the controller PC first captures the surface geometry of the three-dimensional design in a stereolitography (STL) file. Next, a slicing software, e.g., Slic3r, takes the STL file as input and outputs the tool-path instructions for the 3D-printer. We show the work flow to find tool-path instructions in Fig. 2.

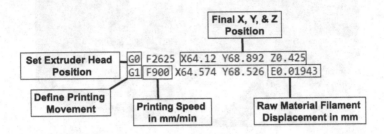

Fig. 3. Labeled G-Code example.

The tool-path instructions can be represented in several different formats. In this work, we will focus on the G-code format. Specifically, tool-path instructions coded in the G-code format specify the end position of the extruder head, the speed of movement, and the position of the extruder gear, which determines the amount of deposited material. Besides movement, G-code instructions can also be used to set the temperature of the heaters. Figure 3 shows an example of a set of G-code tool-path instructions initialize the position of the extruder head and then move the extruder head while depositing material.

3.3   Extruder Head Movement Model

We model the movement of the extruder head based on the tool-path instructions described in Sect. 3.2. The objective is to describe the expected direction and speed of movement of the extruder head based on the tool-path instructions. Since a single tool-path instruction only specifies the final position of the extruder head, we need two consecutive tool-path instructions to determine the extruder head movement. In particular, let $P_k = \{X_k, Y_k\}$ be the final position of the extruder head specified by the kth tool-path instruction, where X_k and Y_k are the X and Y coordinates, respectively. Thus, the extruder's initial position for movement k is defined as X_{k-1} and Y_{k-1}. Moreover, the change in position of the extruder head during the kth tool-path instruction along the X and Y axes is given by:

$$\delta X = X_k - X_{k-1}, \quad \delta Y = Y_k - Y_{k-1} \tag{1}$$

The movement of the raw material filament through the extrusion head can be similarly modeled. Let E_k be the final position of the extruder filament after the kth instruction. Then, the length of the raw material filament that is extruded by the 3D-printer is given by:

$$\delta E = E_k - E_{k-1} \tag{2}$$

Moreover, the speed at which the raw material filament moves during the kth tool path instruction is usually directly specified by the G-code command. We denote it by F_k. If F_k is not specified, we use the speed specified in the most recent tool-path instruction where the speed was specified.

Note that the extruder head moves along the Z-axis to raise the gantry after a layer is finished. However, the movement along the Z-axis requires the operation of two-stepper motors instead of one as it is the case with movement along the X and Y planes. Since operating two motors results in a vastly different power consumption, we leave the study of the Z-axis movements for future work.

3.4   Power Consumption Measurement Model

To build objects, the 3D-printer transforms alternating current (AC) from its power source to direct current (DC) power, which is then routed it to the step-per motors. Previous works, e.g., [12], attempt to detect defect injection attacks by measuring the power consumption of the individual stepper motors, which requires disassembly of the 3D-printer. Instead, to avoid retrofitting of the 3Dprinter, we directly measure the overall AC power consumption of the 3D-printer using an AC current sensor that is placed between the 3D-printer and the AC power source.

Since the AC current consumed by the 3D-printer follows a sinusoidal shape whose amplitude varies proportionally to the total power consumed by the 3Dprinter, we can use information about the magnitude of the peaks and valleys to determine the power consumed to execute specific tool-path commands. Specifically, let $|I_k^p| = [i_k^1, i_k^2, ..., i_k^N]$ be the vector of absolute peak AC current samples taken by the sensor during tool-path instruction k, where N is the total number of samples. Then, the average AC current peak during tool-path instruction k is given by:

$$\bar{I}_k^p = \frac{1}{N} \sum_{j=1}^{N} i_k^j \tag{3}$$

We note that although the average peak AC current $\bar{I}_k^p$ discards the non-peak current values, our experiments show that using $\bar{I}_k^p$ provides enough information for our deep neural networks to effectively detect the defect injection attacks.

3.5   Threat Model

We consider an adversary that aims to introduce a defect into the additively manufactured objects by maliciously modifying the original tool-path instructions. To avoid detection, the adversary intercepts the sensor measurements taken by the 3D-printer and replaces them with sensor measurements that match the

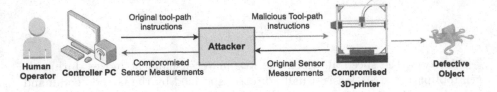

Fig. 4. A 3D-printer architecture under a defect injection attack.

tool-path commands of the original object design. To this end, the adversary can launch one of several cyberattacks, including compromising the controller PC or the firmware installed the 3D-printer. Moreover, the adversary seeks to avoid detection by choosing to inject defects into the manufactured object that are difficult to notice by visual inspection, e.g., a small modification to the dimensions of the object. This threat model is shown in Fig. 4

The adversary can maliciously modify the original tool-path instructions in several ways. In this work, we consider the following tool-path instruction modification attacks

1. **Insertion Attacks.** In this type of attack, the adversary inserts one or more additional tool-path instructions into the machine code that is executed by the 3D-printer. The inserted command could be solely movement, or it could also contain a command to deposit material with movement. This attack introduces defects by printing material in unintended locations or by manipulating the start position of the extruder for the next tool-path instruction.
2. **Deletion Attacks.** The adversary launches a deletion attack by removing one or more tool-path instructions from the machine code executed by the 3D-printer. This attack can introduce a defect by removing commands which print material at specific locations, or set the extruder position for the next instruction.
3. **Reordering Attacks.** In this attack, the adversary swaps the order in which two tool-path instructions are executed. The instructions need not be consecutive. The swapped instructions lead to defects during the swapped commands as well as the commands that follow, as the starting location of the extruder head for those commands will now be modified.
4. **Void Injection Attack.** In this attack, the adversary prevents the 3Dprinter from depositing material at certain positions and layers in such a way that a cavity is introduced into the printed object. Voids lead to a modified cross-section of the printed object, which will affect the stresses and strains that object undergoes. This could ultimately lead to an object with less physical integrity than the intended print [11].
5. **Printing Speed Attack.** In a printing speed attack, the adversary changes the printing speed parameter of the 3D-printer. This attack can result in a raw material filament pressure change that causes an alteration in its diameter as it is extruded. This can affect the surface morphology and integrity of the printed object [25].

We assume the adversary does not compromise any other devices such as the AC current sensor that we use in our proposed detection method. We also assume that the operator can perform destructive testing on multiple manufactured objects to collect power measurements while the printer builds objects when there is no attack. This ensures that enough power consumption measurements are available to train our proposed deep neural network.

4   Power-Based Deep Learning Attack Detection Method

In this section, we describe the proposed deep learning attack detection methodology.

To detect defect injection attacks in real-time, we propose to design a deep neural network that takes the original tool-path instructions as input to output a prediction about the power consumption of the 3D-printer. By comparing the power consumption predicted by a deep neural network to the power consumption observed by a sensor installed on the power line that feeds the 3D-printer, we can determine if the 3D-printer is deviating from the original tool-path instructions. If the predicted and observed peak current consumptions differ by more than the threshold, then we conclude that the printer is implementing a tool-path instruction different from the original tool-path instruction used as input to the deep neural network. We show our overall defect injection attack approach in Fig. 5.

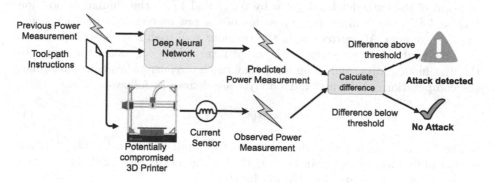

Fig. 5. Proposed attack detection procedure.

In the rest of this section, we explain in detail each step of our proposed defect injection detection scheme.

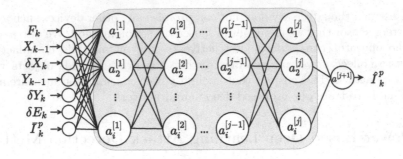

Fig. 6. Neural network architecture.

4.1 Deep Neural Network Architecture

We first present a deep neural network that predicts the power consumption of a 3D-printer while it executes a specific tool-path instruction. The deep neural network follows a multi-layer perceptron feedforward architecture as shown in Fig. 6.

As described in Sect. 3.4, we use the average peak AC current $\bar{I}_K^p$ to measure the overall power consumption of the 3D-printer. Thus, our deep neural network generates a prediction of the average peack AC current using the tool-path instruction characteristics specified in the G-code command as described in Sect. 3.3. Specifically, it uses as input the extruder head speed F_k, the previous position of the extruder head given by X_{k-1} and Y_{k-1}, the change in position δX_k and δY_k, the changes in the position of the raw material filament δE_k, and the average peak AC current from the previous tool-path instruction $\bar{I}_k^p$.

The input values are given to the input layer, which calculates the inputs to the first hidden layer, and so on until they reach the output layer. In particular, the computations of the first hidden layer are defined as follows:

$$\mathbf{a}^{[1]} = \sigma\big(\mathbf{w}^{[1]} \cdot \mathbf{x}\big) \tag{4}$$

where $\mathbf{x} \in \mathbb{R}^{7 \times 1}$ is a vector that contains the input values, $\mathbf{a}^{[1]} \in \mathbb{R}^{i \times 1}$ is the output of first hidden layer, and $\mathbf{w}^{[1]} \in \mathbb{R}^{i \times 7}$ is the matrix of weights for the first layer, and σ is the sigmoid activation function.

The hidden layer is fully connected to another hidden layer of the same size i. The computations performed by the following hidden layers are defined as:

$$\mathbf{a}^{[j]} = \sigma\big(\mathbf{w}^{[j]} \cdot \mathbf{a}^{[j-1]} + \mathbf{b}^{[j]}\big), \forall j = 2\ldots, j, \tag{5}$$

where $\mathbf{a}^{[j]} \in \mathbb{R}^{i \times 1}$ is the output of jth hidden layer, $\mathbf{w}^{[j]} \in \mathbb{R}^{i \times i}$ and $\mathbf{b}^{[j]} \in \mathbb{R}^{i \times 1}$, are the matrices of weights and biases for the jth layer respectively, and i is the size of the jth hidden layer. This hidden layer is connected to another hidden layer up to j layers.

Finally, the last hidden layer j is fully connected to a dense output layer with one node. The computations performed by the last layer are as follows:

$$\hat{I}_k^p = \sigma\big(\mathbf{w}^{[j+1]} \cdot \mathbf{a}^{[j]} + \mathbf{b}^{[j+1]}\big) \tag{6}$$

where $\hat{I}_k^p$ is the final scalar output of the network and represents the predicted average AC peak current for tool-path instruction k.

The ability of the deep neural network to accurately predict $\hat{I}_k^p$ depends on the parameters $\mathbf{w}^j$ and $\mathbf{b}^j$ (for all j). To find these parameters, the network is trained using average peak AC current samples taken when the printer is building an object without defect as we later describe in Sect. 5.3.

4.2   Detection of Abnormal Average Peak Current

To detect defect injection attacks against the 3D-printer, we propose to compare the predicted average peak current $\hat{I}_k^p$ to the observed one $\bar{I}_k^p$. Specifically, we calculate the square error loss function for each tool-path instruction used to build an object [26], i.e.,

$$D_k = (\hat{I}_k^p - \bar{I}_k^p)^2 \tag{7}$$

for all k. We then compare D_k to a threshold value t to determine if there is a defect injection attack. If D_k is less than the threshold value (for any k), we conclude the printer is following the original tool-path instructions used as input to the deep neural network. Otherwise, we conclude it is executing different tool-path instructions, and thus it is under attack.

5   Experimental Evaluation

In this section, we implement our proposed defect injection attack detection mechanism and evaluate its performance.

5.1   Testbed Implementation

To closely replicate a real-world 3D-printing scenario, we used a general-purpose PC connected via USB to a LulzBot Mini 3D printer, as shown in Fig. 7. To take AC load current measurements, we clamped a YHDC SCT-013 current sensor around a single wire coming from the 120V power source (i.e., the wall outlet) into the printer. This current sensor outputs voltage measurements that are linearly proportional to the magnitude of the current flowing through the wire. The output voltage resolution of the sensor is .033V/1A. We used an oscilloscope to observe the voltage output of the current sensor and collected the measurements with the general-purpose PC. In practice, the controller PC would be different from the PC collecting the measurements. However, to simplify the control of the 3D-printer and the measurement collection, we used the same PC for both functions.

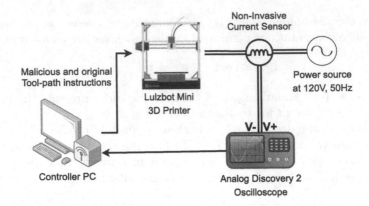

Fig. 7. Diagram of our experiment testbed for defect injection attack detection.

To control the 3D-printer and collect measurements, we developed a Python application that sends tool-path instructions for a specific object design to the printer, collects AC current measurements from the sensor. We also use this application to implement the defect injection attacks by changing the tool-path instructions as described in Sect. 3.5. We also developed an application that processes the AC current measurements and implements the deep neural network detection mechanism. We use PyTorch version 1.4, an open-source machine learning library, to train and implement the deep neural network. Both applications are run on a general-purpose PC with an Intel i7-7700HQ CPU, 16 GB RAM, and an NVIDIA GeForce GTX 1050 graphics card.

5.2 Power Consumption Measurement Preprocessing

Before we can use the current consumption measurements to train the deep neural network, we need to preprocess the raw AC current measurements. Specifically, we first extract the peaks from the AC current measurements to form the vector I_p^k as described in Sect. 3.4. Since some of the peaks stored in I_p^k may correspond to the operation of the extruder heater, which does not contribute information about the movement of the extruder head, we remove peaks that are greater than a threshold. The threshold can be easily set due to the peaks corresponding to the heater being several mA higher than the peaks that correspond to stepper motors. After removing the peaks due to the heater, we can calculate the average peak AC current $\bar{I}_k^p$ as described in (3). We show an example of raw and preprocessed data in Fig. 8

5.3 Deep Neural Network Training

To train the deep neural network, we collected average peak current measurements of the 3D-printer while executing different types of tool-path instructions. Specifically, we first built the test object in Fig. 9 and collected the average peak

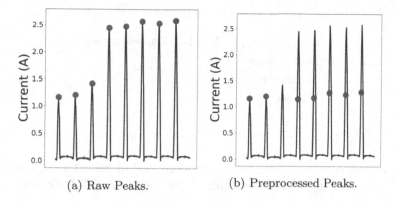

(a) Raw Peaks.   (b) Preprocessed Peaks.

Fig. 8. Effects of preprocessing.

current measurement for each of its 84 tool-path instructions. This process was repeated 10 times. This test object results in tool-path instructions that contain both single-plane instructions, i.e., movements parallel to one of the planes, and double-plane instructions where the extruder head moves along two planes at the same time, i.e., diagonal movements. The length of the movements required by the tool-path instructions varies between .707 and 105.8 mm. We then paired the pre-processed power consumption measurements with their corresponding tool-path instructions to create a training data set for the deep neural network described in Sect. 4.1. Table 1 summarizes the types of tool-path instructions in our data set.

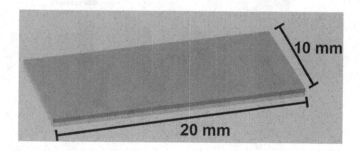

Fig. 9. 3D-model of the test object.

After building the training data set, we train the deep neural network described in Sect. 4 in Pytorch. We used the ADAM optimizer algorithm to find the parameters of the deep neural network. The loss function was set to the mean square loss, with a learning rate of .0015.

Moreover, we also build a testing data set that we later use to analyze the performance of our deep neural network. Specifically, we build the test object 50

Table 1. Types of tool-path instructions for the test object.

Instruction type	Number of appearances
No Movement	1
X-axis only	30
Y-axis only	14
X, Y-axis	39

times under each defect injection attacks described in Sect. 3.5, and measured the average peak current of the 3D-printer for each tool-path instruction.

5.4   Hyperparameter Tuning

To find the deep learning network architecture that could best predict the power consumption of the 3D-printer, we measured the performance of the neural network under several hyperparameter combinations. Specifically, for each network configuration, we re-trained the deep neural and measured the training loss, i.e., how well it predicts the average peak current, and the training time. We tested several networks with a varying number of hidden layers, and a varying number of neurons in each layer between 25 and 100.

We show the results in Fig. 10 and observe that the best performing architecture has 2 hidden layers of 100 neurons.

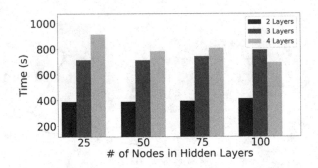

Fig. 10. Training loss under best performing hyper-parameters.

We also measured the training time for each network model tested. Figure 11 shows the training time of the proposed neural network for varying number of layers and layer sizes. We see that adding layers generally increases the training time, while the size of the layers has little effect.

Based on the training loss and training time results above, we chose a deep neural network with 2 hidden layers of 100 neurons to detect defect injection attacks in our experiments.

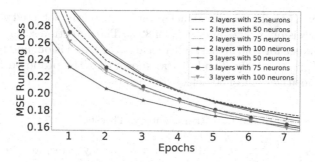

Fig. 11. Training time under varying parameters.

5.5 Results

We first evaluate the performance of the proposed deep neural network in detecting the attacks described in Sect. 3.5 under varying values for threshold t. As described in Sect. 4.2, after calculating the the square error value in (7), we need to compare it to a threshold t. Figure 12 shows the accuracy of the deep neural network to identify attacks for varying values of the threshold t. We see that choosing a threshold of .73 gives a high accuracy for all attack types.

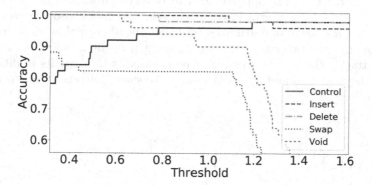

Fig. 12. Attack detection accuracy.

Table 2 shows the performance of the proposed detection scheme when the threshold $t = 0.7$ for each of the attacks. The first column shows the type of attack launched against the test object or if it was a defect free print. The second column indicates the number of times our detection scheme correctly classified the test object print as either defect-free or compromised. The third column shows the number of types it incorrectly classified the object print. Columns four, five, and six show the accuracy, precision, and recall of the proposed detection scheme under each type of attack. We observe that the deep neural network is able to correctly detect the insertion and deletion attacks in all 50 trials of the test object printing.

We also observe that the reorder attacks can be correctly detected with an accuracy of 82%, precision of 95%, and recall of 82%. The detection scheme shows even better performance for void attacks with an accuracy, precision, and recall of 98%, 96%, and 98%, respectively. The last row shows that the proposed method only had two false positives out of 50 defect-free prints.

Table 2. Detection accuracy. Threshold = .73.

Attack	Correct	Misclassified	Accuracy	Precision	Recall
Insertion	50	0	1.00	0.96	1.00
Deletion	50	0	1.00	0.96	1.00
Reorder	41	9	0.82	.95	.82
Void	49	1	0.98	.96	.98
Control Print	48	2	0.96	NA	NA

The reason why our deep neural network has a high-accuracy in detecting the insertion and deletion attacks is that they result in high differences between the predicted and observed average peak current not only during the affected tool-path instruction but through the entire object build. This allows the neural network to have more opportunities to observe an abnormal average peak current. Under a reorder attack, our deep neural network also achieves a high accuracy but has fewer opportunities to detect the abnormal average peak current since only the two swapped instructions will result in abnormal readings. In void attacks, the extruder motor stops running, which results in differences between the predicted and observed values. We show differences caused by void attacks in Fig. 13.

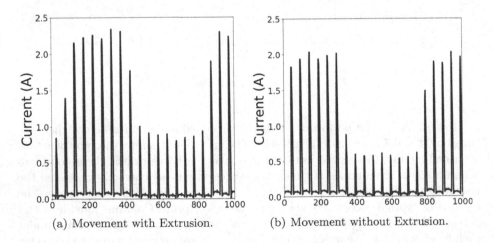

(a) Movement with Extrusion.   (b) Movement without Extrusion.

Fig. 13. Effects of void attack

6   Conclusions and Future Work

In this paper, we have investigated the problem of detecting defect injection attacks against 3D-printers. Since the adversary can compromise the sensor measurements reported by the potentially compromised 3D-printer, we use an external sensor that measures the power consumption of the 3D-printer. We then use a deep neural network that takes as input the object design and the previously observed power consumption measurements and predicts the power consumption measurement for the current tool-path instruction. If the difference between the predicted power consumption and the observed one is large, we can determine that the 3D-printer is deviating from the known object design, and injecting defects into the object. Previous works use sophisticated hardware that is difficult to install and often requires the operator to disassemble the 3D-printer. In contrast, our proposed detection technique only requires a low-cost power sensor that can be easily installed without retrofitting the 3D-printer. Our extensive experimental evaluations show that the proposed method can detect several defect injection attacks with up to 96% accuracy.

In the future, we plan to investigate the application of our proposed attack detection method in substractive manufacturing. Similarly to AM, substractive manufacturing processes design files to produce G-Code or M-Code commands that define the movement of the machine's tools. However, instead of depositing material in specific locations as in AM, substractive manufacturing uses CNC machines to shape blocks of raw material into the manufactured parts using a number of tools (drills, saws, etc.). Our proposed method could be used to monitor CNC machine power consumption, and detect malicious variations in tool-path commands. Additionally, we plan to imporove the accuracy of the system to more closely monitor indivudal stepper motors.

References

1. Dodziuk, H.: Applications of 3d printing in healthcare. Kardiochirurgia i torakochirurgia polska = Polish J. Cardio Thoracic Surg. **13**(3), 283–293 (2016)
2. Sandström, C.: Adopting 3D printing for manufacturing - the case of the hearing aid industry. In: Ratio Working Papers 262, The Ratio Institute, December 2015. https://ideas.repec.org/p/hhs/ratioi/0262.html
3. Wood, J.: 3d printing's soaring impact on aviation and aerospace. Forbes, September 2019. http://www.forbes.com/sites/mitsubishiheavyindustries/2019/09/24/3d-printings-soaring-impact-on-aviation-and-aerospace/#1b3d57a7269c
4. Sculpteo: automotive and 3d printing: the complete guide to the 3d printed car (2020). https://www.sculpteo.com/en/3d-learning-hub/applications of 3d printing/3d-printed-car/
5. Shahrubudin, N., Lee, T., Ramlan, R.: An overview on 3d printing technology: technological, materials, and applications. Procedia Manufact. **35**, 1286– 1296 (2019). http://www.sciencedirect.com/science/article/pii/S2351978919308169, the2nd International Conference on Sustainable Materials Processing and Manufacturing, SMPM 2019, 8-10 March 2019, Sun City, South Africa

6. Tao, F., Cheng, Y., Xu, L.D., Zhang, L., Li, B.H.: CCIoT-CMfg: cloud computing and internet of things-based cloud manufacturing service system. IEEE Trans. Ind. Inf. **10**(2), 1435–1442 (2014)

7. Buckholtz, B., Ragai, I., Wang, L.: Cloud manufacturing: current trends and future implementations. J. Manufact. Sci. Eng. **137**(4), 040902 (2015)

8. Verizon: Data breach digest (2019). http://www.verizonenterprise.com/resources/breports/rp_data-breach-digest-2017-perspective-is-reality_xg_en.pdf

9. U.S. Department of Homeland Security: ICS-CERT monitor-incidence response activity (2015)

10. Stouffer, K.: Guide to industrial control systems (ICS) security. NIST Spec. Publ. **800**(82), 16 (2011)

11. Belikovetsky, S., Yampolskiy, M., Toh, J., Gatlin, J., Elovici, Y.: dr0wned – cyber-physical attack with additive manufacturing. USENIX Association, Vancouver, BC, August 2017. https://www.usenix.org/conference/woot17/workshop-program/presentation/belikovetsky

12. Gatlin, J., Belikovetsky, S., Moore, S.B., Solewicz, Y., Elovici, Y., Yampolskiy, M.: Detecting sabotage attacks in additive manufacturing using actuator power signatures. IEEE Access **7**, 133421–133432 (2019)

13. Langner, R.: Stuxnet: dissecting a cyberwarfare weapon. IEEE Secur. Priv. **9**(3), 49–51 (2011)

14. Wu, M., Song, Z., Moon, Y.B.: Detecting cyber-physical attacks in cybermanufacturing systems with machine learning methods. J. Intell. Manuf. **30**(3), 1111–1123 (2019). https://doi.org/10.1007/s10845-017-1315-5

15. Song, C., Lin, F., Ba, Z., Ren, K., Zhou, C., Xu, W.: My smartphone knows what you print: exploring smartphone-based side-channel attacks against 3d printers. In: Proceedings of the 2016 ACM SIGSAC Conference on Computer and Communications Security, CCS 2016, pp. 895–907. Association for Computing Machinery, New York (2016). https://doi.org/10.1145/2976749.2978300

16. Belikovetsky, S., Solewicz, Y.A., Yampolskiy, M., Toh, J., Elovici, Y.: Digital audio signature for 3d printing integrity. IEEE Trans. Inf. Forensics Secur. **14**(5), 1127–1141 (2019)

17. Gao, Y., et al.: Watching and safeguarding your 3d printer: online process monitoring against cyber-physical attacks. Proc. ACM Interact. Mob. Wearable Ubiquit. Technol. **2**(3) (2018). https://doi.org/10.1145/3264918

18. Monroy, S.A.S., Li, M., Li, P.: Energy-based detection of defect injection attacks in IoT-enabled manufacturing. In: 2018 IEEE Global Communications Conference (GLOBECOM), pp. 1–6 (2018)

19. Yampolskiy, M., Schutzle, L., Vaidya, U., Yasinsac, A.: Security challenges of additive manufacturing with metals and alloys. In: Rice, M., Shenoi, S. (eds.) ICCIP 2015. IAICT, vol. 466, pp. 169–183. Springer, Cham (2015). https://doi.org/10.1007/978-3-319-26567-4_11

20. Sturm, L.D., Williams, C.B., Camelio, J.A., White, J., Parker, R.: Cyber-physical vulnerabilities in additive manufacturing systems: a case study attack on the.stl file with human subjects. J. Manufact. Syst. **44**, 154–164 (2017). http://www.sciencedirect.com/science/article/pii/S0278612517300961

21. Graves, L.M.G., Lubell, J., King, W., Yampolskiy, M.: Characteristic aspects of additive manufacturing security from security awareness perspectives. IEEE Access **7**, 103833–103853 (2019)

22. Do, Q., Martini, B., Choo, K.R.: A data exfiltration and remote exploitation attack on consumer 3d printers. IEEE Trans. Inf. Forensics Secur. **11**(10), 2174–2186 (2016)

23. Sturm, L., Albakri, M., Williams, D.C.B., Tarazaga, D.P.: In-situ detection of build defects in additive manufacturing via impedance-based monitoring, pp. 1458–1478 (2016)
24. Spoerk, M., Gonzalez-Gutierrez, J., Sapkota, J., Schuschnigg, S., Holzer, C.: Effect of the printing bed temperature on the adhesion of parts produced by fused filament fabrication. Plast. Rubber Compos. **47**(1), 17–24 (2018). https://doi.org/10.1080/14658011.2017.1399531
25. Geng, P., et al.: Effects of extrusion speed and printing speed on the 3d printing stability of extruded peek filament. J. Manufact. Process. **37**, 266–273 (2019)
26. Kravchik, M., Shabtai, A.: Detecting cyber attacks in industrial control systems using convolutional neural networks. In: Proceedings of the 2018 Workshop on Cyber-Physical Systems Security and PrivaCy, pp. 72–83 (2018)

Session 4

A Proposal for Monitoring Grass Coverage in Citrus Crops Applying Time Series Analysis in Sentinel-2 Bands

Daniel A. Basterrechea[1](✉), Lorena Parra[1,2], Mar Parra[1], and Jaime Lloret[1]

[1] Instituto de Investigación para la Gestión Integrada de Zonas Costeras, Universitat Politècnica de València, C/Paraninf, 1., 46730 Valencia, Grao de Gandia, Spain
{dabasche,maparbo}@epsg.upv.es, loparbo@doctor.upv.es, jlloret@dcom.upv.es
[2] IMIDRA, Finca "El Encin", A-2, Km 38, 2, 28800 Alcalá de Henares, Madrid, Spain

Abstract. The growing trend in the world population causes an increment in the demand for food as fruits like oranges. In this context, crop grass coverage becomes essential to reduce the resources in tree maintenance and improve the harvest. In this paper, we propose the use of remote sensing for monitoring the grass coverage. To do so, we have compared in times between plots with and without initial coverage. In our work, we present image-processing techniques that consist of using different bands of Sentinel-2 images for different periods of the year, of obtaining reliable information for changes in the grass-coverage of the selected plots. The pixels of the selected images have a resolution of 10 m × 10 m wherein our experiment represents information about orange trees plus grass coverage or soil. In addition, we present the results of the study, demonstrating the best behaviour of the presented technique. For this experiment, we use five different brands of the satellite: red band, green band, blue band, near-infrared band, and water vapour band. As well as normalised vegetation index using combinations of red and infrared bands. The significance values are obtained applying Single Analysis of Variance, a Statistical analysis. In this case, the higher results are located in WVP band with F- Reason of 42.56 and P-Value of 0.000 blue bands with F-Reason of 38.61 and P-Value of 0.000.

Keywords: Image treatment · Image processing · Sentinel 2 bands

1 Introduction

Taking into account the ever-growing trend in population, as well as the socio-economic issues we are living, there is no doubt there will be a food problem [1]. We have been headed for a long time towards a future in which the availability of resources may not be as easy as we thought. Although, it is to be noted that, we have also been focusing on finding new techniques in order to subvert this situation. To better manage our resources and secure that everybody is provided of them.

L. Peñalver and L. Parra (Eds.): Industrial IoT 2020, LNICST 365, pp. 193–206, 2021.
https://doi.org/10.1007/978-3-030-71061-3_12

The world we would deal with in case we were not trying to find solutions for these problems such as hunger, scarce resources and the consequences of both factors, would be a terrible one. That is the reason behind many technological advances humankind has achieved in the past century. It is also, what motivated this paper.

Precision agriculture is the name given to the techniques and methods aimed to enhance the management of the agricultural stock. It is a crucial element for sustainable use and production of resources. Another option to improve the sustainability of agriculture is implementing alternative management solutions such as conservation agriculture, which promotes minimum soil disturbance and the maintenance of grass coverages.

Precision agriculture aims to improve the use of resources through technological advances [2]. The technical developments which came from the pursue of precision agriculture range from the creation of new materials and improvement of devices to new techniques and methodologies. The importance of imaging techniques is to be noted in precision agriculture. They can be used for many purposes, from detecting plant diseases [3] and weeds [4] to calculate the yield [5]. They can even be combined with terrestrial techniques [6]. Although the issue with these techniques is the pixel size, satellite images can have different pixel sizes, which affect the resolution of the image. The smaller the pixel size, the more information an image holds. Nonetheless, the resolution of the image determines its price, images becoming more expensive as the pixel size gets smaller [7]. In order to measure small changes, such as the presence of grass coverage, using large pixel sizes, images from different moments must be used [8].

In this paper, we will use images from Sentinel 2 from different moments to determine the maintenance or removal of grass coverage in citrus plots. We will be focusing on orange groves, which are predominant on the east of Spain. Using images from summer and winter, which present a difference in the presence of grass coverage, a method will be created. In order to create the method, different bands and the Normalised Difference Vegetation Index (NDVI) [9] will be analysed. Not only that but also images from different moments will be used in a multitemporal approach since the change we want to detect is small compared to the pixel size. We use these images because they are free, obtaining a low-cost system.

The rest of the paper is structured as follows. Section 2 presents some research related to the one developed in this paper. Then, the techniques used, as well as the process, is shown in Sect. 3. Next, results are explained in Sect. 4. Finally, Sect. 5 deals with the conclusions and presents the future line of this research.

2   Related Works

In this section, some methodologies used for precision agriculture are explained, focusing on those who deal with image processing techniques. In addition, the NDVI is explained. Moreover, they are contrasted with the experiment developed in this paper in order to ascertain their differences and point out the strengths of imaging techniques.

Zhang et al. [9] compared the use of Landsat-8 and Sentinel-2A images to calculate the NDVI. Both satellites have similar resolutions and coverages. Nevertheless, they present angular, spectral and spatial differences. It was proven that it is essential to adjust the sensitivity of filtering and atmospheric correction, as well as the adjustment to the nadir Bidirectional Reflectance Distribution Function (BRDF), adjusted reflectance. Both datasets presented similar results after applying the adjustments. Mahlein [3] used optical techniques such as 3D scanning, which can collect information related to crop plant vitality. The developed work focused on the reliable and accurate identification of plants infected with diseases. One of the strong points highlighted in this paper is the non-destructive nature of this method. Moreover, it also discusses the phenotypical use of these techniques besides precision agriculture use.

Parra et al. [4] used imaging techniques in order to detect weeds, which can be harmful to other plants, in lawns. The early detection of said weeds is critical to assess the problem before it gets out of hand. To do so, they used a mathematical combination of the red, green, and blue bands, as well as edge detection techniques. Nevertheless, some post-processing operations had to be done in order to reduce false positives. The combination of both methods (band combination and edge detection) also reduced the false positives. Parra et al. [5] used images from Sentinel-2, the same used in this paper, to estimate the performance of different varieties of an oil-producing plant. They used six varieties of said plant, grown during the months from February to June, being harvested in June. Only one image from every month was used in order to determine productivity. Using the differences in spectral signatures and the correlation using vegetation indices, they were able to estimate the yield accurately.

Kharuf-Gutierrez et al. [10] highlighted the importance of imaging techniques to analyse several parameters regarding crops. Factors such as hydric stress, nitrogen levels and vegetal strength can be monitored through the use of imaging techniques. They proved the use of those techniques to calculate the number of stems, the foliar mass, and the level of vegetal strength. Nevertheless, an Unmanned Aerial Vehicle (UAV), not from a satellite, obtained the images they used. Müllerova et al. [11] used different types of remote sensing, among them satellite imagery, to detect plant invasions. They tested their methods with four different plant species. For satellite images, with less resolution, they used pixel and object-based approaches. These methods were useful for species with complicated architecture.

The use of UAVs can be combined with the use of Unmanned Ground Vehicles (UGVs), as proven by Tokekar et al. [6]. They developed a symbiotic system, which solved the two main problems the use of both vehicles presents. These problems are the time-consuming soil measurements done by the UGVs and the limited energy or UAVs. Using both technological advances as well as new algorithms, the problems were solved, both theoretically and on real soil experiments. Ezenne et al. [12] developed an Unmanned Aerial System (AUS), which could estimate the water needs of crops using specific indices. They were able to determine the water stress through thermal imagery. Moreover, the UAS could be adapted for real-time irrigation. Taha et al. [13] proposed the use of mobile cameras for environmental surveillance. To provide better QoS for ultra-high definition (UHD) mobile users in the handoff process, they propose an intelligent handover algorithm model to decide on the handover process and the load balance among the network devices in the coverage area.

These fine researches show many applications of imaging techniques as well as prove the usefulness of the NDVI and Sentinel-2 images. Nevertheless, it is essential to note the importance of pixel size and economic availability of these techniques. Those that deal with small changes need either high resolution (small pixel size) or a multitemporal approach to make them economically viable.

This paper presents a method for the detection of grass coverage, which could disturb the growth of cultures, namely, orange trees. That is achieved by using images from different time series and using indexes to help identify the coverage. Creating a tool as useful as the one proposed in this paper could help farmers improve the managing of their crops.

3   Materials and Method

In this section, we are going to present the different materials and the methodology that we use in the performance of this experiment. Likewise, we have framed this section in different subsections as characteristics of the satellite, studied zone, and performance of the experiment.

3.1   Characteristics of the Satellite

The experiment aims to analyse and detect temporal changes in the grass coverage of the citrus crops. In this context, it will be necessary the use of image treatment of images from different temporal frames. To perform this experiment, the use of satellite images will be necessary.

We determinate to use the Copernicus Sentinel-2. This system is based on two polar-orbiting satellites placed in the same sun-synchronous orbit, phased at 180° to each other. Likewise, this allows the monitoring variability in land surface conditions and its full swath width of 290 km. Moreover, it has a high revisit time of 10 days at the equator with 1 satellite, and five days with 2 satellites under cloud-free conditions with results in 2–3 days at mid-latitude. Likewise, this characteristic allows this project to monitor Earth´s surface changes [14], with coverage limit from latitudes 56° south and 84° north.

Furthermore, this satellite has a Multispectral Imager (MSI) providing 13 different spectral bands from 10 to 60 m of pixel size. Table 1 represents the ranges of the bands that we use in the experiment and their characteristics. This will be useful to extract specific information from the image using different combinations of the bands. Moreover, some of the operations that we can perform with these images include the achieve of Natural Colour, combining red, green and blue bands (B4, B3, B2); Colour Infrared, that is composed by B8, B4 and B3 are used to obtain a reflecting of chlorophyll; Short-Wave Infrared using B12, B8a, and B4 detects vegetation. Besides, other applications will be the agricultural use to detect the health of crops by combining B11, B8, and B2; the geological use to detect faults and lithology using B12, B11, and B2; and the bathymetric use (B4, B3, and B1) whitch is optimum to estimate sediment in the water.

Table 1. Sentinel-2 spectral bands.

Bands	Wavelength (nm)	Resolution (m)	Description
B2	490	10	Blue
B3	560	10	Green
B4	665	10	Red
B8	842	10	Visible and near infrared (VNIR)
B9	945	60	Water vapour

Finally, the last two applications are for obtaining the Vegetation Index and Moisture index. Furthermore, the Copernicus Sentinel-2 offers two types of products (images). Firstly, we have "Level-1C" products, which give information on the top of atmosphere reflectance in cartographic geometry. Otherwise, "Level-2A" offers data of the bottom of the atmosphere reflectance in cartographic geometry.

3.2 Studied Zone

The working zone is situated in Spain, specifically in Gandia (Valencian Community). This is one of the communities with higher areas of orange tree crops. Likewise, this area represents an optimum scenario to apply the proposed system for monitoring the changes in the grass coverage. This coverage has considerable benefits in these harvests as moisture retention that is very necessary because of the climate. In this case, we decide to use Sentinel-2 images because they have a resolution of 10×10 m each pixels in some bands. This cannot be considerate as an excellent resolution, but it is the best pixel size that we can find in open source images. This pixel resolution will contain information about the different surfaces included in this 10×10 m. Although it will not be possible to distinguish the trees, grass (coverage) and soil, we expect to find differences in pixels when they contain grass coverage (GC = 1) or no grass coverage (GC = 0) as it is defined in Fig. 1.

We hypothesise that during the period in which the grass of the agriculture plots is green the values of the pixel of the plots will be different than in summer when the grass is dead and is not present. The summary of the expected differences (subtraction between data from winter and data form summer), based on our hypothesis, is depicted in Table 2.

For the performance of this study, we use the software ArcGIS [15]. This software is needed to apply image treatment to the selected images. Figure 2 represents the selected orthoimage of Gandia, where we determinate the orange plots that we will evaluate. To do this, we select 21 plots, and we classify the plots in two categories, No-Cover (with number 0) and Covered (with number 1). The classification was done using some criteria: trees should be separated, grass cover should be visible, and the plot should be in productions (cannot be abandoned). This would be necessary to determine changes in grass coverage.

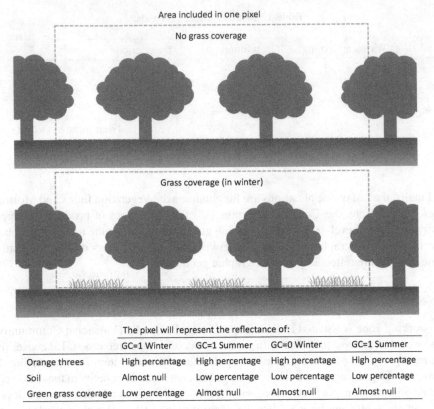

Fig. 1. Scheme of our hypothesis

Table 2. Summary of expected changes according to our hypothesis.

Bands	Reflectance GC = 1	Reflectance GC = 0	Differences in reflectance GC = 1	Differences in reflectance GC = 0
B2	Low	Low	Low	Low
B3	Higher	High	High	Low
B4	Low	High	High	Low
B8	High	High	Low	Low
B9	Higher	High	High	Low

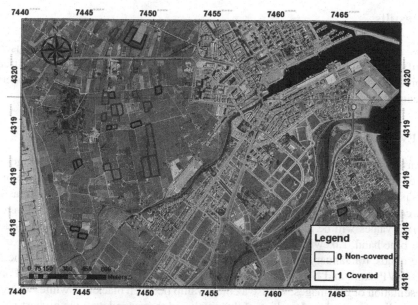

Fig. 2. Plots classification of the studied zone.

3.3   Performance of the Experiment

In this monitoring system, we select Sentinel- 2 images from January and July, taking into account the tree life cycle and situation of grass coverage in the different seasons of the year. These variables have a high relevance when it comes to detecting changes in coverage. In this context, oranges trees need 5 to 7 years to grow up and be productive. Likewise, this could cause different leafiness in the plots obtaining different results in the experiment. These two images will allow us to obtain the possible differences of coverage in citrus crops. We perform the test, evaluating the different changes between all of the bands, including NDVI. In this context, we use B2 (Blue), B3 (Green), B4 (Red), WVP, and NVDI. To do this, we applied the command of "Raster Calculator" to obtain the differences between the bands for the two images. In the case to achieve the vegetation index firstly, we use a combination of B8 that represents the VNIR, and B4 that is the red band. The purpose of these operations is to obtain two types of pixels: the tree with soil and tree with coverage. Finally, we use a "Zonal Statistics table" to get quantifiable information instead of qualitative information.

The obtained results in this proposed monitoring system are to provide an economical device for counselling the farmers in the monitoring of the citrus crops, analysing grass coverage changes in the harvests.

4   Results

In this section, we show the obtained pictures and the processing techniques used to quantify the evolution of grass coverage in citrus crops. First, we evaluate the different combinations of bands. Finally, we quantify and analyse the changes in grass coverage between winter and summer images.

4.1   Evaluation of Different Band Combination

To start, for this proposal it is necessary to evaluate which bands of the images can be used to detect grass covereage changes in the crops. In this context, the size of the pixels is about 10 m. This causes that some pixels will contain values from the areas with grass-coverage, and some from the areas without. In the case, in the plots with covereage the pixel values will be high in the green band, intermediate in the red band, and low in the blue band. Likewise, in Fig. 3 the RGB composition, the representation of the single bands, for January and July are presented. Otherwise, Fig. 4 illustrates the NIR band, WVP band, and NVDI image obtained by a combination of B8 and B4. For the representation of the images, we use a colour ramp between black and white, where the first one displays the lowest values of the pixel; and the second one, the highest values.

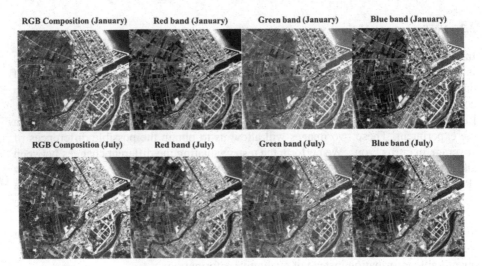

Fig. 3. Single bands of the January and July.

Furthermore, it is necessary to combine the individual bands of different dates to obtain the differences in the grass coverage for all the plots. The purpose of this paper is to maintain the system operation as simple as possible. In this case, we applicate only one command with "Raster Calculator" using the mathematical operation subtract in all of the bands. Moreover, Fig. 5 displays the different image results using greyscale. From those combinations, the covered plots should have low values (black colour pixels) because this pixel contains information about the orange trees and grass coverage. On

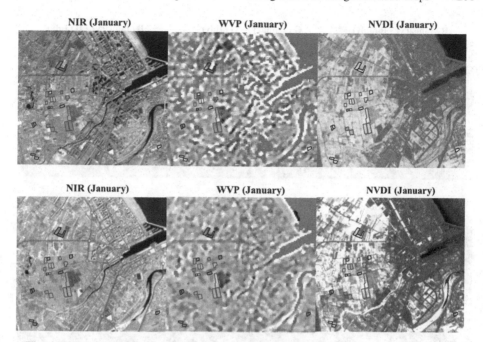

Fig. 4. Near-infrared band, water vapour band, and vegetation index of January and July.

the contrary, non-covered plots, in which orange tree information is combined with the soil without coverage, have high values (white colour pixels). Besides, visually, it is difficult to find differences due to the resolution of the image (10 × 10 m). Figure 5 represents the band combination results. Moreover, the visible spectral bands as red, green, and blue bands encompass the wavelengths that have optically fewer changes between plots marked in blue and red. Otherwise, the combination bands of NIR, WVP, and NVDI represent more clearly the possible changes between both classifications of crops. To obtain more reliable data from the images, we decide to evaluate the values using statistical analysis.

4.2 Analysis of Data

The next step is to obtain a statistical analysis of the obtained results. Our purpose is to evaluate if the values of non-covered crop and covered crops have significate differences. In our case, we use the specific statistical software Statgraphics [16] to analyse the values to obtain more information from the resultant images. Tables 3 and 4 represent the "MEAN" of the pixel values for both types of classified crops in the six images. In this table, the changes between the plots covered and non-covered are better appreciated. Moreover, the blue band, infrared band, and vegetation index bands are three of the bands that represent more unstable values between classifications.

Otherwise, the red band, the green band, and the WVP displayed some changes in the range of covered and non- covered crops. These values will have a marked pattern being minimum in classification 0 and maximum in 1.

R (January) - R (July)   G (January) - G (July)   B (January) - B (July)

NIR (January) - NIR (July)   WVP (January) - WVP (July)   NVDI (January) - NVDI (July)

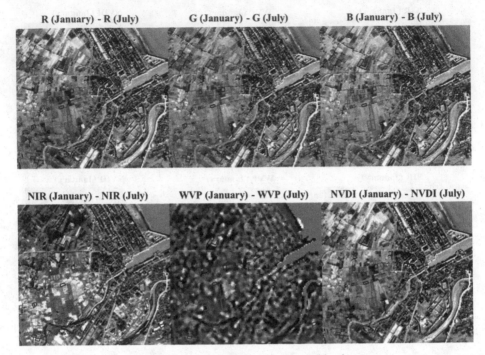

Fig. 5. Resultant images of band combination.

In addition, some of the data do not correspond to their classification being in some cases higher in covered plots or lower in non-covered crops. This will be caused by the different variables of the land and human uses, such as different sizes of the orange trees (old or young trees), the separation between the trees, or unexpected human actions in the crops. To minimise these errors is required to apply this technique in crops with more information and with the participation of the farmers that can contribute with the necessary data of the crops to use this image treatment technique with more efficiency.

In this context, it is necessary to run a more thoroughly evaluation to determinate the values for each band which are more statistically significant. To obtain these results, we applied a Single ANOVA procedure.

Figure 6 illustrates graphics where the differences between the two classifications of plots can be appreciated. For example, the more overlapping there is between the grey boxes for covered and non-covered plots values, the higher similarities the data presents between them. The excessive overlapping is considered as the values are not being significant, which means the limited validity of the band to detect changes in grass coverage for orange trees.

Table 3. Mean of the pixel values of different band combinations for covered plots.

Plots	B2	B3	B4	B8	B9	NVDI
1	−172	−239	−503	349	−1454	0.29
2	−62	−158	−356	−238	−1417	0.2
3	−76	−165	−239	−330	−1416	0.14
4	−119	−228	−317	650	−1482	0.14
5	−183	−250	−557	12	−1383	0.31
6	−150	−328	−448	370	−1569	0.24
7	−204	−320	−584	313	−1497	0.28
8	−227	−289	−548	528	−1457	0.33
9	−229	−257	−594	1039	−1450	0.37
10	−132	−167	−526	−823	−1335	0.28

Table 4. Mean of the pixel values of different band combinations for non-covered plots.

Plots	B2	B3	B4	B8	B9	NVDI
12	−419	−340	−145	214	−1491	0.23
13	−554	−410	−214	−783	−1676	0.18
14	−546	−368	−189	−760	−1670	0.2
15	−470	−311	−153	−310	−1733	0.2
16	−796	−410	−215	−439	−1704	0.25
17	−752	−450	−296	−417	−1701	0.2
18	−721	−379	−202	−518	−1732	0.26
19	−528	−400	−211	−569	−1608	0.18
20	−608	−430	−247	−568	−1662	0.23
21	−882	−474	−325	−20	−1558	0.34

Furthermore, to determine the statistical signification of the values, we use F-Reason and P-Value parameters. In this case, there will be a significant difference between the data for "Mean" and "Plots type" when the P-Value of F-Reason is smaller than 0.05 with a level of significance of 5%.

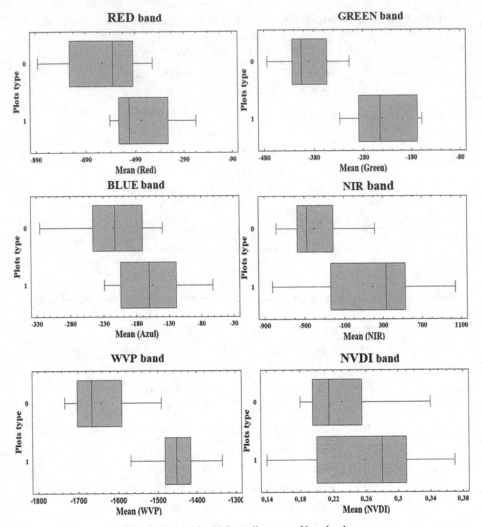

Fig. 6. Box and whiskers diagram of band values.

Moreover, Table 5 represents these two parameters for all band combinations. In this context, we verify that only the NVDI combination band is not significant because the P-Value is higher than 0.05 with a value of 0.3366. Otherwise, the rest of the bands fulfilled the required parameters to be considered significant values. Besides, the WVP band displayed the best results obtaining 0.0000 for P-Value and 42.56. Otherwise, the green value showed fascinating results with 0.0000 of P-Value and 38.61. It can be considerate that the best band combination is located in the green WVP bands. For this case, the data confirmed our hypothesis of monitoring grass coverage in orange crops. Besides, we verify the possible use of the NIR band in this experiment.

Table 5. F-Reason and P-Value parameters.

Bands	F-Reason	P-Value
B4	6.68	0.0177
B3	38.61	0.0000
B2	5,83	0.0254
B8	10.57	0.0040
B9	42.56	0.0000
NDVI	0.97	0.3366

5 Conclusions

We propose a system to evaluate the changes in grass coverage between covered plots and non-covered plots between summer and winter. The proposed monitoring system aims to obtain an economical device for farmers to consult the status of grass coverage in crops to obtain more quality and quantity of harvest. We use Sentinel-2 imagery to obtain images in the different bands of RGB, NIR, WVP, and NDVI for different times of the year to evaluate changes between plots with coverage and plots without grass coverage. The changes between the different classifications of crops are not easy to see in the band combination images. Nevertheless, they are observed in the statistical analysis of the pixels values. The highest differences are located in the combination of green bands and the WVP band. The obtained results are impressive because the NDVI has the lowest functionality when this band combination is one of the most used band to monitor vegetation. Furthermore, the result will be improved, increasing the information on studied plots and cooperating in person with the farmers. The developed system is useful to differentiate between orange trees and grass coverage. Nevertheless, is not optimum for differentiating between diverse plants.

For future works, we will improve new studies using drones as well as developing this monitoring system, collaborating with the farmers, and applying new image operations to obtain better results when consulting the crops.

Acknowledgement. This work has been partially funded by the European Union through the ERANETMED (Euromediterranean Cooperation through ERANET joint activities and beyond) project ERANETMED3–227 SMARTWATIR, and by Conselleria de Educación, Cultura y Deporte with the Subvenciones para la contratación de personal investigador en fase postdoctoral, grant number APOSTD/2019/04.

References

1. Prosekov, A.Y., Ivanova, S.A.: Providing food security in the existing tendencies of population growth and political and economic instability in the world. Foods Raw Mater. **4**(2) (2016)
2. Narvaez, F.Y., Reina, G., Torres-Torriti, M., Kantor, G., Cheein, F.A.: A survey of ranging and imaging techniques for precision agriculture phenotyping. IEEE/ASME Trans. Mechatron. **22**(6), 2428–2439 (2017)

3. Mahlein, A.K.: Plant disease detection by imaging sensors–parallels and specific demands for precision agriculture and plant phenotyping. Plant Dis. **100**(2), 241–251 (2016)
4. Parra, L., Parra, M., Torices, V., Marín, J., Mauri, P., Lloret, J.: Comparison of single image processing techniques and their combination for detection of weed in Lawns. Int. J. Adv. Intell. Syst. **12**(3–4), 177–190 (2019)
5. Parra, M., Parra, L., Mostaza-Colado, D., Mauri, P., Lloret, J.: Using satellite imagery and vegetation indices to monitor and quantify the performance of different varieties of Camelina Sativa. In: GEOProcessing 2020 The Twelfth International Conference on Advanced Geographic Information Systems, Applications, and Services. IARIA, Valencia, Spain, pp. 42–47 (2020)
6. Tokekar, P., Vander Hook, J., Mulla, D., Isler, V.: Sensor planning for a symbiotic UAV and UGV system for precision agriculture. IEEE Trans. Rob. **32**(6), 1498–1511 (2016)
7. Sozzi, M., Marinello, F., Pezzuolo, A., Sartori, L.: Benchmark of satellites image services for precision agricultural use. In Proceedings of the AgEng Conference, AgEng, Wageningen, The Netherlands, pp. 8–11 (2018)
8. Sagawa, T., Yamashita, Y., Okumura, T., Yamanokuchi, T.: Shallow water bathymetry derived by machine learning and multitemporal satellite images. In: IGARSS 2019–2019 IEEE International Geoscience and Remote Sensing Symposium, Yokohama, Japan, pp. 8222–8225. IEEE (2019)
9. Zhang, H., Roy, D.P., Yan, L., Li, Z., Huang, H.: Comparison of Landsat-8 and Sentinel-2A reflectance and normalised difference vegetation index. In: AGUFM 2017, vol 2017 EP23B–1919
10. Gutierrez, S.K., Morales, R.O., Díaz, O.D.L.C.A., Ruiz, E.P.: Multispectral aerial image processing system for precision agriculture. Sistemas Telemática, **16**(47) (2018)
11. Müllerová, J., Brůna, J., Dvořák, P., Bartalo, T., Vítková, M.: Does the data resolution/origin matter? Satellite, airborne and uav imagery to tackle plant invasions. In: International Archives of the Photogrammetry, Remote Sensing & Spatial Information Sciences, vol. 41 (2016)
12. Ezenne, G.I., Jupp, L., Mantel, S.K., Tanner, J.L.: Current and potential capabilities of UAS for crop water productivity in precision agriculture. Agric. Water Manag. **218**, 158–164 (2019)
13. Taha, M., Parra, L., Garcia, L., Lloret, J. An Intelligent handover process algorithm in 5G networks: the use case of mobile cameras for environmental surveillance. In 2017 IEEE International Conference on Communications Workshops (ICC Workshops), Paris, France, , pp. 840–844. IEEE (2017)
14. Sentinel ESA. https://sentinel.esa.int/web/sentinel/missions/sentinel-2. Accessed 25 May 2020
15. ArcGis Software. https://www.arcgis.com/index.html. Accessed 19 Feb 2021
16. STATGRAPHICS Centurion XVIII Software. https://statgraphics.net/descargas/. Accessed 28 May 2020

Correlation of NDVI with RGB Data to Evaluate the Effects of Solar Exposure on Different Combinations of Ornamental Grass Used in Lawns

José F. Marín[1], Lorena Parra[2,3], Jaime Lloret[3], Salima Yousfi[2], and Pedro V. Mauri[2(✉)]

[1] Area verde MG Projects SL., C/Oña, 43, 28933 Madrid, Spain
jmarin@areaverde.es

[2] Instituto Madrileño de Investigación y Desarrollo Rural, Agrario y Alimentario (IMIDRA),
Finca "El Encin", A-2, Km 38, 2, 28800 Alcalá de Henares, Madrid, Spain
loparbo@doctor.upv.es, {salima.yousfi,pedro.mauri}@madrid.org

[3] Instituto de Investigación para la Gestión Integrada de Zonas Costeras, Universitat Politècnica de València, Valencia, Spain
jlloret@dcom.upv.es

Abstract. In the urban areas, the use of water to irrigate the green areas must be improved by the use of technology to reach water efficiency. Normalized Difference Vegetation Index (NDVI) is the most important indexes to evaluate the vegetation vigour, but the required equipment for its gathering have a high cost. In this paper, we present the use of NDVI and pictures taken with a regular camera to evaluate the status of two groups of plots under different solar exposure. Besides, we study the possibilities to correlate data obtained from regular pictures with NDVI, offering a low-cost option for monitoring plant status. From the 18 evaluated plots, which include 3 different grass combinations, the mean value of NDVI and one picture is taken. Then, we obtain the red, green, and blue histograms of each picture using Matlab software. The histograms were included in Statgraphics to search for correlations between histograms and Normalized Difference Vegetation Index of each plot. The highest correlation was found with the data of red histogram ($R^2 = 0.58$ and high significance level). Finally, the variance of both evaluated variables is analyzed, and we have determined that both variables are useful in determining the solar exposure of studied plots. Significance level was higher in NDVI than with data of the histogram, but both of them have a P-Value lower than 0.05 in the analysis of variance.

Keywords: GreenSeeker · Matlab · Camera · Solar radiation · Turf · NDVI · RGB

1 Introduction

In urban areas, water management is critical, especially given the future previsions of climate change. A reduction of 40% on the rainwater might be expected in the following

L. Peñalver and L. Parra (Eds.): Industrial IoT 2020, LNICST 365, pp. 207–220, 2021.
https://doi.org/10.1007/978-3-030-71061-3_13

50 years [1]. Thus, it is essential to maximize the efforts to reduce the water waste and enhance the efficiency in the water use. Several efforts are being made to reach water efficiency, in which the use of technology, are becoming priceless tools. The use of sensors for water distribution network [2] and the creation of systems to achieve water efficiency in water distribution network [3] are some examples.

However, there are several aspects in the urban areas linked to water use which must be addressed to attain true water efficiency. One of these aspects is the proper maintenance of green areas. Traditionally, the irrigation of green areas, mainly composed by grasses, is performed considering the climatic and agronomic parameters (such as temperature and expected evapotranspiration) [4]. Nonetheless, there are other parameters which can affect the water requirements of turf and have to be considered to program the irrigation. One of those parameters is the changes in solar radiation caused by the shade projected by buildings and trees or different orientation. Differences in solar radiation lead to different water need of the lawns.

With regards to the use of technology for plants monitoring and its irrigation needs, we can identify the Wireless Sensor Network (WSN) as one of the most useful solutions in agriculture. Precision Agriculture (PA) is mainly based on the use of sensors and remote sensing for archiving the sustainability of agriculture. In different papers, we can see the use of similar systems for Precision Gardening (PG). Although, the WSNs are very important in agriculture, in PG the remote sensing can have a better performance. In view of the periodicity of required mows to maintain the gardens, and the mowing equipment, remote sensing can be implemented in the lawnmowers.

In PA, the Normalized Difference Vegetation Index (NDVI) is one of the most used indexes for plant vigour monitoring. The regular cameras, or RGB cameras, can be an excellent alternative to estimate the greenness of plants. In previous papers, we have estimated the plant coverage in lawns by using RGB pictures and operating with their histograms [5]. Although the use of RGB images might not be as precise as NDVI to detect alterations of the health of plants (water stress, pests, diseases, etc.), they should be considered as a good alternative for daily monitoring. The RGB cameras are much cheaper than the equipment required for NDVI calculation. In addition, a microprocessor can be included to calculate the histograms and derived products.

In this paper, we present the use of NDVI and RGB histograms to detect changes in grass lawns when they have different sun exposure. A total of 18 plots have been analyzed, from which we can divide two subgroups. The first subgroup (plots 1 to 9) receive lower solar radiation than the second one (plots 12 to 18). Two technological solutions have been used to evaluate the changes between two subgroups of plots, the GreenSeeker, which measures the NDVI, and an RGB camera. From each picture, the red, green, and blue histograms are analyzed. Then, multivariate analyses to search correlations between the NDVI and the histogram of the 18 analyzed plots are carried out. From the regions of the histograms in which correlations are found are studied in detail. Finally, analysis of variance is performed to determine if there are differences between plots with different solar exposure in NDVI and RGB data.

The rest of the paper is structured as follows; Sect. 2 outlines the related work and highlight the differences between existing studies and the proposed analysis. The material and methods are defined in Sect. 3. Section 4 presents the results and discussion of the proposed analysis, including the statistical correlations and analyses of variance. Finally, the conclusions and future work are detailed in Sect. 5.

2   Related Work

In this section, we summarize the current solutions for monitoring plant status, focusing on the use of NDVI, other indexes and RGB images. In addition, a comparison between the proposed analysis and existing ones is presented.

The NDVI is widely used for plant monitoring, and several papers demonstrate its benefits. It can be measured in-situ with specialized equipment with remote sensing. Following we include a series of papers that have used the NDVI information for monitor plant status. First of all, the NDVI is highly used in PA, in [6] authors proposed the use of optical and analogue sensors for vineyard monitoring. They propose to change the remote sensing information by data gathered by proximal sensing technologies. Authors develop the idea of creating a mobile lab which includes GreenSeeker RT100, ultrasonic sensors to estimate canopy thickness, and DGPS receiver. Their results showed that NDVI data and ultrasonic lectures where highly correlated and NDVI was used to estimate the real vine phytosanitary status.

In [7], authors propose to obtain the NDVI data using an unmanned aerial vehicle in wheat agronomy and breeding trials. They use a multispectral camera in the unmanned aerial vehicle, and the handheld GreenSeeker to obtain data. Then, they correlate data of both methods and use the gathered information for phenotyping the crop. They were able to identify the d flowering time and maturity with the NDVI. Authors of [8] have exposed the use of NDVI with remote sensing to determine the drought. Their results point out that the NDVI is highly correlated with the standardized precipitation index. Finally, they show the use of NDVI to predict the yield.

The use of NDVI in rice was presented in [9]. The authors demonstrate the effectiveness of NDVI to estimate the yield of rice in dry and wet seasons. In the conclusions, authors indicate that the measurement of NDVI during the early reproductive stages is the measure with the highest correlation with yield in dry seasons. The use of NDVI in pastures has also been reported in [10]. In that paper, authors present the use of NDVI for rapid determination of evapotranspiration coefficient. The evapotranspiration coefficient is vital for irrigation management, and it is measured with vaporation chambers. Its correlation with the NDVI allows rapid estimation of the evapotranspiration to adjust the irrigation. The test performed in [10] were carried out with *Festuca arundinacea* during two consecutive growing seasons. Results showed a high correlation between NDVI and evapotranspiration coefficient of *F.arundinacea*.

Finally, the use of RGB data has also been presented for plant monitoring. We are going to detail some examples. In [11] authors propose the use of RGB data for Assessing Early Plant Vigor in Winter Wheat jointly with GreenSeeker and hyperspectral camera. Their results indicate that the RGB data can be used as a low-cost option in the very early growth stages. After this moment, the use of other methods is recommended. On the other hand, we also found the use of RGB data in lawns monitoring to assess the plant coverage using the data of green histogram [5].

After analyzing the related work, and as far as we know, no work has been published aimed to relate the RGB data and NDVI in grass crops. Besides, no publications focused on the effect of solar exposure on the NDVI have been found.

3   Materials and Methods

The description of used equipment to gather data from the plots, and software selected to analyze the data is shown. In addition, the plots, its composition, and differences are detailed in this section.

3.1   Equipment Used to Gather the Data

For data collection, two different devices have been used. On the one hand, for the RGB pictures acquisition, a reflex camera was used. On the other hand, specific equipment, the GreenSeeker [12], was used for the obtention of NDVI data of plots.

The camera selected for gathering the RGB pictures was the Canon EOS 77 [13]. Several parameters of the camera can be modified; the configuration of the camera can be seen in Table 1. The pictures were taken at a distance of 1.5 m from the soil. One picture is gathered for each plot, and we ensure that 100% of the picture contains the plot. To avoid including the variability of the edges of the plot, the borders are not included in the picture. Therefore, the picture contains the centre of each plot. The pictures were taken without flash in a day with no clouds.

With regard to the NDVI data, the GreenSeeker Handheld, see Fig. 1, has been used. This device is able to measure the NDVI of a surface (the plots) in dynamic mode, and after the measurement, the mean value is displayed in the screen. To obtain the mean value, the device was located at 1.5 m from the soil and moved along the plot to gather the NDVI of several points.

Table 1. Configuration of Canon EOS 77 Camera in the moment of taking the pictures.

Characteristics	Canon EOS 77
Size of the image	6000 × 4000 pixels
Horizontal and vertical resolution	72 ppp
Bit depth	24
F point	f/5
Focal distance	18 mm
Exposure time	1/160 s
ISO velocity	ISO - 100

Fig. 1. Device used to gather data from NDVI of each plot.

3.2 Software for Data Analysis

Once the data were gathered in the field, the pictures have to be processed to extract the histograms before obtaining any existent correlation between NDVI and RGB data or find variances between plots with high and low solar exposure. After processing the image, statistical analyses were done to find correlations.

To extract the histograms form the pictures, the Matlab software [14] was selected due to its high capacity and the option to implement it in the future in the Raspberry nodes. The code used to obtain the histograms, based on the code described in [5], is saved in a script. This code generates a series of matrixes and vectors that contain the information about the value of each pixel in RGB and the histograms themselves. The Red, Green and Blue files contain the value of each pixel for the specified colour, and the histograms are contained in files h_R, h_G, and h_B. The rest of the generated files are elements needed to calculate the histograms.

The other used software is a statistical tool which is used first to find correlations between NDVI and the histograms, and then to analyze the variance between plots with different solar exposure. The selected software was the Statgraphics Centurion XVI [15] due to its easy-to-use interface and its powerful capabilities. First of all, multivariate analysis to search for correlations is conducted. In this analysis, the data of NDVI and the number of pixels for each value of brightness for red, green, and blue histograms are included. The objective of this analysis is to find which region or regions of histogram have a high correlation with NDVI data. The second set of analyses was aimed to find the linear regression between the NDVI values and the part of the histogram, which has the greatest correlation. Finally, ANalysis Of VAriance (ANOVA) with NDVI and the data of histogram with better linear regression was performed to determine if evaluated factors are affected by the different solar exposure.

3.3 Plots Description

The studied area is composed of 18 small plots which contain different grass combinations. The plots are placed in the fields of Instituto Madrileño de Investigación y Desarrollo Rural, Agrario y Alimentario (IMIDRA) in the Finca el Encín (Alcalá de Henares). Half of these plots are located in an area with higher solar exposure; there is no shadow over those plots along the day. The rest of them are closer to the trees, which project a shade over the plots in the first hours of the morning.

The differences in solar exposure are the sole differentiating parameter. The soil characteristics, irrigation, and fertilization remain equal in both groups of plots since its seed. The plots were seed on 4th of Abril of 2019, and the pictures were taken after 204 days (25th of October of 2019).

All the included plots are formed by a combination of two grass species, a C3 and a C4 plant. More information about the aim of these combinations can be found in [16]. As a C3 plant, *Festuca arundinacea* is included in all the plots. Meanwhile, different C4 species are used (*Brachypodium distachyon*, *Zoysia japonica*, and *Cynodon dactylon*). Thus, we can find three grass combinations in the plots: *Festuca Arundinacea* with *Brachypodium distachyon* (F+B), *Festuca Arundinacea* with *Zoysia japonica* (F+Z), and *Festuca Arundinacea* with *Cynodon dactylon* (F+C). Each combination is repeated three times for each solar exposure regime (R1, R2 and R3). A picture of the location is depicted in Fig. 2. A scheme of the combinations and its location with regard to the path of the Sun can be seen in Fig. 3. The plots are located in a single row almost perpendicular to the path of the Sun and parallel to the road and the ornamental trees responsible for the shade projection.

Fig. 2. Picture of the studied area.

4   Results

The description of used equipment to gather data from the plots, and software selected to analyze the data is shown. In addition, the plots, its composition, and differences are detailed in this section.

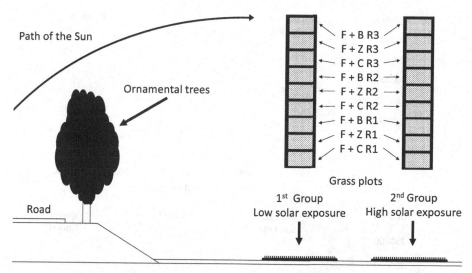

Fig. 3. Scheme of the plots, grass combinations and path of the Sun.

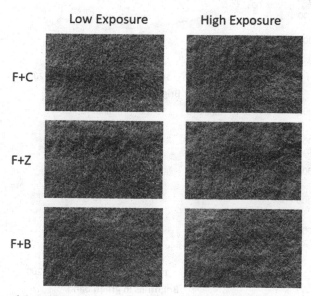

Fig. 4. Example of the taken pictures in the plots including the three grass combinations under high and low solar exposure

4.1 Histogram Analysis

Part of the taken pictures is shown in Fig. 4. We present the first replica of the three compositions with high and low solar exposure. It is important to note that no differences are observed in the pictures, or the plots can be identified to the bare eye.

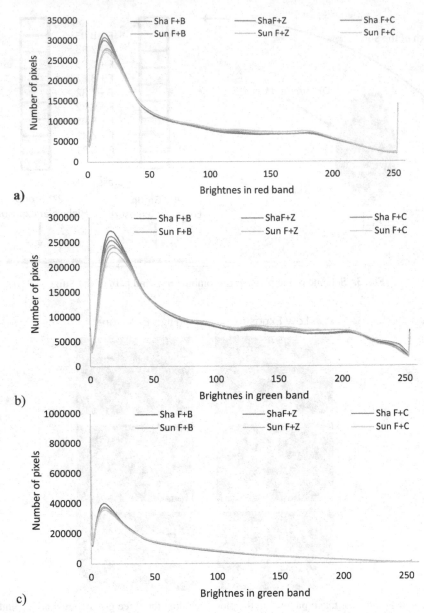

Fig. 5. Mean of red (a), green (b), and blue (c) histogram for each grass combination with high (Sun F+X) and low (Sha F+X) solar radiation exposure (Color figure online)

Next, we apply the code presented in Fig. 2 to extract the data for the histograms from each picture. The three histograms (red histogram a), green histogram b), and blue histogram c)) are displayed in Fig. 5. In the histograms, we have presented the mean values of the three repetitions for each grass combinations in the same solar exposure. They are identified as Sun or Sha according to the high and low solar exposure, respectively. Therefore, a total of 6 histograms are represented for each colour.

Concerning the red histogram, see Fig. 5a), it is possible to note that in the first region of the histogram (brightness values between 10 and 25) the plots with different solar exposure have different values. After this region, the data of plots remain similar until brightness value of 70. Then, the values of brightness are different for plots under high and low solar exposure until the brightness value of 180. Thus, we can identify two regions of the histogram in which the brightness values change with solar exposure.

With regards to the green histogram (Fig. 5b)), we can find similar results than in the red histogram. There is a region with low values of brightness (13 to 29) where the values of brightness are different for plots with different solar exposure.

In addition, we can identify another region (values of brightness from 150 to 200) with differences. Finally, for the blue histogram, see Fig. 5c), there is only one region where we can differentiate the plots (from 8 to 16) under high and low solar exposure.

4.2 Correlation Between NDVI and RGB Data

Following, we are going to present the results of analyses to found correlations between Normalized Difference Vegetation Index (NDVI) data and histograms. For these analyses, we include the mean value of NDVI for each plot obtained with the GreenSeeker as the first column of data in Statgraphics and the number of pixels for each value of brightness as the rest of the columns. Thus, for each analysis, we have included 257 values for each plot. The multivariate analysis search for correlations between each column of data. In this case, we only consider the correlations between first column (NDVI) and the rest (histogram). In general terms, we consider that there is a correlation between two variables when the P-value of the correlation is lower than 0.05. In our analyses, we focus on the correlations with P-values lower than 0.002. Table 2 outlines the results of these analyses. First, we indicate the number of cases with P-value < 0.002 (62 for red, 4 for green, and 7 for blue histograms). Then, we specify the values of the brightness of those cases, which represent two regions in red, one in green and blue histograms. Finally, we portray the case with the highest correlation and the P-Value for this case. For the red histogram, the value of brightness equal to 86 is the point with the most significant correlation. For green and blue histograms, the values of brightness are 24 and 13.

Once the specific value of brightness for each colour which is highly correlated with the NDVI data, we plot both variables (number of pixels with the selected value of brightness as a percentage and NDVI). The fact of using the percentage instead of as the summation of pixels allows us to apply our results (equations and models) for further analysis using other pictures with different size in the future. For the regressions, a lineal model and the method of least squares.

Figure 6a) presents the linear regression for NDVI and the percentage of pixels in the red histogram with brightness value equal to 86. The indicators of the goodness of this linear regression can be seen in Table 3. The regression model with data of red histograms is the one that has the better correlation in terms of R2, standard and absolute errors and P-Value of the variance analyses. The error and the P-Value are lower with data from the red histograms, and the R2 is higher than in the data of green and blue histograms. The obtained models have a negative correlation between variables.

The regression models for green histograms, in which the percentage of pixels with a brightness value equal to 24 is used, is presented in Fig. 6b). With these data, we have a positive correlation between NDVI and data from the histogram. With blue histogram, see Fig. 6c), we also found a positive correlation.

Table 2. Summary of multivariate analyses to search correlation between NDVI and RGB data from the histograms. For each colour cases (values of brightness) from 0 to 255 are included. Significance levels: ns, not significant; *p < 0.05; **p < 0.01 and ***p < 0.001.

	Red	Green	Blue
Number of cases with P-value < 0.002	62	4	7
Cases (values of brightness)	9–22, 73–121	21–24	10–16
Case with the highest correlation	86	24	13
Level of significance	0.0001***	0.0012**	0.0001***

According to the results of the regressions, we can affirm that it is possible to interfere with the NDVI data from simple RGB picture. Hence, we have demonstrated that with equipment which has a lower cost than GreenSeeker, we can monitor the grass vigour.

4.3 Effectiveness of NDVI and RGB Data for Assessing Grass Status Concerning Different Solar Exposures

After analyzing the three obtained regression models, the one that relates the red histogram presents better results than green and blue histograms. Therefore, we are going to use this data for the last part of the paper in which we compare the results of both groups of plots to evaluate the suitability of NDVI and percentage of pixels with brightness values equal to 86 in the red histogram to differentiate the plots under high and low solar exposure. Thus we present the results of two Box-and-whisker diagram and two ANOVAs. From the diagram of Box-and-whisker we can affirm that the data of NDVI, see Fig. 6a) is more accurate to differentiate both group of plots than data from the red histogram, see Fig. 6b).

Nevertheless, to affirm if the variance between plots under high and low solar exposure is caused by the differences in solar exposure of just by the randomness of the data, the results of ANOVAs must be analyzed. The first ANOVA has been performed with the NDVI data of both groups of plots, identified as Low and High solar exposure. The results of ANOVA with NDVI data, see Table 4, indicate that this variable (NDVI) is suitable to differentiate both groups of plots and the observed differences on the NDVI data is caused by the different solar exposure of plots. The results for the ANOVA performed with the percentage of pixels from the red histogram is also significant. Nonetheless, the level of significance of the ANOVA performed with the red histogram (P-value of 0.0452) is lower than with the data of NDVI histogram (P-value of 0.0001). Thus, both

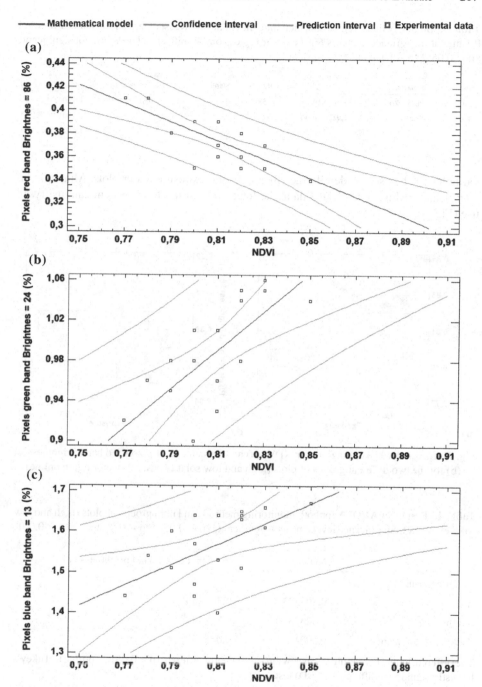

Fig. 6. Linear regression for selected data from red (a), green (b), and blue (c) histograms. (Color figure online)

Table 3. Summary linear regression, including the equations, R2, standard and absolute errors and P-value of the variance analyses for the linear regression. Significance levels: ns, not significant; *p < 0.05; **p < 0.01 and ***p < 0.001.

Colour	Equation	R2	Standard error	Absolute error	P-value
Red	Pixels (%) = 1,02 − 0,798 * NDVI	0.58	0,013	0,011	0,0002***
Green	Pixels (%) = −0,57 + 1,922 * NDVI	0.49	0,039	0,032	0,0012**
Blue	Pixels (%) = −0,47 + 2,514 * NDVI	0.32	0,073	0,057	0,0142**

variables can be used to identify the effects of solar exposure in our plots. Although the significance is higher for NDVI data, the lower cost of the RGB system can justify its use (Fig. 7).

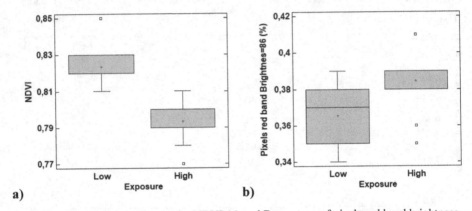

a)   b)

Fig. 7. Box-and-whisker diagram for NDVI (a) and Percentage of pixels red band brightness = 86 (b) for the two different groups of plots (high and low solar exposure) (Color figure online)

Table 4. Results of ANOVA for both monitoring methods and both groups of plots (high and low solar exposure). Significance levels: ns, not significant; *p < 0.05; **p < 0.01 and ***p < 0.001.

	NDVI	% of pixels red band brightness = 86
Solar exposure		
Low	0,793333[a]	0,365556[a]
High	0,823333[b]	0,384444[b]
Level of significance	0,0001***	0,0452*

The different letter succeeding the means are significantly different (p < 0.05) according to Tukey's honestly significant difference (HSD) test.

5   Conclusions

In this paper we have studied the relation between NDVI and RGB picture for 18 grass plots which are maintained under different solar exposure with the aim to find in the RGB data can be used to evaluate the plant vigour. The importance of using RGB is justified by the low cost of the systems to gather this type of data compared with the equipment required for NDVI data. It is important to note that the data included in these analyses correspond to different grass combinations, which implies a greater variability in the data.

The results of our analyses portray that there are correlations between some areas of the red, green, and blue histogram and the NDVI data. The highest correlation and the best lineal regression was found in the red histogram with the number of pixels which has brightness value equal to 86. It should be pointed out that although the variability between different grass combinations, the data of NDVI and a specific region of the red histogram can be used to differentiate the plots under low and high solar exposure.

In future work, we want to include data of other grass combinations, having variability in the C3 specie (including the specie *Poa pratensis*). Furthermore, we plan to implement the same analysis with pictures gathered with a drone and evaluate the suitability of the RGB histograms to monitor changes in plant vigour due to water scarcity and use a Raspberry as a node to process the data.

Acknowledgement. This work has been partially funded by AREA VERDE-MG projects, Projects GO-PDR18-XEROCESPED funded, by the European Agricultural Fund for Rural Development (EAFRD) and IMIDRA, by the European Union through the ERANETMED (Euromediterranean Cooperation through ERANET joint activities and beyond) project ERANETMED3-227 SMARTWATIR, and by Conselleria de Educación, Cultura y Deporte with the Subvenciones para la contratación de personal investigador en fase postdoctoral, grant number APOSTD/2019/04.

References

1. Mapedza, E., Tsegai, D., Bruntrup, M., McLeman, R. (eds.): Drought Challenges: Policy Options for Developing Countries. Elsevier, Amsterdam (2019)
2. Rocher, J., Parra, L., Lloret, J., Mengual, J.: An inductive sensor for water level monitoring in tubes for water grids. In: 2018 IEEE/ACS 15th International Conference on Computer Systems and Applications (AICCSA), pp. 1–7. IEEE, October 2018
3. Parra, L., Rego, A., Femenía, J.S., Mauri, J.L.: The use of IoT and AI to achieve the water efficiency in urban environments. In: Health, Wellbeing and Sustainability in the Mediterranean City, p. 11. Routledge (2019)
4. Litvak, E., Pataki, D.E.: Evapotranspiration of urban lawns in a semi-arid environment: an in situ evaluation of microclimatic conditions and watering recommendations. J. Arid Environ. **134**, 87–96 (2016)
5. Marín, J., et al.: Urban lawn monitoring in smart city environments. J. Sens. **2018**, 1–16 (2018)
6. Mazzetto, F., Calcante, A., Mena, A., Vercesi, A.: Integration of optical and analogue sensors for monitoring canopy health and vigour in precision viticulture. Precis. Agric. **11**(6), 636–649 (2010). https://doi.org/10.1007/s11119-010-9186-1

7. Duan, T., Chapman, S.C., Guo, Y., Zheng, B.: Dynamic monitoring of NDVI in wheat agronomy and breeding trials using an unmanned aerial vehicle. Field Crops Res. **210**, 71–80 (2017)
8. Dutta, D., Kundu, A., Patel, N.R.: Predicting agricultural drought in eastern Rajasthan of India using NDVI and standardized precipitation index. Geocarto Int. **28**(3), 192–209 (2013)
9. Phyu, P., Islam, M.R., Sta Cruz, P.C., Collard,B.C.Y., Kato, Y.: Use of NDVI for indirect selection of high yield in tropical rice breeding. Euphytica **216** (2020). Article number: 74. https://doi.org/10.1007/s10681-020-02598-7
10. Alam, M.S., Lamb, D.W., Rahman, M.M.: A refined method for rapidly determining the relationship between canopy NDVI and the pasture evapotranspiration coefficient. Comput. Electron. Agric. **147**, 12–17 (2018)
11. Prey, L., Von Bloh, M., Schmidhalter, U.: Evaluating RGB imaging and multispectral active and hyperspectral passive sensing for assessing early plant vigor in winter wheat. Sensors **18**(9), 2931 (2018)
12. GreenSeeker Information. https://trl.trimble.com/docushare/dsweb/Get/Document-475150/022503-1123A_GreenSeeker_DS_MarketSmart_USL_0415_LR_web.pdf. Accessed 19 Oct 2020
13. Manual of Canon EOS 77D Camera. https://gdlp01.c-wss.com/gds/3/0300026603/01/EOS_77D_Instruction_Manual_EN.pdf. Accessed 10 July 2020
14. MATLAB Software. https://www.mathworks.com/products/matlab.html. Accessed 28 May 2020
15. STATGRAPHICS Centurion XVIII Software. https://statgraphics.net/descargas/. Accessed 28 May 2020
16. Marín, J., Yousfi, S., Mauri, P.V., Parra, L., Lloret, J., Masaguer, A.: RGB vegetation indices, NDVI, and biomass as indicators to evaluate C3 and C4 turfgrass under different water conditions. Sustainability **12**(6), 2160 (2020)

Deployment and Assessment of a LoRa Sensor Network in Camelina [*Camelina sativa* (L.) Crantz] Culture

David Mostaza-Colado[1]([✉]) [iD], Pedro V. Mauri Ablanque[1] [iD], and Aníbal Capuano[2]

[1] IMIDRA Agro-Environmental Research Department (Madrid Institute for Rural, Agrarian and Food Research and Development), Ctra. A2 Km. 38.200 – Finca El Encín, 28805 Alcalá de Henares, Madrid, Spain
`david.mostaza@madrid.org`
[2] Camelina Company Spain, Fuente el Saz de Jarama, Madrid, Spain

Abstract. The use of LoRa sensors and IoT in farming is increasing progressively. For this study, we installed a series of LoRa soil moisture and conductivity sensors at 5 cm and 30 cm depth in a *Camelina sativa* (L.) Crantz cultivar. The information gathered by the sensors show how rain or irrigation water infiltrates in the soil. This allows the farmer to take decisions regarding the use of water in a very effective, cheap and reliable way. Although the use of LoRa sensors is more common in irrigated crops of high economic value and yield, the use of cheap sensors in rainfed agriculture can be a great contribution to manage the crop and add additional value to the production. It could provide information on the water stress and needs of the crop and be decisive in assessing whether, in large areas of dry land, it will be economically profitable to cultivate.

Keywords: Camelina · Smart agriculture · Precision farming

1 Introduction

The growing demand of new techniques for developing intelligent agriculture implies the adoption of technologies such as the Internet of Things (IoT) on farms. This kind of IoT technology allows the farmer to monitor his crop in real time and to identify the fundamental factors of agricultural production. The IoT sensors are connected to the Internet and transmit the information to a platform where it is collected and can be analyzed automatically [1].

There are several IoT systems, but currently the aim is to send certain environmental data such as temperature, soil moisture or irrigation water conductivity. Although these systems are useful for farmers, they can be useless if the crops are not in the right plot or have been affected by events such as a natural disaster or pests. Therefore, a monitoring system like this is an important factor in agriculture: 1) ensures and reduces the loss of productivity in high-yielding crops; 2) provides accurate and visual information to

L. Peñalver and L. Parra (Eds.): Industrial IoT 2020, LNICST 365, pp. 221–230, 2021.
https://doi.org/10.1007/978-3-030-71061-3_14

farmers; 3) improves decision-making in short time; 4) and ensures the right soil and plant conditions, thus increasing the value and yield of the crops [2, 3].

On the other hand, modern agriculture aims to answer the increasing worldwide need for food production. Thus, new technologies and solutions in the agricultural field provide an optimal alternative to collect and process information while improving productivity. At the same time, the alarming climate change and the growing water crisis require new and improved methodologies for the agricultural and farming fields of the modern era. Automation and intelligent decision-making are also becoming more important to fulfill this mission. Therefore, the combination of IoT with other technologies such as Big Data Computing or remote sensing is becoming increasingly popular and more often [4].

Consequently, IoT is an environment where objects, animals or people are equipped with unique identifiers capable of data transmission over Internet network without the need for human interaction. Thus, it has great potential and is one of the key areas for future development of internet services. New uses of IoT are being searched for and established, but most of the effort is in the area of solution standardization [2, 5, 6].

1.1 LoRa Technologies

The challenge arises when implementing a real-time visual monitoring system to control an entire farm and increases as the farm grows bigger or is in places with difficult access. It is not possible to wire the entire farm to deploy sensors, so IoT and technologies such as LoRa (short for long range) take advantage. This radio information packet handling technology is characterized by high tolerance to interference, low power consumption, long range and low data transfer rate. This allows the deployment of low-cost sensor networks in large areas like farms or woods. Thus, LoRa provides long-range and low-power consumption, a low data rate, and secure data transmission. It can be used with public, private, or hybrid networks to achieve a greater range than cellular networks. LoRa technology can easily integrate with existing networks and enables low-cost, battery-operated Internet of Things (IoT) applications. A single gateway can cover huge areas of square miles/kilometers. Therefore, LoRa networks are considered low-power wide area networks (LPWANs). The nodes can be battery powered, and the lifetime of the battery is about ten years, plus they transmit data in small amounts over long distances and a few times per hour (for example, every ten minutes), thus enhancing the battery stamina. LoRa-based environmental sensing system enables farmers to remotely monitor the status of a large farm in near real-time. On the other hand, coverage is highly dependent on obstructions (buildings, trees, hills), environment (heavy rain) and technical factors (high-level radio interference, antenna type), so it is necessary to design the system deployment correctly to achieve full performance [1, 3, 7–9].

1.2 Camelina Culture

An example of the use of LoRa sensors in precision agriculture is the CAMEVAR project of the CAMELINA Operational Group (OG), which focuses on the cultivation of *Camelina sativa* (L.) Crantz. Oil crops such as camelina are one of the major plant groups with the highest production, research, experimentation and marketing worldwide. They are very useful and generate seeds with a high percentage of fatty acids and proteins of high quality that can be used in the chemical, pharmaceutical, cosmetic or animal and human food industries, among others. Its fruit is shaped like a small siliqua with 6–16 seeds with an oil content of between 30% and 40% in dry weight. Oil is very rich in alpha-linolenic acid (ALA), omega-3 fatty acids and high levels of gamma-tocopherol (vitamin E) [10–14].

Camelina cultivation stands out for its high resistance to drought and the reduced need for inputs. Therefore, it is an alternative crop when compared with more demanding rainfed crops. Moreover, among other advantages, it can be adapted as a rotation crop in semi-arid and arid rainfed regions, thus minimizing fallow, where other oilseed alternatives are less competitive [15–18]. In addition, it can be used in crop rotations, as it can grow without fertilization by exploiting residual nitrogen (N), phosphorus (P) and potassium (K) in the soil from previous crops [19–22].

The OG, composed by Camelina Company Spain (CCE), IMIDRA, ASAJA and the farmer, Julián Caballero de la Peña, aims to research on the improvement of the varieties of this oil crop in the central Spain area. To this extent, research is carried out on combining traditional cultivation techniques with new technologies such as remote sensing using Sentinel-1 and Sentinel-2 images or crop monitoring using IoT technologies [23, 24].

1.3 Related Works

The selection of LoRa technologies sensors for the CAMEVAR project was due to the ease of its implementation and its proven performance in other experiences, measuring the soil moisture and soil temperature. This kind of IoT networks have a prolonged lifetime at lower cost compared to other sensors due to the optimized sleep time of sensor nodes and less power consumption. In addition, the use of solar-powered features on sensor nodes extends the lifetime of the network. Thus, this kind of LoRa based gateway is demonstrated to solve power problems and cover large areas in agriculture fields [7].

In addition, it is more suitable for battery-powered devices such as the soil moisture sensors. Reliable communication over long distance is possible because of techniques like adaptive data rate, LoRa's chord spread spectrum radio modulation scheme, and gateways that decode data received on multiple channels modulated with different spreading factors. In precision agriculture, LoRa technology provides low-cost low-power communication solution for prolonged monitoring operations [25].

The rest of the paper is organized as follows: Sect. 2 presents the methodology employed to deploy the LoRa sensors network and collect data. Section 3 depicts the raw results gathered from the sensors and the weather station. This data is discussed in Sect. 4. Lastly, the conclusions and future works are presented in Sect. 5.

2 Materials and Methods

We selected a 2.5-hectare plot (plot X), located on Finca El Encín IMIDRA, in the municipality of Alcalá de Henares, Madrid, Spain. On January 23, 2020, we seeded the plot with camelina's V1 variety (provided by CCE). We used a conventional Solà cereal seeding machine, calibrated at a dose of 8 kg/ha to 10 kg/ha. Later, since rainfall was scarce during the germination period, we performed two short irrigations on plot X to boost the growth of the seeds. The plot is technically divided into 5 sectors that have an independent sprinkler irrigation system, which allows differential irrigation of the crop and soil. On February 13, 2020, we installed sensors in each sector to measure soil moisture (sM) and soil conductivity (sC) (at a depth of 5 cm and 30 cm), as well as ambient temperature (T). We placed the LoRa network hub-gateway close to these sensors (<200 m), on the border of the field. Additionally, as a control plot (plot Y), we installed sensors on another camelina rainfed plot 2000 m away from the experimental plot (Fig. 1 and Fig. 2). We gathered information from the sensors every 15 min. The meteorological data was extracted from the weather station located on the farm, which collects daily data on rainfall and maximum and minimum temperatures.

The monitoring system was formed by LoRa wireless nodes, a local gateway with 3G connectivity, and a cloud data server provided by Plantae®.

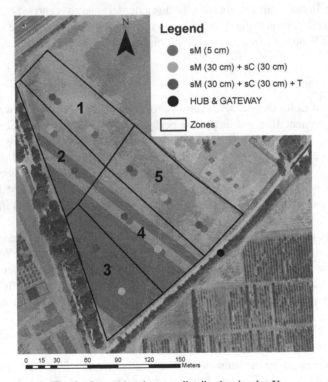

Fig. 1. Sensors and zones distribution in plot X.

The final goal was to perform different stages of irrigation in each sector and to compare the data on soil moisture and conductivity with the rainfed plot. We aimed to assess how the changes in the soil moisture and conductivity took place along with the rainfall or irrigation periods. Thus, even though it is a rainfed crop, we would be able to simulate different rainfall scenarios and evaluate how the soil moisture or conductivity affects the growth and final yield of the camelina.

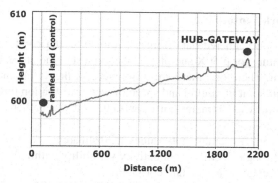

Fig. 2. Average slope between the rainfed control sensor and the hub-gateway.

Unfortunately, because of the COVID 19 situation we were not able to proceed with the differential irrigation calendar in plot X, so all the zones (1 to 5) where rainfed, as in plot Y.

3   Results

In this section, we provide an overview of the data collected by the LoRa sensors and the weather station and explain the possible variables that may have affected the results.

3.1   Meteorological Data

To assess the rainfall and estimate how was its availability for the crop through the infiltration, we processed the meteorological data from the weather station. We calculated the total (68 mm) and diary rainfall (2.16 mm/day), as long with the average temperature since the day we sowed the camelina crop (11.90 °C).

Rainfall was concentrated in the first weeks after the camelina was seeded and in final weeks, where the crop's water demands are higher because it is growing and developing the fruits and seeds (Fig. 3).

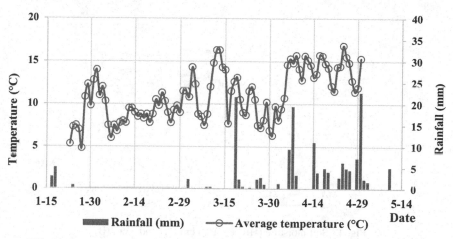

Fig. 3. Finca El Encín weather station (from January 23, 2020, to April 30, 2020).

3.2 LoRa Network Sensors Data

LoRa network sensors gathered data from soil moisture and conductivity along with superficial temperature for plot X and plot Y. We harvested moisture data from the soil at 5 cm and 30 cm. Therefore, there are differences in the variation of soil moisture mainly due to the amount of rainfall and speed of water infiltration through the soil. On the other hand, conductivity remains quite constant, as it was gathered at 30 cm (Fig. 4 and Fig. 5).

In both plots (X and Y) conductivity values at 30 cm are related to moisture at 30 cm, as it is calculated through electrical conductivity variability within the sensor probes, so the graphical representation has certain correlation.

Although the two plots were finally rainfed, because we were unable to apply differential irrigation to plot X, the plot Y "rainfed" sensor showed a remarkable decrease in conductivity. Probably due to the installation method or differences in the soil composition (Fig. 5).

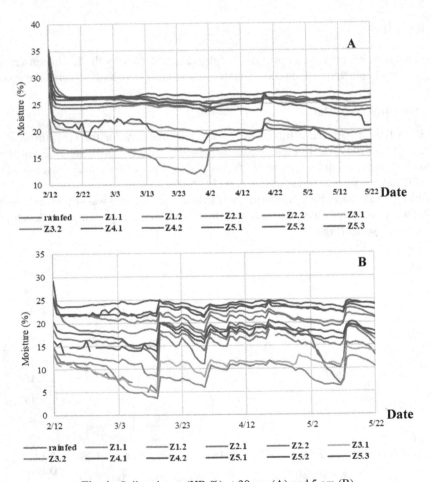

Fig. 4. Soil moisture (HR %) at 30 cm (A) and 5 cm (B).

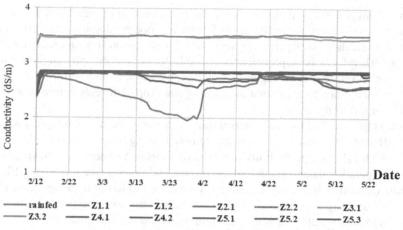

Fig. 5. Soil conductivity (dS/m) at 30 cm.

4 Discussion

Camelina crop is a rainfed culture, thus it only needs rainwater as input, and it is enough to make the crop grow healthy and profitable. In this situation, as OG CAMELINA works to research in best camelina varieties, we wanted to test the behavior of V1 variety in different irrigation scenarios, to simulate several rainfall areas. However, because of the COVID 19 situation we were not able to proceed with the differential irrigation calendar, so all the zones (1 to 5) from plot X where rainfed. This is the reason why the graphs do not show differences in terms of soil moisture, and have a similar behavior. The collected data is based only on the water provided by the rain. Even so, some interesting patterns appear, that may help in understanding soil and crop behavior.

The graphs plot shows how the sensors effectively and quickly detect the increase of moisture in soil at 5 cm because of rainwater; although some differences are appreciated related to the soil texture or the placement of the sensors. In addition, intraday variations in soil moisture are shown because of the day-night cycle, solar radiation and temperature variations.

If this was a conventional irrigation process with sprinklers, this information would allow the farmer to determine when the water begins to infiltrate and is already available for the roots. Every time a rainfall is recorded, there is an increase in the soil moisture at 5 cm, but not at 30 cm. This only happens when rain exceeds certain threshold. Furthermore, there are no significant variations in the soil conductivity, so there is no water infiltration generating soil washing.

Therefore, the rain regime in this central Spain area is not generating water infiltration since moisture is retained in the soil or being used by camelina crop and it is enough for the crop to grow. This fact is important for a rainfed crop like camelina, as we can be sure that the water needs of the plant are fully covered.

Water management is paramount in countries with water scarcity like Spain. This also affects agriculture, as a large amount of water is dedicated to this use. The rising concerns about global warming have led to the consideration of creating water management measures to ensure the availability of water for food production and consumption. Thus, the researches on water usage reduction for irrigation have increased over the years [26]. Therefore, the deployment of cheap LoRa sensors has proven to be a useful system of controlling and managing irrigated crops, but it is also a convenient way to manage rainfed crops to guarantee the yield of the crop or foresee future problems in the development of the plant.

Also, as the future of precision agriculture lies upon modern technological advancements, different kind of smart sensors and remote sensing techniques using Unmanned Aerial Vehicles (UAV), profitability in production farming depends on making correct and timely operational decisions based on current conditions and historical data [27, 28]. Precision agriculture is a comprehensive system designed to optimize agricultural production by carefully tailoring soil and crop management to correspond to the unique conditions found in each field while maintaining environmental quality [28].

5   Conclusions

The use of LoRa sensors for estimating soil moisture and conductivity proves to be a cheap and effective tool as it provides real-time data. This allows the farmer to make decisions about his crop that can be fundamental for its good development and productivity. The installation of a pool of sensors below and under the plants root makes it possible to assess when it is necessary to stop irrigation. If irrigation keeps flowing when moisture increases below the roots, we would be losing water, fertilizers and money.

Gathering data every 15 min in a rainfed field has proven to be enough to understand the behavior of the soil and moisture as a large amount of information is provided. Therefore, increasing the threshold to 1–2 h would not be a problem in rainfed systems were the speed of the physical changes (temperature, moisture, conductivity) is slow.

Although the use of LoRa sensors is more common in irrigated crops of high economic value and yield, the use of cheap sensors in rainfed agriculture can be a great contribution to manage the crop and add additional value to the production. It could provide information on the water needs of the crop and be decisive in assessing whether, in large areas of dry land, it will be economically profitable to cultivate.

As a future work, we aim to install sensors in upcoming rainfed camelina plantations, alternating different varieties of plants and soil management. Therefore, we will be able to gather data on the variation of soil moisture and the final crop yield.

Acknowledgements. PDR18-CAMEVAR project is co-founded by the European Union through the European Agricultural Fund for Rural Development (EAFRD) - Europe invests in rural areas, MAPAMA and the Community of Madrid through IMIDRA, within the framework of the PDR-CM 2014–2020 call.

References

1. Seneviratne, P.: Introduction to LoRa and LoRaWAN. In: Beginning LoRa Radio Networks with Arduino. Apress, Berkeley, CA (2019). https://doi.org/10.1007/978-1-4842-4357-2_1

2. Stočes, M., Vaněk, J., Masner, J., Pavlík, J.: Internet of Things (IoT) in agriculture - selected aspects. Agris On-line Pap. Econ. Inform. **8**, 83–88 (2016). https://doi.org/10.7160/aol.2016. 080108

3. Ji, M., Yoon, J., Choo, J., et al.: LoRa-based visual monitoring scheme for agriculture IoT. In: SAS 2019 - 2019 IEEE Sensors Applications Symposium Conference Proceedings, pp. 1–6 (2019). https://doi.org/10.1109/SAS.2019.8706100

4. Ray, P.P.: Internet of things for smart agriculture: technologies, practices and future direction. J. Ambient Intell. Smart Environ. **9**, 395–420 (2017). https://doi.org/10.3233/AIS-170440

5. Gluhak, A., Krco, S., Nati, M., et al.: A survey on facilities for experimental internet of things research. IEEE Commun. Mag. **49**, 58–67 (2011). https://doi.org/10.1109/MCOM.2011.606 9710

6. Jazayeri, M., Liang, S., Huang, C.-Y.: Implementation and evaluation of four interoperable open standards for the Internet of Things. Sensors **15**, 24343–24373 (2015). https://doi.org/ 10.3390/s150924343

7. Heble, S., Kumar, A., Prasad, K.V.V.D., et al.: A low power IoT network for smart agriculture. In: IEEE World Forum Internet Things, WF-IoT 2018 – Proceedings, January 2018, pp. 609–614 (2018). https://doi.org/10.1109/WF-IoT.2018.8355152

8. Mekala, M.S., Viswanathan, P.: A survey: smart agriculture IoT with cloud computing. In: International Conference on Microelectronic Devices, Circuits and Systems (ICMDCS), pp. pp. 1–7. IEEE (2017)

9. Nguyen Gia, T., Qingqing, L., Peña Queralta, J., et al.: Edge AI in smart farming IoT: CNNs at the edge and fog computing with LoRa. In: IEEE AFRICON-2019 (2019)

10. Imbrea, F., Jurcoane, S., Hălmăjan, H.V., et al.: Camelina sativa: a new source of vegetal oils. Rom. Biotechnol. Lett. **16**, 6263–6270 (2011)

11. Zubr, J.: Oil-seed crop: Camelina sativa. Ind. Crops Prod. **6**, 113–119 (1997). https://doi.org/ 10.1016/S0926-6690(96)00203-8

12. Berti, M., Wilckens, R., Fischer, S., et al.: Seeding date influence on camelina seed yield, yield components, and oil content in Chile. Ind. Crops Prod. **34**, 1358–1365 (2011). https:// doi.org/10.1016/j.indcrop.2010.12.008

13. Pilgeram, A.L., Sands, D.C., Boss, D., et al.: Camelina sativa, A Montana Omega-3 and Fuel Crop. In: Proceedings Sixth National Symposium Creating Markets for Economic Development of New Crops and New Uses, pp. 129–131 (2007)

14. Usher, S., Haslam, R.P., Ruiz-Lopez, N., et al.: Field trial evaluation of the accumulation of omega-3 long chain polyunsaturated fatty acids in transgenic Camelina sativa: making fish oil substitutes in plants. Metab. Eng. Commun. **2**, 93–98 (2015). https://doi.org/10.1016/j. meteno.2015.04.002

15. Zanetti, F., Eynck, C., Christou, M., et al.: Agronomic performance and seed quality attributes of Camelina (Camelina sativa L. crantz) in multi-environment trials across Europe and Canada. Ind. Crops Prod. **107**, 602–608 (2017). https://doi.org/10.1016/j.indcrop.2017.06.022

16. Zanetti, F., Monti, A., Berti, M.T.: Challenges and opportunities for new industrial oilseed crops in EU-27: a review. Ind. Crops Prod. **50**, 580–595 (2013). https://doi.org/10.1016/j.ind crop.2013.08.030

17. Dobre, P., Jurcoane, Ş.T.: Camelina crop - opportunities for a sustainable agriculture. Scientific Papers, UASVM Bucharest LIV, pp. 420–424 (2011)

18. Guy, S.O., Wysocki, D.J., Schillinger, W.F., et al.: Camelina: adaptation and performance of genotypes. Field Crop Res. **155**, 224–232 (2014). https://doi.org/10.1016/j.fcr.2013.09.002

19. de Imperial, M., Hornedo, R., Martín Sánchez, J.V., Lobo Bedmar, M. del C., et al.: Respuesta del rendimiento biológico y agrícola de plantas de Camelina (Camelina sativa) y del contenido de proteína y aceite de sus granos al afecto residual de la fertilización orgánica y mineral. Rev Int Contam Ambient **31**, 377–387 (2015)

20. del Mar Delgado, M. Lobo, C., Plaza, A., et al.: Efecto residual provocado por dos lodos de depuradora procedentes de un ensayo de fitorremediación con cardo en un cultivo de camelina (Camelina sativa (L.) Crantz) en Madrid. Rev la Fac Ciencias Agrar **48**, 13–30 (2016)
21. Moore, A., Wysocki, D., Chastain, T., et al.: Camelina Nutrient Management Guide for the Pacific Northwest. Pacific Northwest Ext (2019)
22. McVay, K.A., Lamb, P.F.: Camelina Production in Montana (Report). Bull MT200701AG 8 (2008)
23. Parra, M., Parra, L., Mostaza-Colado, D., et al.: Using satellite imagery and vegetation indices to monitor and quantify the performance of different varieties of Camelina Sativa. In: GEO-Processing 2020: The Twelfth International Conference on Advanced Geographic Information Systems, Applications, and Services Using, pp 42–47 (2020)
24. Mostaza-Colado, D., Mauri Ablanque, P.V., Capuano, A.: Assessing the yield of a multi-varieties crop of Camelina sativa (L.) Crantz through NDVI remote sensing. In: 2019 Sixth International Conference on Internet of Things: Systems, Management and Security (IOTSMS), pp. 596–602. IEEE (2019)
25. Vuran, M.C., Salam, A., Wong, R., Irmak, S.: Internet of underground things in precision agriculture: architecture and technology aspects. Ad Hoc Netw. **81**, 160–173 (2018). https://doi.org/10.1016/j.adhoc.2018.07.017
26. García, L., Parra, L., Jimenez, J.M., et al.: IoT-based smart irrigation systems: an overview on the recent trends on sensors and IoT systems for irrigation in precision agriculture. Sensors (Switzerland) **20** (2020). https://doi.org/10.3390/s20041042
27. Triantafyllou, A., Sarigiannidis, P., Bibi, S.: Precision agriculture: a remote sensing monitoring system architecture. Information **10** (2019). https://doi.org/10.3390/info10110348
28. Gsangaya, K.R., Hajjaj, S.S.H., Sultan, M.T.H., Hua, L.S.: Portable, wireless, and effective internet of things-based sensors for precision agriculture. Int. J. Environ. Sci. Technol. **17**(9), 3901–3916 (2020). https://doi.org/10.1007/s13762-020-02737-6

Author Index

Printed in the United States
by Baker & Taylor Publisher Services